Art and Expressive T
Within the Medical Model

Art and Expressive Therapies Within the Medical Model explores how to best collaborate across disciplines as art and expressive therapists continue to become increasingly prevalent within the medical community. This collection of diverse chapters from seasoned practitioners in the field introduces readers to art therapy interventions across a variety of artistic approaches, patient demographics, and medical contexts, while paying special attention to new approaches and innovative techniques. This is a cutting-edge resource that illustrates the current work of practitioners on a national and global level while providing a better understanding of the integration of biopsychosocial approaches within art and expressive therapies practice.

Deborah Elkis-Abuhoff, PhD, LCAT, ATR-BC, ATCS is director and associate professor in the creative arts therapy counseling program at Hofstra University and an assistant investigator in the Center of Neuroscience at the Feinstein Institute for Medical Research.

Morgan Gaydos, MA, LCAT, ATR-BC is an art therapist for Nassau University Medical Center and an adjunct instructor at Hofstra University.

Art and Expressive Therapies Within the Medical Model

Clinical Applications

Edited by Deborah Elkis-Abuhoff and Morgan Gaydos

NEW YORK AND LONDON

First published 2019
by Routledge
52 Vanderbilt Avenue, New York, NY 10017

and by Routledge
2 Park Square, Milton Park, Abingdon, Oxon, OX14 4RN

Routledge is an imprint of the Taylor & Francis Group, an informa business

Library of Congress Cataloging-in-Publication Data
Names: Elkis-Abuhoff, Deborah, editor. | Gaydos, Morgan, editor.
Title: Art and expressive therapies within the medical model : clinical applications / edited by Deborah Elkis-Abuhoff and Morgan Gaydos.
Description: New York, NY : Routledge, 2019. | Includes bibliographical references and index.
Identifiers: LCCN 2018036312 (print) | LCCN 2018037535 (ebook) | ISBN 9780429400087 (eBook) | ISBN 9780367023409 (hbk) | ISBN 9780367023416 (pbk) | ISBN 9780429400087 (ebk)
Subjects: LCSH: Arts—Therapeutic use. | Medicine and art. | Art therapy.
Classification: LCC RM931.A77 (ebook) | LCC RM931.A77 A74 2019 (print) | DDC 616.89/1656—dc23
LC record available at https://lccn.loc.gov/2018036312

ISBN: 978-0-367-02340-9 (hbk)
ISBN: 978-0-367-02341-6 (pbk)
ISBN: 978-0-429-40008-7 (ebk)

Typeset in Bembo
by Apex CoVantage, LLC

This book is dedicated to Ron, Alexandra, and Samantha, and in memory of Mom, Dad, and Scott Abuhoff. Thank you for always believing in me, I love you always.
Deborah Elkis-Abuhoff

This book is also dedicated to Scott Gliniak, Mom, and Dad. Last, but certainly not least, this book is dedicated to Isabella Rita and Michael Charles. I have no doubt that the legacy of always wanting to learn and helping others will live on through both of you.
Morgan Gaydos

Contents

Editors

Deborah Elkis-Abuhoff, PhD, LCAT, ATR-BC, ATCS, BCPC, is Associate Professor and Director of the Creative Arts Therapy Counseling program at Hofstra University. She holds both Creative Arts Therapy and Psychology licenses in New York State, is Registered and Board Certified Art Therapist, Art Therapist Certified Supervisor, Board Certified Professional Counselor, and teacher certification in Art Education (K–12). Dr. Elkis-Abuhoff holds an appointment at Northwell Health's Feinstein Institute for Medical Research as an Assistant Investigator in the Center for Neuroscience. Her research interests bring together behavioral medicine and creative/medical art therapy and neuroscience. Her recent research projects involve art therapy with those diagnosed with Parkinson's disease and cancer and connecting the creative process to neurological responses. She and her research team have published in peer-reviewed journals and in edited volumes and have presented to national and international audiences. Dr. Elkis-Abuhoff and Morgan Gaydos received the American Art Therapy Association's 2016 Rawley Silver Research Award for their work with clay manipulation art therapy and Parkinson's disease research.

Her diverse experiences include medical, geriatric, psychiatric, child, adolescent, and family populations. She is an active member of the review board for *Art Therapy: Journal of the American Art Therapy Association* and the *Canadian Art Therapy Journal*, as well as an invited reviewer for several journals that focus on expressive therapies and psychology. She is a member of the American Art Therapy Research Committee and an active committee member for the Art Therapy Credentials Board.

Morgan Gaydos, MA, LCAT, ATR-BC, is Art Therapist for Nassau University Medical Center and Adjunct Instructor at Hofstra University. She currently practices clinical art therapy within a forensic psychiatry unit located in a hospital setting, with a foundation in psychodynamic theories and behavioral modification. Her work experience also includes art therapy within inpatient/detoxification chemical dependency programs, child psychiatry, and children diagnosed within the autism spectrum. In addition, she is a therapist within a group private practice for children and families on Long Island.

Her teaching experience focuses on the importance of mixed-method approaches, with both quantitative and qualitative components, in art therapy research. Ms. Gaydos' past and current research efforts, as a member of an interdisciplinary research team, focus on art therapy with Parkinson's disease, neuroscience, and cancer. She has published in international and national journals as well as in edited volumes within the field of art therapy in collaboration with neuroscience and education, and has also presented at national and international conferences on mental health, medicine, and art therapy. She is an active member of the American Art Therapy Research Committee and the Art Therapy Credentials Board. Ms. Gaydos was also a joint recipient, with Dr. Deborah Elkis-Abuhoff, of the American Art Therapy Association's 2016 Rawley Silver Research Award for her ongoing involvement with art therapy and Parkinson's disease research.

Contributing Authors

Joan Alpers, MPS, ATR-BC, LCAT, CCLS, currently directs the Child Life Program at Stony Brook Children's Hospital and holds adjunct graduate faculty appointments in both art therapy and child life. With over 30 years of experience, she has given numerous presentations and in-services to the child life, art therapy, and allied health communities. She maintains a private practice as an art therapist and sandplay practitioner, employing a unique combination of child life philosophy, sandplay theory, and art therapy applications for children and adults struggling with medical illness, trauma, divorce, and related issues of loss and bereavement.

Yasmine J. Awais, MAAT, ATR-BC, ATCS, LCAT, LPC, is an art therapist and scholar with clinical and supervisory experience in the United States, Japan, and Saudi Arabia with a wide range of individuals, families, and communities: adjustment/acculturation, homeless/housing insecure, impacted by community violence, infected/affected by HIV/AIDS, medical rehabilitation, and schools. Awais' practice and teaching is informed by multicultural feminist counseling, with a focus on collaboration and communication via art-making. Awais is currently Assistant Clinical Professor at Drexel University's College of Nursing and Health Professions, Creative Arts Therapies Department and serves on the board of directors for Artistic Noise.

Melanie Biscuiti, MA, LCAT, ATR-BC, currently practices art therapy within an adult psychiatric unit in a hospital setting within the state of New York. Her work experience also includes art therapy with forensic psychology, the incorporation of individual art therapy and Reiki sessions with children and adults, and art therapy with Alzheimer's patients and caregivers in a community group setting. Her research efforts are focused on healing and empowerment through art therapy, and she has dedicated her career to helping patients increase mindfulness and self-awareness through art therapy, music, meditation, and Reiki.

Wendy Case, LPC, ATR, CAADC, MAC, is the director of the Ascension Brighton Center for Recovery (BCR) art therapy program. BCR, a

99-bed inpatient substance abuse treatment facility located northwest of Detroit, is part of Ascension Health and has the distinction of being the second oldest treatment facility in the country. The program serves adults with a variety of co-occurring mental health diagnoses and occupational functioning concerns. Trauma accompanies the majority of issues that these clients are grappling with. Case is a 'process' art therapist, and is very interested in the integration of expressive therapies with principles of polyvagal theory.

Joanna Clyde Findlay, MA, MFT, ATR, is a licensed marriage and family therapist and registered art therapist. She is an adjunct professor at the California Institute of Integral Studies, San Francisco, California, publishing and presenting nationally and internationally on the clinical application of art therapy and relational neuroscience; her most recent book is *Art Therapy and the Neuroscience of Relationships, Creativity, and Resiliency*. English by birth, Joanna has studied and practiced in London, Paris, and Los Angeles. Joanna integrates family therapy, art therapy, and mindfulness practices in her clinical work in private practice in San Rafael and San Francisco.

Tracy Councill, MA, ATR-BC, LCPAT, started an art therapy program for patients and families in pediatric hematology-oncology at Georgetown University Hospital's Lombardi Comprehensive Cancer Center in 1991. That highly successful program evolved into Tracy's Kids, a nonprofit organization dedicated to creating art therapy programs for pediatric hematology-oncology patients and their families, with programs in seven locations. She earned her MA in Art Therapy from The George Washington University in 1988, having received a BFA in Painting and Printmaking from Virginia Commonwealth University in 1978. She teaches Art Therapy at the George Washington University, Eastern Virginia Medical School, and Florida State University.

Irene Rosner David, PhD, LCAT, ATR-BC, HLM, began her art therapy career in 1973 at Bellevue Hospital Center in New York, where she conceived and implemented programs for physically ill adults, including trauma, brain injury, rehabilitation, chronic illness, oncology, and palliative care. As Director of Therapeutic Arts, she expanded creative art therapies for a range of hospital services including for victims of 9/11. Her research includes the benefits of art therapy for brain injured patients in cultivating cognition, and has taught, presented, and published on artistic expression and medicine, including paralysis, tuberculosis isolation, AIDS, dementia, and TBI. She has served on the board and numerous committees of the American Art Therapy Association and is the recipient of the AATA's Clinician, Distinguished Service, Advocacy, and Honorary Life Member Awards.

Michelle L. Dean, MA, ATR-BC, LPC, CGP, is an art psychotherapist who has over 20 years of expertise in treating individuals who struggle with addictions, eating disorders, relationship issues, and traumatic experiences. She cofounded the Center for Psyche & the Arts, LLC, with two locations in the Philadelphia area, and is an author, artist, supervisor, educator, and consultant. She is the Director of the Art Therapy Program at The University of the Arts. Her publications include, *Using Art Media in Psychotherapy: Bringing the Power of Creativity to Practice*. Her clinical work has been recognized through many distinguished awards.

Daisy Fancourt, MA, MM, PhD, FHEA, FRSPH, is a Wellcome Research Fellow in the Department of Behavioural Science and Health at University College London. She specializes in psychoneuroimmunology and epidemiology, exploring the effects of arts and cultural engagement on neuroimmune responses, clinical conditions, and population health outcomes. She is Deputy Chair of the Royal Society for Public Health's Special Interest Group in Arts and Health, Chair of the International Arts Health Early Career Research Network, and Codirector of the UK-Florida Arts Health Research Intensive training program. She is also a World Economic Forum Global Shaper and BBC New Generation Thinker, through which she presents radio and TV programs on arts and science.

Yvonne Farquharson, BA, Hons, is the Managing Director at Breathe Arts Health Research, London, UK. She has gained international recognition in the arts and health world, receiving several awards for her work across the healthcare and social enterprise sectors. In addition, she founded and led Breathe to win multiple national awards and gain recognition as a service provider to the UK National Health Service. She has coauthored papers published in medical journals and frequently speaks at health, arts, and social enterprise conferences and events globally. She studied at Lancaster University and the School for Social Entrepreneurs, and has held a variety of roles for the BBC and ITV. She also has experience as a Performing Arts Manager for Guy's & St Thomas' Charity, the largest NHS Charity in the UK.

Holly Feen-Calligan, PhD, ATR-BC, has worked in inpatient detoxification and rehabilitation facilities treating substance use disorders. She earned her PhD in Higher Education at the University of Michigan. Her doctoral program included a practicum that was devoted to understanding how recovering people experienced art therapy. Holly presently serves as Director of the Art Therapy Program at Wayne State University in Detroit, Michigan. She also teaches in the doctoral art therapy program at Mount Mary University in Wisconsin.

Sharon W. Goodill, PhD, BC-DMT, NCC, LPC, is Clinical Professor and Chairperson of the Department of Creative Arts Therapies in the College of Nursing and Health Professions at Drexel University, and a Past-President of the American Dance Therapy Association. She holds a PhD in Medical Psychology with a concentration in Mind/Body Studies. Her

2005 volume, *An Introduction to Medical Dance/Movement Therapy: Healthcare in Motion*, has supported the application of dance/movement therapy for people living with medical conditions worldwide. Her professional interests concern psychosocial aspects of medical conditions and the development of evidence for the creative arts therapies in the broad spectrum of healthcare.

Noah Hass-Cohen, ATR-BC, PsyD, developed the art therapy relational neurobiology (ATR-N) theoretical model. In her publications and frequent national and international presentations, she explores the advantages of therapeutic art-making from integrated interpersonal neuroscience perspectives. She highlights how sensory expressive practices can provide solid opportunities for softening relationships, increasing empathy, mending attachments, and repairing trauma. She is on the faculty at the California School of Professional Psychology at Alliant University Los Angeles. She is a psychologist, art therapist, and certified mindfulness instructor in clinical practice. Originally from Israel, she and her family live in Los Angeles, California.

Mariya Keselman, MA, is an art therapist in the Philadelphia area, with a MA from Drexel University and a BA from the University of Pennsylvania. Keselman has worked in medical, psychiatric, and community settings with individuals who have experienced medical, mental health, or complex trauma; collective trauma; persecution; or acculturation or who have identity concerns. Keselman uses intersectional and social justice lenses and a person-centered, trauma-informed approach. She is currently an art psychotherapist at Einstein Medical Center, a mobile therapist with Horizons Behavioral Health, a teaching artist with BuildaBridge International, and is involved with program development to increase access to social supports for underrepresented communities.

Juliet L. King, MA, ATR-BC, LPC, LMHC, is an Associate Professor of Art Therapy at The George Washington University and Adjunct Associate Professor at the Indiana University School of Medicine Department of Neurology. She has two decades of experience as a clinician, administrator, and educator. Ms. King created and implemented the graduate art therapy program at Herron School of Art and Design, IUPUI, Indianapolis, Indiana. Her research explores the integration of arts, neuroscience, and related therapeutics, focusing on the brain–computer interface as a method of understanding creative expression and its contributions to the psychotherapeutic process. Her edited textbook is *Art Therapy, Trauma, and Neuroscience: Theoretical and Practical Perspectives*.

Sabine C. Koch, BC-DMT, holds a doctorate in Psychology and is a Dance Movement Therapist, Director of the Research Institute for Creative Arts Therapies at Alanus University Alfter, and Professor and the head of the dance/movement therapy (DMT) Master Program at SRH University

Heidelberg, Germany. She specializes in embodiment research, evidence-based research, Kestenberg Movement Profiling, and active factors across the creative arts therapies with studies on DMT for schizophrenia, autism, and depression. Research interests include DMT, body–mind approaches, embodiment, nonverbal communication, body memory, movement and meaning, DMT for trauma, dance for Parkinson's disease, and creative arts therapies.

Linda Levine Madori, PhD, LCAT, ATR-BC, CTRS, is a two-time Fulbright Scholar, Professor, Author, Trainer and Researcher of a non-pharmaceutical approach utilizing the creative arts for brain stimulation, which can be found in her first book, *Therapeutic Thematic Arts Programming*. Her second book; *Transcending Dementia Through the TTAP Method: A New Psychology of Art, Brain, and Cognition*, expands on the current significant research demonstrating the cost-effectiveness of this innovative multimodal approach for psychiatric settings, geriatric populations, and those diagnosed with Alzheimer's.

Richard McDougall, MIMC, one of the founding magicians of Breathe Magic, is a Member of the Inner Magic Circle with Gold Star and a former World Open Champion for Close-Up Magic. He performs for private and corporate clients worldwide and feels fortunate to have appeared at several events hosted by HM The Queen, including a private party to celebrate her Diamond Jubilee, which was attended by royalty from around the world. He lectures on the performance and presentation of magic at prestigious international magic conventions, and was a guest presenter on the first live global online magic event, EMC. He now teaches and speaks on the impact of body language and has worked with senior oncologists helping them to deliver scientific data more effectively and improve awareness and interpersonal skills with patients.

Jill McNutt, PhD, ATR-BC, ATCS, practices as an art therapist specializing in cancer care at Aurora Healthcare in Milwaukee, Wisconsin. Her professional practice centers on a postmodern approach to art therapy through social and personal narratives. For personal art expression, she prefers the less predictable properties of media like paint and wet clay as these help to evolve her own narrative. Jill also serves as Director and Associate Professor of the Master of Arts in Art Therapy program at St. Mary of the Woods College. This chapter included elements from dissertation research through Lesley University, Cambridge, Massachusetts.

Robert M. Pascuzzi, MD, was born in Council Bluffs, Iowa, and received his undergraduate degree from Indiana University, an MD degree from Indiana University School of Medicine, and completed his neurology residency and fellowship training at the University of Virginia. In 1985, he joined the faculty at Indiana University School of Medicine and has served as Chairman of the Department of Neurology since 2004. Dr.

Pascuzzi directs the Amyotrophic Lateral Sclerosis Program at IU Health and the ALSA Multidisciplinary Clinic. Professional emphasis relates to general adult clinical neurology and neurological education.

Libby Schmanke, MS, ATR-BC, ATCS, LCAC, MAC, has more than 25 years of experience in a range of settings, including inpatient, prison, community outpatient, long-term residential, and private practice. Libby has been on the faculty of the graduate art therapy program at Emporia State University for over 15 years, and served for over 12 years in several roles for the Art Therapy Credentials Board. She has provided numerous national and regional presentations, and her publications include the single-author text *Art Therapy and Substance.*

Vered Zur and Boaz Zur, both MA, CAGS, are Expressive Arts Therapists from the European Graduate School (EGS). Founders of Expressive Arts Ireland, they work with individuals and groups of all ages in the areas of therapy, education, social change, self-development, performance, and community arts around the world. Their focus and passion are connected with the arts of storytelling, nature, landscape art, ritual, and drama. They believe in the healing process and self-growth that can be achieved through the intermodal arts and enjoy traveling and engaging with local people, collecting stories, and experiencing richness in cultures. They love telling stories that connect to different cultures, and they apply them to supporting people who suffer from various illnesses (cancer, acquired brain injuries, mental illness, special needs with emotional/behavioral/cognitive and autism spectrum) to find connection and meaning within life's journey. Boaz and Vered are a married couple with four children, and have developed unique work that allows them to live their passion and dreams for the past 33 years.

Keshet Zur, MA, holds a Master's Degree in Expressive Arts with a minor in Psychology from the European Graduate School (EGS). She has a strong background in fine art with experience in performance art. She is a cofounder of Expressive Arts Ireland; an organization invested in facilitating therapy sessions and training via the intermodal therapeutic approach, in Ireland and internationally. In addition to her work with Expressive Arts Ireland, Keshet is working as an Outreach Facilitator and Arts Coordinator with Autism Initiatives.

Preface

It all started in January of 2006 when, as professor and student, we began to delve into the depths of medical art therapy research. Together we explored the impact of clay manipulation art therapy for those diagnosed with Parkinson's disease, how spontaneous mandala drawing could give insight into the journey of women diagnosed with breast cancer, how tablet technology could allow art therapy into places such as chemotherapy and blood transfusion treatment rooms, and how to best address the needs of medically ill patients through the incorporation of art and expressive therapies. We published in academic journals and chapters in textbooks, traveled, and presented at professional conferences both nationally and internationally. During this time, the student became the colleague, and together we became a team.

About 3 years ago, we started our journey to develop this edited text. The goal is to bring to the forefront how art and expressive therapies are being incorporated into treatment to support the needs of the medically ill patient. We realized that there were so many amazing and creative things happening in the areas of art and expressive therapies within the medical realm, and that the need to share the expertise was ever so important. As art and expressive therapists become more prevalent within the medical practice, it becomes crucial to collaborate within an interdisciplinary community. This edited volume will offer diverse chapters, composed by seasoned professionals, and is intended to introduce the reader to a variety of medical populations and corresponding art and expressive therapy approaches.

Together we gathered authors from places such as England, Ireland, Germany, and around the United States, who have created unique approaches and innovative applications, as well as those who bring their knowledge and experiences to share their insights into the profession. Through this collaboration of such great contributing authors, we bring you this edited volume of ideas, applications, and thought-provoking topics.

The aim of art and expressive therapies within a medical setting is to allow a patient to experience control within a diagnosis, emotionally heal, and have an opportunity to feel positive physical effects on specific symptomology. We hope you find the included collection of chapters to be educational, and that you are able to add some ideas and approaches to your toolbox of applications when working with, and supporting, those who are challenged by a medical illness.

Deborah Elkis-Abuhoff and Morgan Gaydos

Acknowledgments

This project never would have been possible without the wonderful collaboration that we have formed together for the past 12 years. We have transcended through different roles, and are now close colleagues, but have always maintained our ability to effectively work together and pursue endeavors that aim to strengthen the field of art therapy.

We would like to thank the Routledge team, who have made this edited volume possible. In addition, we would also like to thank educators who have challenged us, and close colleagues who have supported us along the way, all of which who have brought a higher level of inquisitiveness and learning into our practice. We would like to thank fellow researchers, specifically Dr. Robert Goldblatt, for his creative thinking—you will always be considered part of the team.

We would also like to highlight and acknowledge our contributing authors, without whom none of this could have ever happened. Your knowledge, experiences, and passion to help those challenged with medical illness is invaluable. This has been both a learning experience and a means to bring the fields of art and expressive therapies closer together.

Lastly, we are forever thankful and indebted to our spouses, children, and family members who have allowed the formation of this text to take place.

1 Art Therapy in Pediatric Oncology

Tracy Councill

When a child becomes seriously ill, the whole family's sense of well-being is shattered. Preventive medicine has nearly eradicated many causes of childhood mortality, leading most people to assume that all children will grow to adulthood. The diagnosis of a life-threatening illness unleashes a crisis: not only must the family find treatment to restore the child's health, continue to care for siblings, and maintain careers to keep health insurance, but they must also work through profound questions—Why did this happen? How? Is it my fault? What does it mean to the rest of our lives? In the space of brokenness, the power of creativity emerges: Art therapy in pediatric oncology can offer immediate comfort, teach coping skills, and build resilience to help patients and families confront the crisis of illness. Approaching art therapy in pediatric oncology through the lens of the patient experience lends focus and impact to the profession.

What a Medical Diagnosis Means

A medical condition is not the only challenge patients face: becoming a patient can impose its own sense of powerlessness. One of the early reports on childhood cancer survivors includes a compelling description of what it is like to be a patient in a hospital. Being a patient is like visiting a foreign land: The patient is surrounded by a host of strange people, smells, clothing, language, food, behavior, and customs. From the lab-coat dress code to abbreviations for illnesses and procedures, many aspects of the hospital language are designed to exclude the uninitiated (patients and families) from the communications of what may seem like a secret society (medical staff) (van Eys, 1981). Patients and families may feel hospital culture lacks transparency, leading to difficulty trusting the medical team and feeling unnecessarily excluded from their care.

Coping with a serious illness is essentially a process of grief. Feelings of sadness and anger are natural human responses to loss, and a serious illness is a loss that must be mourned. The healthy, autonomous self is harmed by the illness, as well as the physical body. Art therapy offers patients powerful tools for allowing those feelings to emerge, find expression, and be heard—allowing the healthy, whole person to replace the passive 'patient' identity (Councill, 2012). Patients' sense of competency and control are well served by the opportunity to tell their own stories, to invent personal symbols, to express feelings in metaphor, and to reflect on life experiences.

Especially with cancer, the outcome of treatment may only be known over time, and there is often little the patient can do other than to take medicine and wait. Art therapy puts the patient-artist in control—what kind of art to create, whether the product is 'good' or 'bad,' what it means, and whether it is to be saved or thrown away, are decisions that only the artist can make. That small measure of control can help patients step out of their isolation and fear.

Adjustment

Art can be adapted to any age and to almost any level of neurological and developmental functioning. Councill writes of her work with pediatric cancer patients, that,

> offering familiar materials with the skilled therapist's support can reassure the ill child that he or she is still a person with a great deal to offer . . . When a child is ill, words often fail, either because the child's vocabulary does not match the experience or because the ill child feels he must protect the adults around him from his feelings.
>
> (Councill, 2012, p. 228, referencing Bluebond-Langner, 1978)

Art therapy can open the door to metaphorical expression: A dragon made of clay can telegraph a child's anger and confusion, but it can't really hurt anyone. When symbolic artwork is accepted and understood, the child is also validated and encoded messages received.

Cognitive Development, Agency, and Resiliency

A medical diagnosis can affect one's sense of self-esteem and efficacy, and impact cognitive and social development. Separated from daily routines of school, family, and friends, a child's identity is challenged. Children have access to the full range of human emotions, but their ability to reason and understand the curative intent of treatment is determined by their age, cognitive development, and social support:

- *Very young children* sense that their parents are frightened, but they may not be able to understand why. They may try to be 'good,' so as not to further upset the family, and perceive treatment as a punishment for being 'bad.'

- *School-age children* may grasp the seriousness of their illness, but focus on changes in their appearance, such as hair loss and weight gain, due to the side effects of chemotherapy, and missing out on school and friends.
- *Teenagers and young adults* often put their future on hold during treatment, and risk losing opportunities they worked hard to attain. They also give up much of their autonomy and accept care and supervision from parents and medical personnel. Anger and withdrawal are common coping strategies for ill teens and young adults. The question of blame, rooted in the magical thinking of early childhood, echoes throughout all stages of development as patients and parents alike wonder why this happened to them.

An individual case of childhood cancer is seldom the result of any identifiable cause, certainly not the result of anything the patient has done. Such a diagnosis can lead to a sense of hopelessness and depression because it seems that one's actions do not matter. The social science concept of personal agency refers to the ability of an individual to influence his or her life circumstances by taking action. Explaining this concept, Bandura (1999) writes, "unless people believe that they can produce desired effects by their actions, they have little incentive to act or persevere in difficult circumstances" (p. 28). He continues, "those who believe they can relax, get engrossed in engaging activities, calm themselves by reassuring thought and support from friends, family, and others find unpleasant emotional states less aversive than those who feel helpless to relieve their emotional distress" (p. 30). Art therapy can help patients feel a renewed sense of agency by engaging them in processes that are both active and calming—allowing them to take small actions that can make enduring the illness and treatment more tolerable.

A Lesson in Agency

When I invited a 14-year-old boy to participate in the open art studio at the clinic where he received chemotherapy, he repeatedly refused. His main coping strategy seemed to be to isolate himself and ignore everything that was happening. One day when I invited him to the art table he angrily explained to me that he, personally, did not have cancer—only his body did—and that his 'real' self stayed at home while his body received treatment. He would not work with me because that would mean he would have to show up as a person, and he wasn't going to do that. I responded that it must be hard work to divide himself in two like that, and if he ever changed his mind, he was always welcome. Over the next few weeks, he gradually sat closer to the art therapy space and conversed with those who participated; during the last month of treatment, he even led a group art project. As I reflected on that experience, I realized that for some patients participating in art therapy might exact a personal cost: that I was asking patients to allow their hearts, minds, and imaginations to join in their treatment, not just their physical bodies.

A Resilient Response

Though many people regress in the face of illness, cancer treatment may go on for months, and even years, calling on patients to develop new coping strategies to help them move forward in the face of uncertainty. Engaging in creative work at a developmentally appropriate level can be profoundly normalizing and can help young patients reflect on their experiences and explain to others what it is like to cope with a serious illness.

A college student diagnosed with an immature teratoma fell into a coma soon after diagnosis. Though she did not require chemotherapy after hospitalization, she visited the outpatient clinic often to participate in the art therapy open studio.

She was grateful to have a good prognosis and minimal treatment, but was still profoundly shaken by the experience. She related that her friends and family expected her to be *happy* and *get back to normal*, but she felt phony when she tried to agree with them. In a watercolor painting, she depicted herself as a sunflower sheltered between two trees, and concluded that she needed family and friends to give her room to reflect on all she had been through (Figure 1.1).

Figure 1.1 A Patient's Reflection on Moving Forward After Treatment

As the patient became a creator in art therapy, the helplessness she experienced while in a coma was replaced by resiliency and a sense of personal agency. Working creatively and being heard allowed her to give form to her feelings and needs, as she began the process of rejoining her former life of school and friends.

Coping with Symptoms

Relieving, describing, and coping with symptoms are woven into the fabric of care for many people diagnosed with a serious illness. Fear of pain and distress over intrusion on body boundaries are common reactions to medical procedures, especially in children, who may have difficulty understanding the intent of the procedure. Patients with chronic illnesses often must deal not only with acute pain that signals a problem in need of treatment, but also with chronic pain that may be an ever-present part of life. Art therapy offers patients a proactive tool for coping with pain that is not fully relieved by medication and provides a way to gain mastery over frightening events (Councill et al., 2009).

Just as social isolation can exacerbate feelings of depression and hopelessness, a sense of belonging to a community can be a powerful source of support in recovery from trauma (Boss, Beaulieu, Weiling, Turner, & LaCruz, 2003). Illness may separate young people from ordinary activities that connect them to their community. Open studio art therapy in a treatment center brings patients together, creating opportunities to connect with others experiencing similar challenges.

Art Therapy and the Culture of Medicine

The power of art therapy is rooted in the combination of two inseparable elements: the creative process and the therapeutic alliance (Rubin, 1989, 2001). In medicine, a measured, targeted intervention causes a physical change to occur in the patient—an antibiotic clears an infection or a surgery repairs a broken bone.

Medical professionals follow treatment protocols with extreme precision under controlled conditions designed to achieve a desired outcome, but art therapy takes place in the ambiguous, messy, interpersonal side of life, and provides a complement to the precision of modern technology. It is within the witnessed creative process, and mutual reflection between client and therapist, that art therapy occurs. Being allowed to 'get messy' in the very clean hospital environment, and to engage in an open-ended creative process that doesn't have to be 'good' or 'bad,' are among the gifts art therapy brings to hospitalized patients.

Art Therapy and the Medical Environment

One key difference between art therapy in mental health and art therapy in medicine is that most of the time medical patients do not have mental health diagnoses. Pediatric oncology patients are typically "normal children dealing with abnormal circumstances" (Councill, 1993, p. 78). They come to the hospital seeking treatment for a medical condition, not for psychotherapy, and it is important for the art therapist to teach patients and families how art therapy can help.

The building blocks of medical art therapy include psychology, neuroscience, the study of creativity, the relationship between the body and the mind, and the theory and practice of art therapy, which elucidates many approaches to the healing potential of the visual arts. Art therapists may support coping during active treatment, facilitate the transition from treatment to the end of treatment, or work with patients and families at the end of life.

Cancer and other serious medical conditions are so prevalent that it is likely the therapist or a member of her family may one day experience a serious illness. Especially when there is a cancer history in the therapist's family, there may be less emotional distance between therapist and client. Managing one's counter-transference is essential to practicing in medicine. Witnessing the daily suffering of children and adults can bring up feelings of hopelessness and burnout, but helping patients find hope and self-expression during suffering can be extremely rewarding.

Adaptive Models

A great deal of medical art therapy is done in settings that are not very private for the patient. In a clinic or infusion center, much of what is said and created is apparent to everyone in the area. In a hospital room, family members, visitors, and healthcare professionals must be included, excluded, or managed in some way before therapy can begin. The art therapist working at a patient's bedside is essentially a guest in the patient's home (Givens, 2008). Medical art therapists create a safe environment by teaching patients, family members, and healthcare providers to allow open-ended creative work without judging and questioning. Patience, humor, empathy, and humility give the medical art therapist the poise to teach patients, families, and hospital caregivers about art therapy—and the ability to recognize when therapeutic work is not possible at a given moment.

There may be times when simply enduring treatment consumes all the patient's energy, and he or she may not have the capacity to engage in art therapy. The art therapist may be one of the few persons in the hospital to whom the patient can say 'no.' This writer was once 'fired' loudly by an angry teenager, admitted on an inpatient medical unit for five consecutive days, when she was in a dangerous health crisis. After discharge, the art therapist asked why she was so resistant in the hospital. The teen replied, *when I was in the hospital I thought I was going to die, and if you came in I would start talking about it and I would start to cry—and I didn't want to cry, so I had to fire you!* In her medical crisis, the emotional bond between the patient and her art therapist made the patient feel too vulnerable to cope with the crisis at hand. Temporarily 'firing' her art therapist gave the patient a measure of control. The art therapist who models resilience in the face of unexpected challenges joins with the patient in a therapeutic alliance that is both meaningful and malleable.

Stabilization and Processing Trauma

One thing that distinguishes the art therapist from nearly any other medical treatment team member is expertise in processing trauma. Trauma occurs when an event is so overwhelming it cannot be assimilated into long-term memory (van der Kolk, Hopper, Freyd, & DePrince, 2001). Though there may be no conscious memory of the event, it is stored as nonverbal, sensory information that can be re-experienced out of context in the form of 'flashbacks,' panic attacks, and other manifestations of post-traumatic stress (Councill, 2016).

Medical traumas might be major events, such as the diagnosis itself, or small but cumulative experiences, such as needle sticks or painful dressing changes. The ability to express and release medical traumas as they are happening mitigates the collective impact of the trauma moving forward (Chapman, 2014). Regardless of the source of the trauma, its manifestations can affect patients' ability to cooperate with treatment, interrupt sleep, and diminish concentration. Nonverbal techniques for processing trauma can help patients integrate troubling material and promote coping.

Trauma processing in medical art therapy may begin by repurposing radiation masks, painting with syringes, and making found object sculptures using medical items. Displacement into art-making renders medical equipment less threatening, as it puts the patient-artist in control.

Trauma Processing: Post Bone Marrow Transplant Mother–Daughter Art Therapy

A 16-year-old patient experienced a bone marrow transplant to cure her sickle cell disease. Two years later, though the sickle cell disease was cured, the patient still experienced many challenging side effects. She spent much of the year following transplant recovering from graft vs. host disease (GVHD), which altered her appearance, and avascular necrosis (bone death), of her knees and elbows.

In the patient's own words, she sought individual art therapy sessions because *I know I don't have sickle cell anymore, but the transplant was so hard and with all the side effects it doesn't seem like it's really over. I look in the mirror and I still see my puffy face and bald head and my skin GVHD. The thing about art therapy is that when I am creating, I can think of what I want to say and just talk to you about what is on my mind.* The patient herself identified two of her trauma symptoms: re-experiencing and body dysmorphia.

She faced the possibility of going back to school in a wheelchair in the fall, but meanwhile was preparing for an innovative surgical procedure that might enable her to walk again. We set about a process of reflecting on her transplant experiences by creating an altered book. The surgery yielded dramatic success, although the hospital stay was miserable. During her first visit after surgery, she could walk with only crutches (the good news) while working through feelings of frustration at being misunderstood and undertreated for pain in the hospital (the bad news). She added several self-portrait drawings to her altered book and then set the project aside.

She was walking unassisted and beginning to look forward to the prospect of a 'normal' year of school ahead, without medical problems interfering. In art therapy, she moved on to create two fascinating clay sculpture self-portraits. Her process included much wetting, kneading, and folding of the clay, which she described as soothing. She was cautioned that by folding the clay she might incorporate air bubbles that would cause her piece to explode in the kiln. She folded the clay as she worked and reworked it, valuing the tactile process over the potential product. She seemed to experience a developmental regression to the kinesthetic stage that grounded her in her body and in the present moment, allowing her to integrate her traumatic experiences through the art.

When the sculpture (Figure 1.2) was complete, she allowed me to hollow it out as best I could, hoping to prevent it from exploding in the kiln. Nonetheless, a section of the back of the figure's head popped off in the firing. When confronted with the damaged piece, she said *it's ok, I'll just work with what I have. I kind of like it.* She painted the figure with underglazes in a patchwork design, echoing the appearance of her skin discolorations from GVHD, while elevating this quality into a design element that gave meaning to the brokenness of the figure itself.

She invited her mother into art therapy, encouraging her to experience the soothing qualities of working with clay. Our sessions evolved into parallel art-making, with both mother and daughter talking about their feelings and treatment experiences.

Her second small head sculpture (Figure 1.3) renders a similar form in a more abstract way. This time the clay piece fired safely, and she glazed the figure in a more naturalistic skin tone. The pair of sculptures illustrates a process of confronting and transforming loss, and moving toward integration.

Creating a Legacy

When the prognosis is poor, art therapy can give severely ill patients the opportunity to create a legacy, and to gently process feelings of love, gratitude, and impending separation. A teenage patient, whose cancer was extremely aggressive and metastatic at diagnosis, realized a few months into treatment that she was not getting better. She said to the art therapist, *I know I am not getting better. I am going to stop watching television because it is not productive. I want to do art every day and make gifts for my family and friends.* She embarked on a daily creative journey, making clay mugs and bowls glazed using a syringe-painting technique she invented, shrink-art jewelry for friends, and collage-covered water pitchers and canvases to express gratitude to her nurses and her love for her family. This extraordinary young woman died with the materials for a planned collage for her best friend at her bedside.

Figure 1.2 Broken Figure

A 4-year-old boy endured 18 months of treatment, but his aggressive cancer returned. When it became clear that his cancer was growing through every kind of chemotherapy, radiation, and surgery, and that there was no hope of cure, he and his family did an extraordinary thing. Instead of avoiding the awful truth, they pivoted to asking for every possible resource to help prepare him, his older sister, and his parents, for the inevitable loss.

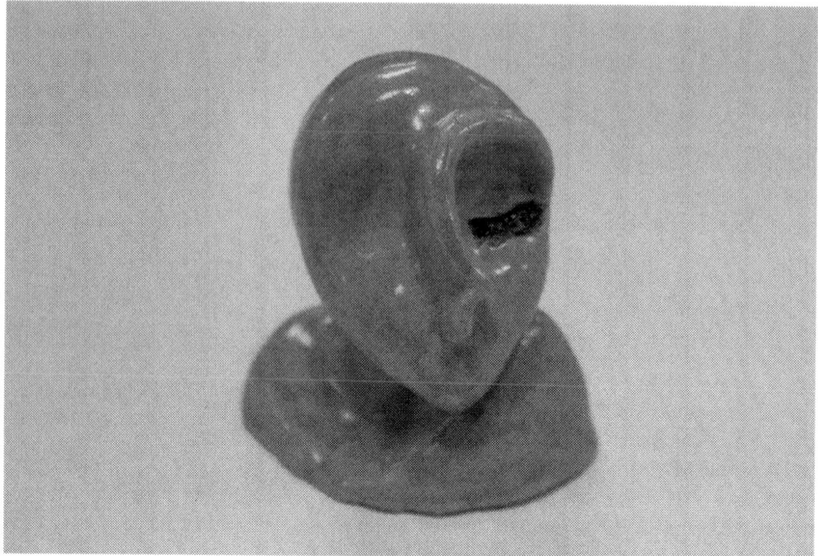

Figure 1.3 Abstraction

The parents asked the art therapy team that had been an integral support to their family to help them explain to their 10-year-old daughter that her brother would never get well. In the days that followed, the sister processed her experience in a series of multimodal art therapy sessions.

After she heard the bad news, she painted a 'police car' as a gift for her brother, finding comfort in doing her best to create a beautiful present for his room (Figure 1.4). The following day, she left the heavy atmosphere of the hospital room to do art therapy in the outpatient clinic. This time, she began by filling a canvas with a regressive, formless pile of glitter, glue, and puff paint, exclaiming repeatedly, *I love puff paint!* In the safety of art therapy, she sensed she could lower her defenses and pour out her pain and confusion and still regain control. She accepted a journal the art therapists offered and decorated it with her brother's name and the gold ribbon symbol for childhood cancer, stating her intention to write down her thoughts and questions whenever they came to mind so she could remember them and ask for help.

Three days before the patient died, the family asked us to help them create handprint artworks and a plaster cast of mom holding the patient's hand—tangible memories of their closeness and love (Figure 1.5).

Conclusion

Advances in modern medicine can cure illnesses that only a few decades ago were almost invariably fatal, but medical science cannot fully address the

Figure 1.4 Police Car

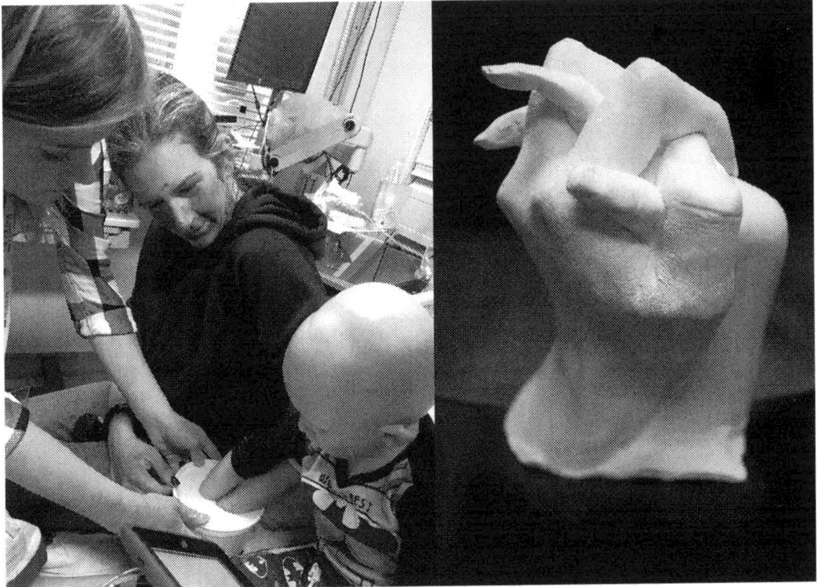

Figure 1.5 Lifecasting in the Hospital

human experience of illness and treatment. Art therapy in pediatric oncology helps patients and families actively engage in medical care, process experiences, and marshal their inner resources to endure and transcend the rigors of childhood cancer and its treatment.

References

Bandura, A. (1999). Social cognitive theory: An agentic perspective. *Asian Journal of Social Psychology, 2*(1), 21–41. doi: 10.1111/1467-839X.00024

Bluebond-Langner, M. (1978). *The private worlds of dying children*. Princeton, NJ: Princeton University Press.

Boss, P., Beaulieu, L., Weiling, E., Turner, W., & LaCruz, S. (2003). Healing loss, ambiguity and trauma: A community-based intervention with families of union workers missing after the 9/11 attack in New York City. *Journal of Marital and Family Therapy, 29*(4), 455–467. doi: 10.1111/j.1752–0606.2003.tb01688.x

Chapman, L. (2014). *Neurobiologically informed trauma therapy with children and adolescents: Understanding mechanisms of change*. New York, NY: W. W. Norton & Company.

Councill, T. (1993). Art therapy with pediatric cancer patients: Helping normal children cope with abnormal circumstances. *Art Therapy: Journal of the American Art Therapy Association, 10*(2), 78–87. doi: 10.1080/07421656.1993.10758986

Councill, T. (2012). Medical art therapy with children. In C. A. Malchiodi (Ed.), *Handbook of art therapy* (2nd ed., pp. 222–240). New York, NY: Guilford Press.

Councill, T. (2016). Art therapy with children. In D. Gussak & M. Rosal (Eds.), *The Wiley handbook of art therapy* (pp. 242–251). West Sussex, UK: John Wiley & Sons.

Councill, T., Barron, K., Padden, J., Rubin, C., Masterson, J., & McCaw, J. (2009). Art therapy and pain. In G. Herman & M. French (Eds.), *Making the invisible visible: Chronic pain manual for health care professionals* (pp. 203–206). Potomac, MN: Pain Connection.

Givens, S. (2008). Home hospice art therapy: Re-storying the therapist as an invited guest. *Art Therapy: Journal of the American Art Therapy Association, 25*(3), 134–136. doi: 10.1080/07421656.2008.10129601

Rubin, J. A. (1989). *The art of art therapy*. New York, NY: Brunner/Mazel.

Rubin, J. A. (Ed.). (2001). *Approaches to art therapy* (2nd ed.). New York, NY: Brunner-Routledge.

van der Kolk, B. A., Hopper, J. W., Freyd, J. F., & DePrince, A. P. (2001). Exploring the nature of traumatic memory: Combining knowledge with laboratory methods. In J. J. Freyd & A. P. DePrince (Eds.), *Trauma and cognitive science: A meeting of minds, science, and human experience* (pp. 9–31). Binghamton, NY: Haworth.

van Eys, J. (1981). The truly cured child. In J. Spinetta & P. Spinetta (Eds.), *Living with childhood cancer* (pp. 30–40). St. Louis, MO: Mosby.

2 The Application of Technology Within the Medical Environment

Tablet, Apps, and Stylus

Deborah Elkis-Abuhoff

In the age of technology, when even our medical records are digitized, art therapy can also find its place. When someone thinks of the application of art therapy, they usually think of materials such as paint, clay, pencils, pastels, canvases, and potter wheels. As technology becomes a staple in our everyday lives, it is important to dovetail this tool into the list of art therapy media available within the therapist's toolbox.

Introduction

Computer technology is everywhere these days, and the use of technology within art therapy is not a new concept. It is amazing that only 40 years have passed since the first home computer was launched, and how quickly it became commonplace during the 1980s. Art therapists were actively considering its impact by the mid-1990s; Parker-Bell (1999) discussed how the future of art therapy might incorporate computer technology, looking at basic computer hardware and software, and the importance of matching the technology correctly to specific populations. In addition, Gussak and Nyce (1999) explored how computer technology can be added to the art therapist toolbox. They, like Parker-Bell, cautioned that the blind acceptance of applications might limit the art therapist from appropriately matching the needs of the client. Gussak and Nyce (1999) suggested the creation of the 'visual toolbox,' which would connect art therapists with program designers working together to develop applications that would bring technology into best practice, and ensure that the needs of the art therapist and the client were met. Although specifically designed art therapy applications are ideal, many creative applications have been developed since 1999, making technology more appropriately available for a wide array of populations. As a tube of paint or clump of clay is not specific media for only art therapy, being brought into the session and adapted to the client's needs, the same can happen with the various creative applications that are presently available.

The Rise of Technology Within the Art Therapy Profession

In 2000, Malchiodi published the first technology-focused text, *Art Therapy and Computer Technology: A Virtual Studio of Possibilities*, that fully focused on the influence of technology within the profession of art therapy. Malchiodi (2000) discussed the impact and opportunities that technology brings to the art therapy profession; for example, the art therapist's toolbox could now incorporate an array of digital media. Approaches such as photography, videotape, computer painting, and photo programs can support innovative ways for the client to engage in creative expression.

In addition to in-session application, the use of computers has allowed for the global art therapy world to connect through email, discussion groups, and real-time cyber chats (Malchiodi, 2000). These advancements have made the art therapy profession connected, allowing for sharing of ideas, knowledge, and information.

A survey was conducted in 2005, and again in 2012, targeting 250 art therapists, assessing how, and to what level, computer technology was being incorporated into practice (Orr, 2012). The outcome of the survey showed that over the 7-year period, the use of computers to manage an art therapy practice remained consistent with the increase in technology across the general population. Although there was also an increase in the use of technology as a tool in practice, art therapists reported that they still have reservations about its use, with the main reservation being ethical implications (Orr, 2012). As a result, the incorporation of technology as a tool in the art therapist's practice has not kept up, and more training and education are needed.

Alders, Beck, Allen, and Mosinski (2011) see the ethical considerations as twofold: first, the use of technology to engage clients in the therapeutic process, and second, through clinical record keeping. In 2011, the American Art Therapy Association (AATA) addressed the growing use of technology within the profession, stating that "art therapy by electronic means is a new and evolving application of art therapy" (American Art Therapy Association, 2011, p. 9). The AATA continued to discuss that technology creates both opportunities and ethical dilemmas that had not been encountered in the past. AATA guidelines state that "art therapists are advised to use caution as the ethical ramifications of providing art therapy services via the Internet and other electronic means emerge" (American Art Therapy Association, 2011, p. 9). The Art Therapy Credentials Board (ATCB) (2011) also addresses the ethical use of technology in the areas of practice management (record keeping, distance art therapy services, and proper assessment of the client, as well as legal ramifications and electronic transmission of clinical records). Although the ethical consideration is focused on practice management, the use of technology to engage the client is growing, and these benefits and opportunities need to be further explored.

The good news is that the conversation has only continued to grow. Gretchen Miller, a leader in utilizing social media to create a virtual art therapy community, has served as web editor for AATA and on the Association's Social Media Committee, as well as initiated online communities such as Art Therapy Alliance and 6 Degrees of Creativity. Through her work, she has brought together art therapists, as well as other expressive therapists, and those interested in the profession on a global scale. In her text, Miller (2018) focused on the impact of the growing virtual community and how it can be utilized to support the art therapy profession, in addition to the impact of social networking to bring connection, develop community, and enhance creativity.

Technology Within Art Therapy Applications

As computer technology continues to grow in professional management and social media, it has also grown within art therapy studios and has become more common in the art therapists' toolbox. Evans (2012) discussed how easily accessible and friendly computers can be, making them perfect to include in the therapeutic repertoire. Software, and/or downloading an application, can be easily obtained and cost-efficient. Creativity software has even been compared on the same level of creativity as traditional art, allowing creative expression in places previously unobtainable, and introducing a new means of expression. Additionally, computer created/virtual artwork is easy to file, it does not take up valuable space in the studio/art therapy room, and yet it is easily available for review and/or assessment evaluations (Evans, 2012). In fact, Kim (2017) introduced the computerization of art therapy, in which art therapists could utilize computerized systems to perform the steps of evaluation and interpretation. Engaging a client in technology-based art therapy also can allow for new discoveries and "expressive spontaneity" (McNiff, as cited in Evans, 2012, p. 52).

Even the simple curiosity of new and different computer programs can increase communication and psychosocial engagement. The use of technology may be less intimidating than being faced with traditional art materials (Evans, 2012). Many times, a client will become overwhelmed by a blank piece of paper or the thought of handling a new medium for fear of making a mistake that will either waste materials or require a need to work around. Because most people are at least minimally exposed to computers, they enter the session with some level of familiarity and comfort when presented with a computer or tablet. Art, design, and creative applications are developed to "buffer frustrations or fears in clients, focusing solely on the creative product without acknowledging the vital importance of the process. A program's ability to respond to a variety of input may increase the likelihood of success" (Evans, 2012, p. 52). This approach allows the process to take place more naturally, without the client feeling stressed or intimidated by a 'not doing it right' type of self-talk. Computers allow the user to explore and create, without worrying about making a mistake that will not allow them to have the final project they hoped for, or waste paper and materials in the process of 'getting it right.'

Brooke (2017) brings together the application of computers through social media, online and in session when working with clients. This allows for the creative arts to be supported by computer technology on many levels. Whether the client is blogging, connected to others through online support groups, cyber counseling or by digital means within the therapeutic session, one thing is for sure, computers have changed the way the art therapeutic process is approached.

The Use of Technology Within the Medical Community

Specifically within medical environments, such as a chemotherapy treatment room or on a pediatric hematology unit, the use of iPad/tablet has allowed for barriers to be broken and art therapy to have its impact. Below is an example of how iPad/tablet technology has been able to do just that, allowing art therapy to go places that have previously been limited.

It is known that medical facilities maintain a clean environment as it is a necessity when receiving chemotherapy or a blood transfusion. Bringing the iPad/tablet into the treatment room is exactly what Elkis-Abuhoff, Gaydos, and Goldblatt (2017) have done. Working within the cancer center of a large health system, and with the support and enthusiasm of the doctors and nurses, art therapy was able to be incorporated in vivo with patients receiving chemotherapy for colon cancer.

Bringing Art Therapy to the Cancer Treatment Center

The standard procedure at the cancer treatment center is to bring the patient into the treatment room, a series of individual cubicles, and assign an oncology nurse who discusses and administers the chemotherapy treatment (Elkis-Abuhoff et al., 2017). As a clean environment, the cubical has a reclining chair for the patient, regular chair for the person accompanying the patient, a meal tray, and an IV pole—nothing more. Patients will remain in the cubical for about 3 to 4 hours from start to finish of their treatment. During this time, no services engage the patient in distraction or supportive emotional therapy.

This is a perfect situation to bring in art therapy; in the past, this facility found that it was not conducive, because art supplies can become messy, even pencils can lead to shavings, and the goal is to maintain as clean an environment as possible. With the use of the iPad/tablet, patients were able to engage in therapeutic artwork during treatment, which allowed the individuals to express themselves while in the moment, not hours or days later. Elkis-Abuhoff et al. (2017) worked in real time with the patient and communicated with the treatment team if there are any concerns.

As art therapists are aware, the engagement in art media and its tactile properties are extremely important for the client to experience. Barber and Gardener (2017) discussed that the use of computer technology creates an opportunity that is new and different, and still allows for tactile engagement; through the manipulation of the keyboard, touchscreens, and styluses, the client can become fully engaged in the tactile experience. The computer as a medium can bring visceral sensations through the creation of virtual artwork. Applications have been developed to allow the user to fully engage in the creative process using painting, drawing, and clay manipulation tools, full color palates, and texture options, which all bring depth and perspective to the creative piece.

The Case of Charles

Charles, a 64-year-old married male, with two married daughters, a married son, and three grandchildren, was recently diagnosed with colon cancer; he was initiating his chemotherapy treatment prior to surgery in hopes of shrinking the tumor that has formed in his colon. Charles arrived at the center for his first treatment accompanied by his wife, who left shortly after to take care of some medical billing. He was quiet and expressed a moderate amount of nervousness and concern.

Charles' treatment had just started when the art therapist arrived to his cubical to introduce herself and offer art therapy through technology. Charles was intrigued, although he stated that he did not really understand the computer, or was he an artist. He took the iPad/tablet and the stylus brush. The art therapist reviewed and demonstrated the three applications loaded onto the iPad/tablet and made sure they were ready for Charles to create artwork.

The tablet had three applications for Charles to explore: ArtRage©, Zen-Brush©, and 123D Sculpt©. ArtRage© (2017) allowed Charles to use the stylus brush to paint and provided a wide variety of virtual painting tools including an oil brush, watercolor brush, paint tube, paint roller, palette knife, inking pen, felt pen, gloop pen, glitter tube, color sampler, fill tool, pencil, airbrush, and wax/chalk pastel. Charles could customize the thickness of the brush stroke, the specific color he wanted, and the amount of blending, among several other options. Zen Brush (2017) creates a more meditative experience. In the tradition of Japanese ink brush, the stylus brush produces easy and fluent strokes while creating the feel and texture of a real ink brush. Charles was also able to choose the brush size, ink density, and the created work was a true expression of feelings and atmosphere. Finally, 123D Sculpt (n.d.) brings the power of clay manipulation (naturally a messy medium) into the chemotherapy treatment room. This app allowed Charles to tactilely engage with his fingers to virtually manipulate a basic clay shape, such as a head, body, airplane, dog, or geometric form, by utilizing the tools within the application to create his own sculpture.

In the first session, Charles explored all the apps and enjoyed finding new ways to paint, draw, and sculpt. At the end of the session, he shared with the art therapist that he really enjoyed exploring the features provided by the iPad/tablet, and it made the treatment time easier to bear. This started a ritual for Charles. As he entered each chemotherapy treatment session, he would settle in and then ask for the art therapist to bring him an iPad/tablet and stylus. He even stated that he often thought about what he wanted to create during the session as part of his preparing for treatment. As the treatments continued, Charles became fully engaged in the creative process.

There were times when he didn't want to talk or discuss his virtual art. While other times he asked if his companion, usually his wife, but there were times that one of his children would accompany him, could have an iPad/tablet to do work also. During those times, he admitted that he wanted to create during the chemo session, and was hoping that the iPad/tablet would distract whoever joined him. There were a few times that he even asked for an additional stylus so his wife could create with him. Then there were days that he would accept the iPad/table, but would put it on the side and never engage. Charles seemed to gain a sense of control through his management of the iPad/tablet. This is an important component because medical patients often feel powerless within the chaotic medical situation. Through all the days Charles honored what he needed to do, and so did the art therapist. Whether it was to discuss the artwork created; catch up with Charles' medical treatments and preparation for surgery; verbally discuss fear, anxiety, and depression; or just sit quietly sharing space and time, the art therapist allowed Charles to guide the sessions for where he was in the moment.

One of the more engaging and meditative apps for Charles was Zen Brush©. He used the stylus to spontaneously let the brush move along the paper (tablet) and watched what developed. Many times, he would just play with the brush to explore different outcomes. If he didn't like it, which was often the case, he would just delete it. The fun part about deleting a drawing on Zen Brush© is that the drawing fades away with a rippling effect, and doesn't just disappear.

In one of the earlier chemotherapy sessions, Charles used Zen Brush© to depict how he was feeling on that specific day. Charles created a visual of another planet where he is alone, and there is no place to hide (Figure 2.1). He continued to say that on this *distant* planet, the ground is flat and there is very little vegetation growing or anything to eat. There was no sun on this planet, so the *temperature is on the cold side, not warm at all, and the sky stays gray and cloudy*. He added that he liked that the app allowed him to create in only black, white, or gray because he couldn't put color to the planet.

When asked to discuss how the drawing connected to how he was feeling, Charles shared that he was very scared, overwhelmed, and depressed. Over the past several years, he had been planning to retire and start traveling—something he and his wife looked forward to sharing as they grew older. However, now he doesn't really know what tomorrow will bring or if he will be able to *defeat* the cancer. He felt alone and that this was his personal fight that no loved one can help him overcome. He said he felt like he let his family down, and that life stopped because he was ill. Charles explained that he presently felt lost, *like being on another planet*, where he's alone and there is no place to hide. Charles and the therapist discussed that his created drawing was not a place that looked comfortable, and that they needed to figure out a way to return to Earth safely. The discussion continued to explore Charles' support systems, understanding of his illness, the reason for the chemotherapy, and attempting to keep Charles focused on the here and now so he doesn't become overwhelmed with attempting to take on planning his long-term future. This helped Charles gain some perspective and control over his present state.

Charles was then asked to create a visual using any of the apps to represent how he's responding to his diagnosis (Figure 2.2). Once again, he chose to

Figure 2.1 Zen Brush: How Charles Sees His Illness Today

Figure 2.2 How Charles Is Responding to His Diagnosis

work in Zen Brush© because he didn't want to think about colors. This time Charles' artwork showed a lot of movement in the upper left, with a burst-like shape, then several lines moving from the upper right to lower left, and finally a small sailboat in the lower right corner.

Charles explained that when he received his diagnosis, it was like a bomb went off. The upper right depicts that moment. After that moment, there had been so many things that occurred, between doctor appointments, chemotherapy treatment, feeling ill in response to treatment, scans, and preparing for the surgery. He felt like the little sailboat on the bottom *hauling ass* to get away from the storm that's after him. It appears that the sailboat has wind in its sails and it is moving quite quickly through the waters.

As the art therapist and Charles discussed this drawing, it became apparent that Charles had great resilience and fight in him. Presently, he was feeling overwhelmed, depressed, and anxious, which are all normal reactions to this abnormal situation. The key was to help Charles to stay focused on small periods of time and connected to resources so he could feel as though he could have control over his situation. Things such as connecting to support, helping him find answers to questions, understanding his illness and medical treatment, and allowing him to have control over which course he felt would lead to the best outcome for himself.

Several weeks later, Charles created Figure 2.3 with the 123D Sculpt application. When discussing it with the art therapist, Charles shared that the egglike shape, to which he added a raised rim and a small indent, represented his body. It was painted in a teal, yellow, and dark blue, with a fractured element near one of the ends and by the indentation.

Charles explained how the egg is a representation of his own body, it is fragile now and is fighting off the cancerous tumor in his colon. Results of his last scan showed improvement, with the tumor reducing in size as hoped. Charles stated that he will always be different and a little broken since he will be having surgery, and a part of his colon will be removed. The fracture lines indicate this vulnerability. However, he kept the other side of the egg a solid dark blue, stating that the blue is his strength and about someday feeling whole again. What is interesting to note is that the fracture is also in the dark blue color. Maybe it is Charles' way of communicating that even though he is never going to be the same, his strength is still coming through.

During the final session, Charles used the ArtRage© app to depict a tree standing alone on the grass with a small sun in the upper right corner (Figure 2.4). Charles enjoyed playing with all the materials available within the application, especially the blending and adding drops of paint, which made it look three-dimensional.

This tree was the only piece Charles created that he wanted to title: "Me." He explained that he completed his chemotherapy, and the tumor has done exactly what the doctors had hoped: it shrunk significantly. He was excited to be finished with this phase of his treatment, but remained extremely apprehensive about the surgery.

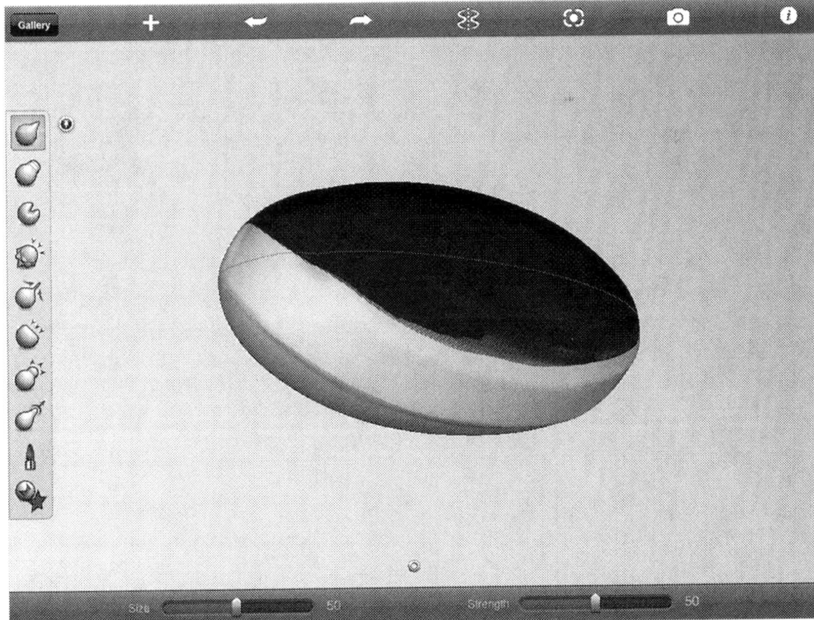

Figure 2.3 123D Sculpt: "My Body, My Life"

Figure 2.4 ArtRage© Application: Tree Titled "Me"

When asked about the tree and the title "Me," Charles said that he felt like he's still alone in this journey, but he is ready to get through the next part, and hopefully become cancer-free. He said he made the leaves with the paint to show some depth, and then noticed that the trunk has a knot in the area that he has the tumor in his colon, and where he will have the surgery.

It was apparent through Charles' discussion that he was ready to move forward. All along, he appeared to have an inner strength and resiliency to his approach. Although he still was scared, anxious, and depressed, he could manage his feelings, become educated about his illness and treatment, take things in small doses, and feel a sense of control over his illness.

Conclusion

Technology, using iPads/tablets, allows a medical patient to engage in art therapy in areas that in the past have been restricted due to the possibility of becoming messy in a medically clean environment. Charles used the iPad/tablet as a distraction during chemotherapy, which lead him to express his thoughts and feelings into something personal through the visual creations. The virtual art therapy experience brought the expressive and creative process into the chemotherapy room, in real time, which allowed Charles to be in the moment with his thoughts and feelings. Through creating virtual artwork and verbally processing with the art therapist, Charles could address the issues related to his diagnosis of colon cancer. This led him to gain insight, tap into resources, and gain a sense of control over his body and his treatment. With new and upcoming design and creative art applications, the use of art therapy through the iPads/tablet technology within the medical community will only grow and add new and exciting options for patients to engage.

References

123D Sculpt©. (n.d.). Retrieved from www.commonsensemedia.org/app-reviews/123d-sculpt

Alders, A., Beck, L., Allen, P. B., & Mosinski, B. B. (2011). Technology in art therapy: Ethical challenges. *Art Therapy: Journal of the American Art Therapy Association, 28*(4), 165–170. doi: 10.1080/07421656.2011.622683

American Art Therapy Association. (2011). *Ethical principles for art therapists*. Retrieved from www.americanarttherapyassociation.org/upload/ethicalprinciples.pdf

Art Rage (2017). Retrieved from www.artrage.com/artrage-ipad/

Art Therapy Credentials Board. (2011). *Code of professional practice*. Retrieved from www.atcb.org/code of professional practice

Barber, B. S., & Gardener, R. (2017). Materials and media: Developmentally appropriate apps. In R. Gardener (Ed.), *Digital art therapy: Material, methods, and applications* (pp. 67–77). London, UK: Jessica Kingsley Publishers.

Brooke, S. L. (Ed.). (2017). *Combining the creative therapies with technology: Using social media and online counseling to treat clients*. Springfield, IL: Charles Thomas Publishers, LTD.

Elkis-Abuhoff, D., Gaydos, M., & Goldblatt, R. (2017). Using tablet technology as a medium for art therapy. In S. L. Brooke (Ed.), *Combining the creative therapies with technology: Using social media and online counseling to treat clients* (pp. 53–73). Springfield, IL: Charles Thomas Publishers, LTD.

Evans, S. (2012). Using computer technology in expressive arts therapy practice: A proposal for increased use. *Journal of Creativity in Mental Health*, 7(1), 49–63. doi: 10.1080/15401383.2012.660127

Gussak, D. E., & Nyce, J. M. (1999). To bridge art therapy and computer technology: The visual toolbox. *Art Therapy: Journal of the American Art Therapy Association, 16*(4), 194–196. doi: 10.1080/07421656.1999.10129478

Kim, S. (2017). *Computational art therapy*. Springfield, IL: Charles Thomas Publishers, LTD.

Malchiodi, C. A. (2000). *Art therapy and computer technology: A virtual studios of possibilities*. London, UK: Jessica Kingsley Publishers.

Miller, G. (2018). *The art therapist's guide to social media: Connection, community and creativity*. New York, NY: Routledge.

Orr, P. (2012). Technology use in art therapy practice 2004 and 2011 comparison. *The Arts in Psychotherapy, 39*(4), 234–238. doi: 10.1016/j.aip.2012.03.010

Parker-Bell, B. (1999). Embracing a future with computers and art therapy. *Art Therapy: Journal of the American Art Therapy Association, 16*(4), 180–185. doi: 10.1080/07421656.1999.10129482

Zen Brush©. (2017). Retrieved from https://itunes.apple.com/us/app/zen-brush/id382200873?mt=8

3 Working with Children Who Encounter Medical Challenges

A Multimodal Approach

Joan Alpers

For hospitalized children, the sights, sounds, and smells associated with medicine and medical care can be foreign, frightening, and overwhelming; the intensity of the hospital experience can threaten a child's continued development and psychological well-being (Malchiodi, 1999; Plank, 1962; Turner, 2009). Children cope in relationship to their developmental level and support systems, beginning with family and extending to the care provider community. The degree to which children can tolerate actual or perceived life-threatening events, and integrate stressful healthcare experiences, is tied to prior experiences dealing with challenges and tolerating anxiety. The ability to regulate emotions is rooted in personality and early attachment (Ainsworth, Blehar, Walters, & Wall, 2015; Siegel, 2010).

This chapter will explore the emotional attitudes and expressions of children who have encountered medical illness and hospitalization through three different lenses of this writer's expertise: as an art therapist, a child life specialist, and a sandplay practitioner working within a child life program and private practice. Children are multimodal and naturally move in and out of different kinds of play, art expression, games, conversation, and sandplay within a very short frame of time when given choices (Gil, 2011; McCue, 2009). How children integrate different modalities, both in the hospital setting and after hospitalization, will be examined.

Child Life

In the North American hospital setting, child life programming has become the leader of psychosocial support for children facing medical challenges (American Academy of Pediatrics, 2014). Art and other expressive therapists for medically ill children are generally employed through child life programs. In a typical day, a child life specialist will prepare children for medical encounters in a language geared to each child's developmental level and provide opportunities for different types of play at bedside or in the hospital playroom. Child life specialists also support children during tests and procedures and offer therapeutic rewards for healthcare accomplishments, such as holding still during venipuncture or enduring a nasty tasting medicine.

Child life plays a significant role in normalizing the environment by celebrating birthdays, holidays, organizing school for lengthy inpatient stays, and hosting special events such as pet therapy or local community athlete and celebrity visits.

Malchiodi and Goldring (2013) defined psychosocial care as focusing on the psychological and social aspects of cognitive and emotional growth and development. This includes the ability to perceive, learn, express, analyze, and experience emotion, as well as to form attachments to caregivers, family members, and peers to maintain stable relationships and learn from the behaviors of one's cultural system (Malchiodi & Goldring, 2013). While psychosocial interventions for medical children are vital, emotional care in hospitals follows medical protocols (American Academy of Pediatrics, 2014). Therefore, the goal of child life is to take a proactive, not reactive, stance that utilizes supportive and therapeutic tools to maintain normalcy, prevent developmental or negative impact during medical care, and to provide a sense of mastery while children undergo experiences that are uncomfortable and overwhelming (McCue, 2009; Rode, 1995).

In addition to proactively preventing injury, child life desires to send children home with an experience that strengthens coping mechanisms, enriches understanding, and promotes new levels of learning and resilience (Child Life Council, 2016). As child life continues to form its own identity, the role of play remains the common denominator across theory, technique, and discipline (Turner, 2009), with the rationale that engaging in pretend play, and including play related to medical settings, can help decrease anxiety and stress (McCue, 2009; Moore & Russ, 2006). In his TEDx talk, Towne (2016), a fellow child life specialist, discussed "the kind of fun that cracks through crisis that comes from deep within and has to do with our spirit, our strength and our resilience." The sacred nature of play goes beyond the preservation of childhood and extends into the inner spirit, reaching deep within when everything else is uncertain, out of control, or sometimes downright depressing (Towne, 2016).

Incorporating Creative Arts Therapy in Child Life Practice

Art therapists are often assigned a caseload or provided referrals by the child life specialist who oversees an area or population of patients. An expressive therapist's understanding of the many interrelated facets of process in a hospital environment can be vital to psychosocial care. As described by Rode (1995), "art therapists can offer play experiences through a wide variety of creative arts modalities to create a transitional space in which the child, the family, and even the healthcare staff can experience a sense of 'order and connectedness' even in the face of serious illness" (p. 106).

Wikstrom (2005) reported three main themes observed in the art and play of hospitalized children: (1) fear/anxiety; (2) powerlessness; and (3) longing for the continuity of home, school, and family. Similarly, Rode (1995) identified the themes of: (1) separation from parents and relocation to a new environment, (2) loss of autonomy and control, and (3) fear of bodily harm and/or death. In the hospital setting, children are often disrupted by both the constant flow of unpredictable intrusions and acute changes in their physical condition. There is a stressful sense of not knowing, and children tend to be developmentally regressive, meaning that their ability to play or to make 'good art' is impaired. It can be hard to fall into an optimal creative mood when you are physically ill, tired, or frightened about who is going to stick you, and which person entering your room is going to do something intrusive or unpleasant to your body. At times, the very act of sitting still with someone in a frenetic world is more important than doing anything. It is not always about the art in the hospital setting, but it is always about the stillness. In other words, there are times where you just need to be present and predictable.

In my experiences supervising graduate art therapy interns, the students who approached patients by offering to sit quietly with them, or those who structured an intervention by playing a nonsense game first, tended to encourage more expressive art-making. One student put paper in a shoebox with a teaspoon of paint and invited children to roll a few marbles through the paint. This made abstract designs on the paper floor, delivering a playful picture that children thoroughly enjoyed. She then offered watercolor painting, and most children agreed to continue exploring.

As an art therapist and child life specialist on an adolescent unit, I would often draw a blank game template (blank squares following a square or circular path) and would ask teens to invent a game, including its title, rules, and how to win. Teens would decide the content in the blank squares and hand-write the game cards. The object of the game was often discharge and teens would write captions in the squares like *move ahead four spaces because you took your medicine, or go back three because you can't find a wheelchair.* On one game card, a boy wrote, *spilled the urinal all over your bed. Go back to start because you are embarrassed.* The power within the cards was that they were anonymously written and when they were read, everyone in the group could share and identify a moment when they felt challenged or distressed within the hospital setting.

Jessee and Gaynard (2009) described play as a child's most powerful tool when confronting the challenges of hospitalization, and enumerated on kinds of play within the healthcare setting. They identified play for enjoyment, which is integral to development in terms of both symbolic play and learning; play as comfort, such as the playroom safe space where no medical procedures are traditionally allowed; play as flow; and play as hope, where "children can take in an attitude toward the possible, explore a range of potential futures, or in effect, travel through time and space to a different or better childhood" (p. 154). Emma Plank (1962), the founder of child life, said, "children do not need diversion to get well, but rather opportunities to participate with all available emotional and intellectual energy in daily living" (p. 73).

Art-making within the hospital setting could be described utilizing the same play-based concepts while incorporating specific approaches for the medical population. Malchiodi and Goldring (2013) described two approaches in the art-making process, *manipulative*, for control and mastery of the environment, and *expressive*, using strategic and specific materials to meet or address affect expression or teach varying affects. Malchiodi (1998) explored two areas of expression with children facing medical challenges: somatic and spiritual. Somatic is defined as "relating to the physical body, distinct from the mind or environment, including characteristics which express or depict physical impairments or disabilities" (p. 173). This includes illnesses that are acute or chronic in nature and invasive treatment methods that result in physical discomfort or injury (Malchiodi, 1998); spiritual aspects of children's art refer to "content or characteristics that reflect children's experiences of God or intangible entities [and] phenomena that may extend beyond personal experience or across cultural experience" (p. 174).

An example of both somatic and spiritual content can be seen in the art of a 12-year-old girl, discharged from the hospital after a routine tonsillectomy. She was subsequently readmitted because of a frightening, primary tonsillar bleed that occurred at home. An art therapy intern, sitting quietly with her at bedside, did very little. Supplies were available for drawing if she wished, but instead, they sat for a while. The child then drew a picture as a gift to the intern (Figure 3.1); the jagged mountains in the picture look like stitches

Figure 3.1 Child Artwork as a Gift; the Writing at the Top of the Page, "Love Your Paintant," is Misspelled but Was Meant to Say "Love Your Patient"

and appear to be a somatic representation of surgery and discomfort. In the center is a sunset filled with unusual spiritual content, perhaps related to the threat of physical loss of life, pain, and the sudden fright of the tonsillar bleed.

Children live fully in their bodies, or are struggling to do so, even when dysregulation or intrusion threatens this natural connection (McCarthy, 2015). The experience of a life threat, real or imagined, is a physical and spiritual/mental experience; for a child who is still developing ego strength, it can be disruptive to further emotional well-being (Malchiodi, 2015). As proactive as child life is, some situations still call for a remedial working through, either after an acute event occurs or with repeat experiences in chronic conditions.

Early in my career, a group of children, all boys and familiar with one another from previous admissions, were hospitalized for asthma and gathered in the playroom on the pediatric unit to *become doctors in the ER.* Their patient, a bear or a doll, would enter the room gasping for air. The boys instantly rushed to their patient's aid and began performing CPR, intubation, and other remedies made up out of spoons, markers, and other objects in the room until one child would finally shout, *it's too late! He's dead.* The children would stand solemnly around the patient for a long 15 seconds until someone would say, *wait, I think I hear a heartbeat*, or *I think he's still breathing!* The boys would begin resuscitation again until the patient survived. This play happened repeatedly, as good play often does, and stretched over multiple admissions. Those same children drew pictures of people with mouths scribbled over or skies marred by scratchy marks that seemed to negate the flow of air (Alpers, 1989) (Figure 3.2).

A recent picture by an asthmatic boy collected by an art therapy intern similarly shows an underwater scene. Stippling around the nose of the shark, and densely colored water that would be difficult to swim through, could indicate trouble breathing (Figure 3.3).

Sandplay Therapy

The idea of doing nothing is a primary theme in sandplay that allows the inner person to stop and rest, in order to find resources for adaptation and creativity (Kalff, 1980; Weinrib, 2004.) Sandplay therapy is a modality consisting of the client's creation of a three-dimensional picture, with miniature figures in a tray of sand, in the protective presence of a trained practitioner. Many different psychodynamic and counseling perspectives make use of play therapy in sand for children and adults; however, only Jungian sandplay is based on the idea that the higher, governing part of our personality, which Jung called the Self, is a tool for psychic order and healing (Jung, 1954). Deeply rooted in sandplay is the notion that by suspending ego, one allows for other wiser and more intuitive healing resources to surface from the unconscious. The therapist refrains from much, if any, interpretation of the imagery, because to do so can impede the reparative power of the nonverbal process (Kalff, 1980; Weinrib, 2004).

Figure 3.2 Example of a Child's Artwork Response to Play

Imagery in sandplay is typically a finished scene of miniatures arranged in the tray, much like a drawing might be arranged on a paper; for younger children, the play can be less static and center around a story where the miniatures act, move around, and sometimes speak. In most cases, the medium combined with the Jungian approach encourages deep play in children. In this Jungian approach, rearranging of the sand and miniatures is considered

Figure 3.3 Underwater Scene

akin to rearranging psyche (Kalff, 1980; Weinrib, 2004). Because sandplay is a tactile medium, it engages the hands and the skin, and is an excellent medium for observing the liminal (transitional or threshold) space where psyche, or mind, touches the body, or soma (Ammann, 1991). In other words, the body speaks through the actions of the hands that are, in turn, willed by the mind

(Amatruda, 2010). In children, mind and body are still mixed and at times undifferentiated (McCarthy, 2015). When children are endangered in body and mind during a collision with serious illness, to ignore the body or not accommodate its expression is to miss the essence of the child (McCue, 2009).

Winnicott (1971) spoke to the value of transitional play space, or the space between, referring to the shared emotional space where the art of playing takes shape. The sharing of a space for play is a container of safety that Winnicott called transitional and Jung referred to as *temenos*, or sacred space. Play in the sand is sometimes referred to as *lila*, or sacred play. The sandbox acts as a *temenos*, a physical play space known as the patient's 'world' (Kalff, 1980), where miniatures arranged in the sand become a visual expression of a personal process, witnessed by the sandplayer and the therapist.

A previously healthy 4-year-old boy contracted a bacterial infection known as scalded skin syndrome, which quickly required a PICU hospitalization. The boy was heavily sedated for pain and was in and out of consciousness, unable to open his eyes for 4 days. His body was blistered and erythematous as his skin peeled away. Because the illness effects the nerves under the skin, any touch was excruciatingly painful. After discharge, his skin continued to peel from head to toes for months, and it hurt to walk.

I first met this boy 6 months after his hospitalization when he came to my private practice as a creative arts therapist and sandplay practitioner. His mother described a change to his temperament; once a calm and easygoing kid, now he would scream at everyone. He had difficulty self-soothing when he became upset and was suffering from nightmares.

In one sandplay session, the boy made images in two trays. In one tray, he kept the sand dry and placed houses laced with skeleton heads. While making the scene he told me about a bad dream, but explained that he could only share some of it because it was too scary. As he told me the dream, he moved to the other tray of sand. He asked me for *all my policemen and firemen* as he poured water into the second tray of sand, eventually drenching it. In the wet, muddy swamp of sand he placed a policeman and sunk him in the goo. When I asked, *what happens now?* he said, *he dies. His parents are home and they don't know, but it is on the news.* He found a miniature TV set and placed it in the tray, sinking it as well until it was symbolically irretrievable. He moved back to the first, dry tray and positioned three ghosts behind the houses before saying *they're dead.* He then took all the bugs in my collection and piled them atop the muddy places where the cop and TV were buried; physically shivering, he picked up some of the more dangly spiders before also shoving their heads into the mud. Finally, he took all the army men, tanks, and Power Rangers he could find and piled them over both trays without arranging them or setting them up to fight. He seemed hypervigilant and overwhelmed as he finished with the scene.

In sandplay sessions, most children move back and forth between expressive play in the sand and other creative modalities. All process follows the child's lead, but as the sandplay experience had ended with such a sense of defeat it seemed time to offer another medium to help facilitate a return to mastery. Because he was a prolific artist, I asked if he would like to try and draw. He initially agreed, but then asked if I would draw Harry Potter for him instead. As I drew, he informed me, *the scar is wrong* and instructed me on how to make it right. He then took a Harry figure from the sandplay shelf, and with the wand pointing outward, ordered *no more bad dreams!*

Giving form to inner experiences through play and imagination are integral to the liminal process of integration of bodily and spiritual/emotional well-being and helps to promote mastery and resilience. As demonstrated, after externalizing an overwhelming and traumatic experience in the sandplay, the boy asked the therapist to create an image of a scarred boy with magical powers. He then took over the play, this time with an increased sense of control, by first directing my artwork. Then, mixing the art-making with the symbolic power of the miniatures, he took on the role of the famous magician and ordered his nightmares away. Adopting a focus on resiliency emphasizes strengths, assets, and capabilities rather than disabilities. It also provides opportunity for a hopeful perspective rather than a trauma-laden and problem-focused viewpoint (Malchiodi & Goldring, 2013), and can be the goal even in the darkest of circumstances.

Terminal Illness

Whether providing art therapy, sandplay, or child life services within a hospital setting, clinicians must be prepared, and trained, to work with terminally ill patients. Figure 3.4 depicts the therapeutic process of a 21-year-old female faced with a life-threatening illness. She drew a scene above the ground line that was chaotic and unbearable. It looked like a raging storm with trees struck by lightning and birds flying off into the darkness.

In a supervision session, I explored the art of this patient with Furth, who believed that psyche and soma work hand in hand, a balancing process in every individual (1988). It seemed to us that while everything was falling apart in the world above ground—and indeed this was the truth for the patient in her real life—below the ground was a very methodical procession of ant trails, animals doing what they needed to do, storing up for winter, calmly going about their routines as if nothing was wrong. On another look, the ant trails formed the shape of a body buried under the earth. I could return to the patient and share that I noticed that there was so much disruption and difficulties going on in her picture; it reminded me of her recent frequent bouts of illness, multiple hospitalizations, and how the comfort of work, school, relationships, and life in general was constantly upended by her diagnosis. Yet, I wondered about the part of her, which was calm, clear, and resilient like the ant trails under the surface, that made me feel as if everyone and everything was proceeding with order and familiarity. Her mood brightened as we looked at the picture together and she replied, *you know, that is true. Everything that is happening to me is horrible and unsettling, but inside I have a certain peace of mind. I am good with myself. I'm OK.* This young woman

Figure 3.4 Artwork Created by a Terminally Ill Female

died 3 months later. The creative spirit in each of us takes as many forms as there are snowflakes in a winter scene. Encouraging all kinds of expression and flow with medically ill children is vital, especially for those transitioning into end of life.

Conclusion

Combined with a strong understanding of the role of development, the child life specialist in me seeks ways to offer mastery in an otherwise chaotic environment where choice and control are almost always limited. The art therapist in me values a psychoanalytic approach, where the unconscious can surface and be valued by another (Cavallo & Robbins, 1980; Robbins, 1998). Finally, it helps me to look at everything I do through the Jungian lens of sandplay, a modality that relies on the natural healing tendencies of psyche as its core philosophy, and where being an attuned witness and sometimes doing nothing is the most important form of presence (Kalff, 1980; Turner, 2009; Winter, 1999). Deep play is the river that runs through all these perspectives, reaching and nourishing the inner spirit, even when everything else is uncertain, out of control, or sometimes just downright depressing.

References

Ainsworth, M., Blehar, M., Walters, E., & Wall, S. (2015). *Patterns of attachment: A psychological study of the strange situation*. New York, NY: Psychology Press.

Alpers, J. (1989). *Art therapy and art diagnosis with chronically and physically ill children in the hospital setting*. Unpublished Master's Thesis, Pratt Institute, Brooklyn, NY, USA.

Amatruda, K. (2010). *The liminal world: Threshold between body and psyche*. Retrieved from Psyche & Soma: Psychotherapy and the Body: http://psychceu.com/psyche&somaintro.asp

Ammann, R. (1991). *Healing and transformation in sandplay: Creative processes become visible*. La Salle, IL: Open Court Publishing.

American Academy of Pediatrics. (2014). Policy statement: Child life services. *Pediatrics, 133*(5), e14711–e1478.

Cavallo, M. A., & Robbins, A. (1980). Understanding an object relations theory through a psychodynamically oriented expressive therapy approach. *The Arts in Psychotherapy*, 7(2), 113–123. doi: 10.1016/0197–4556(80)90017–9

Child Life Council. (2016). *Mission, values, and vision*. Retrieved October 4, 2016, from www.childlife.org/The%20Child%20Life%20Profession/ProfessionMissionVision

Furth, G. M. (1988). *The secret world of drawings: A Jungian approach to healing through art*. Boston, MA: Sigo Press.

Gil, E. (2011). *Helping abused and traumatized children: Integrating directive and non-directive approaches*. New York, NY: The Guilford Press.

Jessee, P. O., & Gaynard, L. (2009). Paradigms of play. In R. C. Thompson (Ed.), *Handbook of child life: A guide for pediatric psychosocial care* (pp. 136–159). Springfield, IL: Charles Thomas Publisher, LTD.

Jung, C. G. (1954). *The collected work of CG Jung*. Princeton, NJ: Princeton University Press.

Kalff, D. M. (1980). *Sandplay: A psychotherapeutic approach to the psyche*. Santa Monica, CA: Sigo Press.

Malchiodi, C. A. (1998). *Understanding children's drawings*. New York, NY: Gilford Press.

Malchiodi, C. A. (1999). *Medical art therapy with children*. New York, NY: Jessica Kingsley Publishers.

Malchiodi, C. A. (2015). Neurobiology, creative interventions and childhood trauma. In C. A. (Ed.), *Creative interventions with traumatized children* (pp. 3–23). New York, NY: The Guilford Press.

Malchiodi, C. A., & Goldring, E. (2013). Art therapy and child life: An integrated approach to psychosocial care with pediatric oncology patients. In C. A. Malchiodi (Ed.), *Art therapy and healthcare* (pp. 48–60). New York, NY: The Guilford Press.

McCarthy, D. (2015). Deep sand: Body-centered imaginative play. In D. McCarthy (Ed.), *Deep play: Exploring the use of depth in psychotherapy with children* (pp. 121–141). New York, NY: Jessica Kingsley Publishers.

McCue, K. (2009). Therapeutic relationships in child life. In R. C. Thompson (Ed.), *Handbook of child life: A guide for pediatric psychosocial care* (pp. 57–77). Springfield, IL: Charles Thomas Publisher, LTD.

Moore, M., & Russ, S. (2006). Pretend play as a resource for children: Implications for pediatricians and health professionals. *Developmental and Behavioral Pediatrics, 27*(3), 237–248.

Plank, E. (1962). *Working with children in hospitals*. Cleveland, OH: Western Reserve Press.

Robbins, A. (1998). *Therapeutic presence*. New York, NY: Jessica Kingsley Publishers.

Rode, D. (1995). Building bridges within the culture of pediatric medicine; The interface of art therapy and pediatric medicine. *Art Therapy: Journal of the American Art Therapy Association, 12*(2), 104–109. doi: 10.1080/07421656.1995.10759140

Siegel, D. J. (2010). *Mindsight: Our seventh sense*. New York, NY: Bantam.

Towne, M. (2016). *Fun in the face of crisis. TedxPeace Plaza*. Retrieved September 8, 2018, from https://www.youtube.com/watch?v=T_Kvefokrpw.

Turner, J. C. (2009). Theoretical foundations of child life practice. In R. C. Thompson (Ed.), *Handbook of child life: A guide for pediatric psychosocial care* (pp. 23–35). Springfield, IL: Charles Thomas Publisher, LTD.

Weinrib, E. L. (2004). *Images of the self: The sandplay therapy process*. Cloverdale, CA: Tamenos Press.

Wikstrom, B. (2005). Communicating via expressive arts: The natural medium of self-expression for hospitalized children. *Pediatric Nursing, 31*(6), 480–485.

Winnicott, D. W. (1971). *Playing and reality*. New York, NY: Tavistock.

Winter, R. (1999). Sandplay and ego development. *Journal of Sandplay Therapy, 8*(1), 91–105.

4 The Use of Magic Therapy for Children with Hemiplegia

Yvonne Farquharson, Richard McDougall, and Daisy Fancourt

A sense of wonder is a feeling one rarely forgets.

I remember feeling that sense of wonder so profoundly when I sat in a small dark theater in London 8 years ago. I had just seen a magician do something seemingly impossible right in front of my eyes. He started by showing us, his captive audience, a normal piece of rope. He gripped both ends with each hand and tugged it strongly to show its strength and solidity. He then took a pair of scissors from a table next to him, and cleanly cut the rope into two equal pieces. The limp pieces of rope fell and swayed from side to side as the magician stood completely still. He put the scissors back on the table, and lifted both pieces of rope towards his mouth. He paused, and then blew gently on the separate strands. As if by the power of his breath alone, it became one length of rope again. He pulled at both ends vigorously to show it had indeed been restored. I let out a belly laugh, mostly through shock. The rest of the audience clearly felt the same, as there followed a prolonged and wild applause.

It was a remarkable performance for many reasons. Firstly, the magician on stage was only 7 years old. He was a small, slight, blonde-haired boy who just 2 weeks earlier had had to opt out of participating in a school assembly due to a lack of confidence. Sat at the back of the school hall in tears, with his teacher by his side, as he watched his classmates and friends continue without him. But now, there he was, standing in front of an audience of over 100 people, grinning with pride, as he confidently stood and accepted his applause.

Secondly, this little boy has a condition called hemiplegia. His condition is the result of a brain injury at birth, and the movement in his right hand and arm had been seriously affected. In fact, his right hand had remained tightly closed and fisted his whole life. This meant that everyday activities were a major challenge for him, as he was unable to get dressed independently and eat using a knife and fork. He could not put on his bike helmet and click it shut by himself or play musical instruments like his friends.

Ten days before walking in to the theater in which he performed, he couldn't extend his fingers and thumb out of a fist position, and so consequently couldn't have even manipulated the grasp pattern required to hold the rope, let alone have the strength to pull both ends of the rope with equal force, without letting go of one end. Even before walking on stage that evening, he had put on his crisp white shirt independently and fastened his buttons unaided. In just 10 days he had not only become a young magician, but he was also on the way to become an independent young boy. Things that seemed impossible 10 days ago, were becoming possible, right before our eyes. This was the real magic.

—Author's account

Introduction

This chapter will introduce the challenges posed by the condition of childhood hemiplegia; a partial or total paralysis on side of the body. It will consider how the therapeutic effects of magic and drama have been combined to provide a unique solution now available within the UK National Health Service: the Breathe Magic program. Breathe Magic was developed by Breathe Arts Health Research, a UK-based social enterprise company that has been using magic within healthcare settings since 2008. The transformative impact of the program will be identified through robust clinical research and the mechanisms by which these effects are achieved.

Understanding Hemiplegia

Childhood hemiplegia (otherwise known as spastic unilateral cerebral palsy) is characterized by predominant unilateral motor impairment. It is the most common type of cerebral palsy, and may be acquired later in childhood through injury or damage to the motor centers in the brain (Bax et al., 2005; Ferriero, 2004). Hemiplegia has approximately the same incidence rate as Down syndrome, with one in two children having an additional diagnosis, such as epilepsy; some children experience challenges such as perceptual problems, learning difficulties, and behavioral or emotional issues (Bax et al., 2005; Ferriero, 2004). Children with hemiplegia have difficulty manipulating objects and performing actions needed for independence in many daily activities.

Hemiplegia is notoriously difficult to treat. Many interventions have an invasive and painful component (e.g., splinting, casting, Botox injections, and surgery) and also require additional physiotherapy, occupational therapy, and home-based therapy, without significant results (Eliasson, Krumlinde-Sundholm, Shaw, & Wang, 2005; Wallen, O'Flaherty, & Waugh, 2007). This continued therapy is typically costly and rarely available on the UK National Health Service (NHS); even when it is, it has limited uptake and no evidence of benefits to functional independence (Eliasson et al., 2005; Wallen et al., 2007; Wallen, Ziviani, Herbert, Evans, & Novak, 2008). Another approach is to use task-focused interventions recommended by the UK National Institute for Health Care and Excellence (NICE) such as constraint-induced movement therapy (CIMT). However, these frequently lead to frustration in participation or lack of motivation, and have not received universally positive responses, and the home-based exercises that accompany CIMT have a low adherence rate (Eliasson et al., 2005; Gilmore, Ziviani, Sakzewski, Shields, & Boyd, 2010).

The most promising therapy for childhood hemiplegia (CH) recommended by NICE is HABIT (hand-arm bimanual intensive therapy) (Charles & Gordon, 2006). This intervention uses a modification of the intensive CIMT treatment regime but delivers 60 to 120 hours of intensive therapeutic input over a 12-day period; this is followed by monthly workshops for 6 months to support consolidation and functional applications as well as psychosocial development (Gordon et al., 2011; Sakzewski et al., 2015). Results have shown clinically significant improvements in hand movement and hand function immediately post intervention and maintained at 6-month follow-up as well as increased goal attainment compared to CIMT treatment. It is estimated that based on the above supporting evidence that the majority of children with hemiplegia could benefit from intensive motor therapy. However, despite receiving a 'green light' (reflecting strong supportive evidence) in a recent systematic review and meta-analysis of interventions for children with cerebral palsy (CP) (Novak et al., 2013) and support in the NICE guidelines, HABIT has not been widely available on the NHS, and challenges in compliance and engagement of children with the intensive hours required for HABIT have also been noted.

The Breathe Magic Program for Those with Childhood Hemiplegia

Consequently, in 2008, Breathe Arts Health Research began work on developing a program that would provide intensive therapy more widely to children in the UK with hemiplegia in a fun and engaging way. Breathe Magic is a HABIT program that delivers 60 hours of one-to-one intensive therapy, within a group setting, over 10 days followed by an additional 18 hours of therapy delivered monthly for the following 6 months. It overcomes the challenge identified in engaging a child's attention for so many hours by using a 'magical' theme: every therapy exercise has been incorporated into a magic trick, so children have a clear incentive and goal to carry out their rehabilitation. Pediatric occupational therapists work alongside professional magicians to teach a vast range of magic tricks and creative skills, all of which have been selected and/or designed to incorporate key hand and arm movements within the performance of the skill, to enable the young person to develop their muscle strength, dexterity, and motor skills. Moreover, this incorporation of magic has another benefit, which is that of providing simultaneous psychosocial support. Within the Breathe Magic program, additional theatrical master classes are taught by magicians and theater performers to help the young people to enhance their communication and social skills, such as understanding the importance of eye contact, posture, and clarity and tone of voice. This supports confidence, self-esteem, and self-identity, meaning that the intervention provides a holistic care package working on the physical, emotional, and social aspects of hemiplegia. The art of magic and theater, both of which are multidimensional in terms of the skills required to perform these creative acts, provides a strong tool for exploring the complex mix of physical and psychosocial challenges faced by young people with hemiplegia.

In addition, a robust research program has run alongside Breathe Magic since 2010. An assessment on each individual participant's abilities is made prior to the start of engagement, as well as at the end of the 2-week intensive program. Further assessments are conducted 6 months later to monitor the program's long-term impact. Breathe Arts Health Research, with research partnerships, has published in peer-reviewed medical journals and presented at conferences internationally (Green et al., 2013; Green & Farquharson, 2013; Green & White, 2014; Weinstein et al., 2016). Research has shown that over this period the young people progress significantly in using their weaker hand to perform two-handed tasks independently, with results comparable to those of the standard HABIT program. These results include clinically significant improvements in bimanual motor skills and independence maintained at 3- and 6-month follow-up; significant reductions in the time required to carry out motor movements; reported improvements in psychological well-being, communication skills, self-esteem, and parent–child relationships; and increases in brain activity, lateralization, and white matter integrity (Green et al., 2013; Green & Farquharson, 2013; Green & White, 2014; Weinstein et al., 2016). In practical terms, this means that for many young people, it is the first time they could use both hands to dress themselves, cut their food using a knife and fork, or tie their shoelaces. In addition, the ability to successfully perform a professional magic trick and accomplish tasks independently, as their friends can, enables greater opportunities for participation across social and motor activities when children return to their daily lives. Interestingly, improvements in bimanual abilities have been found to correlate with improvements in psychosocial functioning, highlighting the interconnectedness of the functional and psychosocial elements of the program (Green & White, 2014). Improvements in independence have also been found to correspond with a reduction in the additional time parents were providing to support their child: *Thanks to the Breathe Magic camp, Jack can now feed himself with his weaker hand—something he was unable to manage previously* (a father of a 9-year-old participant).

Therapeutic Components of the Breathe Magic Program

Of course, a key consideration is *how* Breathe Magic achieves such results. The unique support provided by Breathe Magic and the strength of the results are the combination of a series of program components.

The Magicians

The magicians recruited to work on the program are highly skilled and internationally award-winning. All are driven by a desire to use magic for a greater good, and therefore possess humility and enthusiasm for working within Breathe Magic. This is an important aspect of the delivery, as the young people need a high level of self-motivation, and this comes from being sufficiently inspired by both the magicians and the magic tricks.

The Occupational Therapists

Occupational therapists identify a range of motor movements that are particularly challenging for young people with hemiplegia, including moving their fingers to grasp and hold objects of differing sizes; straightening their elbows and fingers; and bimanual, two-handed, coordination. They work with the magicians to identify suitable magic tricks that can be taught to the children to practice these movements.

The One-to-One Staff Support

Each young person attending Breathe Magic has an assigned staff member to work with them on a one-to-one ratio. The staff member is responsible, under the guidance of the occupational therapists, for working out which aspect of the trick is particularly challenging for the young person, and to ensure from a clinical perspective that the movement is practiced. The occupational therapists, staff member, and the young person work together to ensure the young person's specific global bimanual motor goals are interwoven into the magic tricks where possible. This part of the trick is then repeatedly practiced in isolation of the whole sequence to enable focused and individualized clinical improvements, and the acquisition and refinement of motor movements for every young person. The breakdown of challenging components means that mastery is slow but thorough, with a clearer understanding of what is required in small, digestible steps.

The Magic Tricks

Many of the tricks taught in Breathe Magic are famous traditional tricks, which have the benefit of being particularly engaging to the children, as learning the trick provides them with a unique opportunity to learn a secret of the magic world. For example, the 'cups and balls' is widely regarded as one of the true classics in conjuring, and is one of the earliest recorded magic tricks, stretching back an estimated 2,500 years. The rich history of the trick, and the fact that many people have seen this performed by a professional magician at some point in their life, means that the young people are immediately intrigued and often strongly motivated to master this trick. The trick involves three small balls balanced on cups, which, one by one, pass through the solid cups to rest on the table beneath. It is a 'simple' but classic mystery.

The Magic Show

Breathe Magic works toward young people performing in a stage show, where they can show their newly acquired magic (and bimanual) skills to friends and family. This is an incredibly uplifting part of the program and is important for the family to see and celebrate with the young person all that he or she has have achieved in just 10 days: *For the first time in my life people are looking at me for something I can do, rather than all the things that I can't* (participant, age 15).

Incorporating Daily Life Through the Breathe Magic Program

The above components combine to provide a series of specific training that supports the emotional, social, and physical challenges of hemiplegia. Additionally, Breathe Magic provides transferrable skills that can be incorporated into daily life.

Embedded Fine Motor Skills Exercises

The cup and balls trick, for example, requires several key fine motor movements. Lifting the small ball requires a pinching grip, an essential skill for independent living needed for many everyday tasks, such as manipulating a button on a shirt. The trick also includes lifting and turning the cups over, which develops grasp-and-release hand patterns while also mastering pronation and supination of the hand and forearm. Essential pinching, gripping, and hand rotation skills can be applied to carrying a plate or opening a door. To master this trick, the children must practice this sequence of movements repeatedly, providing intensive motor therapy.

Embedded Gross Motor Skills Exercises

Magic tricks also provide the opportunity to practice very specific gross motor movements; each trick involves a 'magical gesture' or 'magic moment' that has the dual aim of creating a moment of anticipation for the spectator before the magic happens and providing the opportunity for this additional motor exercise. For example, young people are instructed to snap their fingers, followed by a clap of the hands, and a full arm extension over the magical object while wiggling their fingers—four motor movements in one overall gesture. This complex bimanual routine is taught as an essential part of the trick, and therefore is practiced multiple times. The ability to stick to a task, and continue to practice, despite the obvious challenges that this poses, is a key life skill for those diagnosed with hemiplegia to master.

Memory Training

Each trick taught to the young people also requires significant memory. The cup and balls trick is based on a cyclical set of steps that requires patient repetition in small blocks before one sequence can be completed. Simultaneously, the young magician must remember the outer reality of what needs to be seen by the audience while maintaining the secret inner reality of what is covertly happening within the trick. Due to the complex neurological nature of hemiplegia, many individuals have difficulty with complex memory skills and sustained and divided attention. Magic tricks provide the mechanisms to practice these memory skills.

Planning and Multitasking Training

Magic tricks require constant thinking and planning ahead; skills that have tremendous benefits when applied to the daily living activities of young people with hemiplegia. Something as simple as getting on a bus requires planning on how to get onto the bus, open their bag, get out their money, and then hand it over, all while standing up. With hemiplegia, a lot of the young people find multitasking difficult because their motor movements are not subconscious or automatic. Actively practicing multitasking through learning magic tricks has positive ramifications for wider daily living.

Communication Skills Development

Successfully performing magic tricks is dependent on communication, so communications skills are developed across the course of the program. Pauses are strategically embedded throughout the performance of a trick to help strengthen the impact of the magic, and on a deeper level, to give license to the young magician to make eye contact with the audience. Making eye contact with both strangers and friends is an important social skill to develop in young people, specifically those diagnosed with a medical illness. The power of eye contact is regularly enforced throughout all the magic sequences to turn what can initially be viewed as a daunting or exposing act, into one which becomes both habitual, natural, and confident; a skill that can be equally valuable in future communications with adults and with peers at school.

Confidence Development

The program also has a focus on developing confidence in the young magicians. Mastering a skill, such as magic, is something rare amongst their peers. Therefore, when they leave the program having learned a large variety of professional magic tricks to show to family and friends, it is often the first time in their life that they can do something that no one else can. This is an important legacy from the program in improving their self-esteem, which we see transferred into their skills outside the program: *The magic doesn't seem like therapy to the children, it's actually giving them a talent which the other kids don't have at school, and that makes a massive difference to their inner confidence* (father of a 9-year-old participant).

The Individual Impact of the Breathe Magic Program

Breathe Magic is a 'complex' intervention in that many different interlocking components are required, activating several specific mechanisms for the program to have the tangible psychosocial and physical benefits discussed earlier. To illustrate the far-reaching effects of the program, the final section of this chapter will depict a case study of a child within the Breathe Magic program.

Angel, an 8-year-old girl, was born prematurely at 24 weeks and suffered a brain hemorrhage at birth, which caused cerebral palsy and a left-sided hemiplegia. She weighed just 1.7 pounds and was dependent on a life support machine, as her chances of survival were slim. *Her body was the size of a biro pen*, Angel's mother Sumira said. Eight years later, Angel still has very complex medical needs, and mild learning difficulties, but Sumira can't stress enough what a difference Breathe Magic made in Angel's life: *This was a great chance for Angel; all I can say is WOW what a difference it has made for her confidence, all the things able-bodied people take for granted, like tying shoelaces or pulling up your own trousers, were a constant problem for her.*

The Breathe Magic camp addressed an array of Angel's specific therapy needs, from developing fine motor skills to improving social skills and interpersonal behavior. Since taking part in the program, Angel can do magic tricks such as the cup and balls trick with both hands, and it has made a difference in her daily life. Sumira was very pleased that the program also provided an opportunity for her to meet other parents in similar situations and exchange experiences and now finds she is able to relate even more to the challenges Angel faces every day: *I think anything is possible whoever you are. Angel still has a long way to go but it is amazing how well she has improved and to see my little girl looking happy.*

Conclusion

This chapter has considered the psychosocial and physical challenges faced by CH, as well as the unique and effective solution presented by Breathe Magic. Hemiplegia is just one example of the work that Breathe Arts Health Research has been involved with over the past 8 years; other projects can be accessed through www.breatheahr.org. As the research around this program continues to grow, Breathe Magic provides a rich insight into how magic can be applied to help address pressing clinical challenges in everyday life.

References

Bax, M., Goldstein, M., Rosenbaum, P., Leviton, A., Paneth, N., Dan, B., . . . Damiano, D. (2005). Proposed definition and classification of cerebral palsy, April 2005. *Developmental Medicine and Child Neurology, 47*(8), 571–576. doi: 10.1017/S001216220500112X

Charles, J. R., & Gordon, A. M. (2006). Development of hand-arm bimanual intensive training (HABIT) for improving bimanual coordination in children with hemiplegic cerebral palsy. *Developmental Medicine & Child Neurology, 48*(11), 931–936. doi: 10.1017/S0012162206002039

Eliasson, A.-C., Krumlinde-Sundholm, L., Shaw, K., & Wang, C. (2005). Effects of constraint-induced movement therapy in young children with hemiplegic cerebral palsy: An adapted model. *Developmental Medicine and Child Neurology, 47*(4), 266–275. doi: 10.1017/S0012162205000502

Ferriero, D. M. (2004). Neonatal brain injury. *The New England Journal of Medicine, 351*(19), 1985–1995. doi: 10.1056/NEJMra041996

Gilmore, R., Ziviani, J., Sakzewski, L., Shields, N., & Boyd, R. (2010). A balancing act: Children's experience of modified constraint-induced movement therapy. *Developmental Neurorehabilitation, 13*(2), 88–94. doi: 10.3109/17518420903386161

Gordon, A. M., Hung, Y.-C., Brandao, M., Ferre, C. L., Kuo, H.-C., Friel, K., . . . Charles, J. R. (2011). Bimanual training and constraint-induced movement therapy in children with hemiplegic cerebral palsy: A randomized trial. *Neurorehabilitation and Neural Repair, 25*(8), 692–702. doi: 10.1177/1545968311402508

Green, D., & Farquharson, Y. (2013). The magic of movement: Integrating magic into rehabilitation for children with hemiplegia. *Developmental Medicine and Child Neurology, 5*(S2), 19.

Green, D., Schertz, M., Gordon, A. M., Moore, A., Schejter Margalit, T., Farquharson, Y., . . . Fattal-Valevski, A. (2013). A multi-site study of functional outcomes following a themed approach to hand-arm bimanual intensive therapy for children with hemiplegia. *Developmental Medicine & Child Neurology, 55*(6), 527–533. doi: 10.1111/dmcn.12113

Green, D., & White, S. (2014). Perceptions of confidence and competence in childhood acquired hemiplegia or unilateral cerebral palsy. *Developmental Medicine & Child Neurology, 56*(S4), 23.

Novak, I., McIntyre, S., Morgan, C., Campbell, L., Dark, L., Morton, N., Stumbles, E., Wilson. S., Goldsmith, S. (2013). A systematic review of interventions for children with cerebral palsy: State of the evidence. *Developmental Medicine and Child Neurology, 55*(10), 885–910. doi: 10.1111/dmcn.12246

Sakzewski, L., Miller, L., Ziviani, J., Abbott, D. F., Rose, S., Macdonell, R. A. L., & Boyd, R. N. (2015). Randomized comparison trial of density and context of upper limb intensive group versus individualized occupational therapy for children with unilateral cerebral palsy. *Developmental Medicine & Child Neurology, 57*(6), 539–547. doi: 10.1111/dmcn.12702

Wallen, M., O'Flaherty, S. J., & Waugh, M. C. A. (2007). Functional outcomes of intramuscular botulinum toxin type A and occupational therapy in the upper limbs of children with cerebral palsy: A randomized controlled trial. *Archives of Physical Medicine and Rehabilitation, 88*(1), 1–10. doi: 10.1016/j.apmr.2006.10.017

Wallen, M., Ziviani, J., Herbert, R., Evans, R., & Novak, I. (2008). Modified constraint-induced therapy for children with hemiplegic cerebral palsy: A feasibility study. *Developmental Neurorehabilitation, 11*(2), 124–133. doi: 10.1080/17518420701640897

Weinstein, M., Myers, V., Green, D., Schertz, M., Fattal-Valevski, A., Artzi, M., . . . Bashat, D. B. (2016). Exploration of brain and behaviour changes following intensive bimanual therapy in children with hemiplegia/unilateral cerebral palsy. *Developmental Medicine & Child Neurology, 58*, 8–9.

5 Photography as a Natural Therapeutic Process for Medically Ill Patients

Keshet Zur

In the summer of 2016, I worked as a photography activity leader at an international summer camp for children with serious illness based in Ireland. The aim of the camp is to allow children living with a serious illness to simply be children, leaving behind their diagnosis. The focus is a therapeutic recreational model, child centered in its approach, and aims to restore the child's empowerment, confidence, and self-esteem.

It was exciting to work with photography through expressive arts therapy (EXA) within the therapeutic recreational (TR) model with these children and their families. The goal was to incorporate EXA approaches into a recreational structure, while utilizing art as a healing tool. Therapeutic quality is inherent in art, and there is a distinction between something being therapeutic and therapy. The difference perhaps lies in the intention behind the creative process, as well as in the framework the facilitator/therapist creates through boundaries and the therapeutic relationship. Both TR and EXA focus on the process, using art as a means for empowerment, healing, and an agent of change. TR programs address "the challenge of focusing on the process or experience of the participants in the program versus the product of participation" (Kunstler & Daly, 2010, p. 268). Both TR and EXA embody the humanistic perspective that each person has the potential for making positive change in their life. TR promotes healing and change through motivation. The process of making is empowering as one takes ownership over what they create by virtue of their own choices, encouraging individuality, and self-determination, which leads to the overcoming of fears and fostering of independence.

Expressive Arts Therapy and Therapeutic Recreation

In EXA, the arts are the tools that stimulate a deeper nurturing. Simply making art can open bridges to deeper understanding of ourselves, our environment, and the relationship between the two. Art gives this process of change physicality, a means to witness and gain perspective. More than merely a reflection, when one creates, one is in dialogue with the medium/material, and so in EXA the client is not just retelling an experience, he or she is enabling a new notion to be born. Paolo Knill, one of the founders of the EXA method, describes that process of 'decentering' in art-making:

> By decentering we name the move away from the narrow logic of thinking and acting that marks the helplessness around the "dead-end" situation in question. This is a move into the opening of surprising unpredictable unexpectedness, the experience within the logic of imagination.
>
> (as cited in Knill, Levine, & Levine, 2005, p. 83)

In every engagement with art, something new is created. As we shape an art medium, a subsequent shaping happens in our lives. The opportunity for increased sensitivity and openness allows for preconceived notions to dissipate and shifting perspectives to emerge. Art is fluid and allows for new insights with each engagement. Art gives the opportunity to gain new perspectives and develop coping strategies, which is important when working with a medically diagnosed client.

The TR facilitator utilizes the arts, in addition to other chosen activities (i.e., sports, games, cooking, etc.), for recreation, as well as for rehabilitation. This helps clients reach their goals while having fun, deriving meaning from the activity through positive reinforcement. The chosen activity is important in bringing about a positive outcome of both the emotional and physical state of the client. TR "positively impacts one's psychological well-being by enhancing an individual's leisure experiences and developing their resources and capacity to engage in life activities" (Groff, Battaglini, O'Keefe, Edwards, & Peppercorn, 2007, p. 6). When a person is experiencing success, he or she becomes more autonomous, self-confident, and independent. Furthermore, Austin (2011) stated that "the outcomes of Recreational Therapy are not random. They are planned. Recreational Therapy employs an evidence-based approach that involves systematically using interventions to bring about specific therapeutic outcomes for clients" (p. 6).

TR and EXA have similar intentions, to foster optimal health and independence in clients' lives, while also being notably different. EXA sessions are tailored to allow for freedom of expression and the unexpected to emerge, through learning and nourishment, as well as the leisure experience. Every emotion has its place and holds the potential to bring the patient closer to his or her goals in the process of healing with therapy. In contrast, in TR the facilitator strives to have a positive impact on the client's life, building on the foundation established via experiences of joy and achievement through purposeful activities. When working with a medically diagnosed individual, the TR facilitator will choose an activity where the client will succeed; however, the activity cannot be too easy or too challenging. If too easy, it will not yield a high level of satisfaction, and if too challenging, it will have a lower rate of success. The activity needs to have the potential to achieve a level of wellness; improving the client's life despite current and/or ongoing symptomology. TR promotes self-actualization, and through the activity a medically ill client can find motivation and empowerment.

EXA and TR are both resource oriented in how the facilitator/therapist helps the client, specifically when dealing with those diagnosed with a medical illness. Both methods build upon inherent positive foundations and highlight one's resilience, which may have been lost or forgotten after the diagnosis.

Therapeutic Recreation–Focused Camp

With a life-threatening disease, one may experience a lack of control over oneself. Feelings such as helplessness can lead to low self-esteem, depression, stress, isolation, and alienation. During cancer treatment, a patient may experience side effects such as alopecia, weight loss/gain, fatigue, nausea, or anxiety. Changes in social settings, such as being absent from school, results in reduced contact with peers and increased dependency on the parent(s)/caregiver(s). These life-changing disturbances can affect psychological development, as the normal development of adolescents can be disrupted; "identity, independency, social relationships with peers, intimacy" (Barrera, Damore-Petingola, Fleming, & Mayer, 2006, p. 1680). However, investigated interventions for adolescents with cancer, such as annual expressive arts retreats, can help. The value of attending a nonclinical retreat resulted in changes in adolescents' outlook toward their cancer. Social connections and understanding feelings helped adolescents to feel cared for, alleviating isolation and leading to integrating the experience into daily living (Barrera et al., 2006).

Wikström (2005) studied play therapy within a Swedish hospital using expressive arts practices to facilitate a better communication for hospitalized children. While allowing children to express themselves freely through expressive arts, themes of fear, longing, and powerlessness were decreased. The result of the study illustrated the benefits of EXA activities for children to express their feelings, and that children transformed their reality at the hospital into their chosen art activity. Art can give children a safe space to express themselves freely; "children master a situation by displacing their emotion onto an expressive art activity" (Wikström, 2005, p. 484). Art also allows for an important role reversal to take place; the patient becomes the expert, describing what he or she has made and what it means to him or her. Being subjective, art provides the opportunity for a client to revisit an experience, tell it from his or her perspective, and give it meaning.

Children naturally make sense of their experiences, which evolve with cognitive development. Children's ideas of illness might involve punishment, guilt, and self-blame (Perrin & Gerrity, 1981); it is important for children to express freely and incorporate coping tools to counter self-inflicted blame, and to use art to help make sense of their world.

International Camp

The goal of this type of camp is to use a resource-oriented approach with the understanding that each medically diagnosed child has different qualities that he or she may summon with the appropriate encouragement. The camp provides a safe environment, free of judgment, with the focus on the process of the activity, as opposed to skill level or expertise. Encouraging curiosity through exercises that are interesting and challenging allows a child to thrive and realize his or her potential. When a medically ill child is involved in an activity specific to his or her needs, it becomes achievable and enjoyable; allowing the child to meet his or her goal. Overcoming challenges in a group dynamic also helps build confidence and develops coping skills. A collaborative group prompts problem-solving skills, where children end up supporting one another, broadening their perception and understanding and promoting social and personal development (Johnson, Johnson, & Holubec, 1994).

Activities are designed for the medically ill child to step out of his or her comfort zone, allowing for choice and control, so the child feels reconnected with his or her strengths and empowered, as opposed to the passive state of hospitalization. By succeeding, the child finds the motivation to attempt new challenges. The activities are fun, exciting, and enjoyable, while aiming to enhance independence and offer a sense of accomplishment.

When confronting challenging circumstances, such as a medical diagnosis or a change in severity of symptoms, a client can often feel isolated and alienated from peers. The camp experience allows campers to meet others from different parts of the world who are having similar medical experiences, and thus enhance their capacity to empathize. While sharing common experiences with local individuals is beneficial, meeting others from all over the world provides an incredible sense of perspective and broadens a feeling of community. The sense of belonging is an important factor in a client's ability to appropriately cope with, and express, their feelings regarding a medical diagnosis. Unable to speak the same language, children find alternative means to communicate, and by the camp's end have developed lasting friendships. Another valuable aspect that is usually included in this type of camp is the addition of a separate camp for siblings of a medically ill child, understanding that a life-threatening illness affects all members of the family.

Camp activities are structured to prioritize inclusion for children with different mobility challenges (i.e. use of wheelchair/crutches, visual or hearing impairment, and/or cognitive challenges). Activities vary in interest and are developed to include all levels of ability; no child is ever left out. Success is measured on individual terms and journeys, without comparison. Each session begins with developing a comfort level for the group through a warm-up activity.

Different activities allow for a variety of ways to partake (i.e., in theater one could be a performer, director, costume designer, lighting designer, etc.).

The focus is not solely on the outcome, but rather the process. A series of small steps, while maintaining the activity, challenge and ease the participant into taking risks and achieving success. Each camper is encouraged to step out of his or her comfort zone while adapting and redefining new comfort levels. Most campers, within days, choose to be in their 'stretch zone;' wherein they test their abilities and find new successes. Positive reinforcement is consistent and offers encouragement; as a result, the successes allow campers to reflect on their experiences and to link them to everyday reality. As campers become aware of these successes, take ownership of them, and begin to see themselves in a new light, it boosts self-confidence. This process of reflection is extremely important for medically ill children to see themselves as able individuals and rebuild their sense of self.

Although the camp is time limited, campers get to experience and learn about themselves through thoughtful activities, which, in turn, reconnects them with their strengths. Providing an experience packed with positivity, joy, and laughter allows the child to be carefree and more him/herself. Having a life-threatening disease can force children to grow up quickly; the camp does everything to reignite a child's inherent playfulness, which is vital for healthy development.

Photo activities run throughout the summer and are altered according to the campers' needs (i.e., age, camp theme, group size, and stage within the camp). Activities include graphic design, where each camper creates a poster for his or her 'future summer camp' using a variety of objects, such as magnets, stickers, and feathers. The 'hero' theme, where each camper invents a hero with super powers, is processed with the group. A third example, when nearing the end of the stay, is to create an image of their best memory at camp.

The Camp Photography Program

The photography program is 75 minutes of full engagement in creating an effective and meaningful art activity: the development of a photogram. A photogram is a photographic image made in a photo lab without the use of a camera by placing objects on a photographic paper (light sensitive), which is then exposed to light. Areas covered with the objects remain white, while the areas exposed to the light appear black (Figure 5.1).

Working in the photo lab allows each camper to create an image, print it, and keep it in a tangible form. Looking back at the printed image helps reinforce the memory of the experience. Krauss (1983), a pioneer of photography in therapy, wrote that the value of a photograph as an artifact is in "allowing us to reconnect with a past event in the present" (p. 63). As the activity is designed to bring about a feeling of accomplishment and success, the printed images remind the campers of what they have achieved.

The instructions are brief and concise, leaving room for imaginative interpretation. The more time one spends creating with intention, the more

Figure 5.1 Campers Photograms Hanging to Dry

connection there is to what is created; in turn, what is created becomes personal. Imagination is the core of each creation, and the ingredient that makes outcomes individual and unique to the camper. When we make something that is individual to us, we draw upon our own resources, and learn more than just a technique; we emerge empowered, and can relay that sentiment to other activities or aspects of life.

The photogram process proved effective for several reasons, beginning with the notion that working in a photo lab is both a creative and technical process. Making a photogram is not as technically demanding as other printing methods, and is easy to explain. Photogram printing can fit the approach of a low-skill, high-sensitivity activity, wherein the quality of the experience is not measured by the level of skill, but rather by the potential for heightened sensitivity between the participant and material. The exercise is achievable, yet challenging, and campers are urged to be creative and think outside the box. This allows campers the opportunity to be impressed by their outcome, and reflect on the experience, which supports the notion of seeing themselves as both creative and able.

The activity was physically inclusive; campers created at a table, and only stood while exposing and developing images, making it suitable for all, including those in wheelchairs or using crutches. For those with hearing impairment, visual examples helped explain the process, and an adaptation for the visually impaired included a three-dimensional component using pins to make holes to feel the final design.

Although activities open to interpretation, such as a photogram, could increase anxiety for children who are critical of themselves, a supportive setting can enhance a relaxed and enjoyable environment. Structure is important for a child who has experienced hospitalization: the uncertainty regarding illness can cause fear and nervousness, and structure can provide an organized external reality, fostering a sense of control. The combination of freedom of choice within a structured setting can be calming; tapping into an imaginative state within a secure, nonjudgmental environment. When children are fully engaged in the process, they are less critical of themselves, as all their concentration is on the making process itself.

A sense of mystery and curiosity, like storytelling, is created when beginning the photogram process (e.g., *we are going into a photo lab and will be working with photography the same way it was done hundreds of years ago*). Walking into the lab, with objects they had never seen before, children become intrigued and engaged. The photo lab is a new and unusual setting, and by entering the unfamiliar, a 'decentering' can occur that affects personal transformation. Most activities in the camp are high energy and loud, whereas the photo room is quiet. Most sessions happen in low-lit conditions (red light) and indoors. When the children enter, being greeted by a soft calm voice, helps them relax.

Something out of Nothing

Throughout the direct experience of working with the campers, I created a photography activity called *making something out of nothing*. The premise of this activity was to allow space for imagination and enhance each child's strength and resilience. In the initial photogram activity, campers designed an image using a variety of objects; this activity involved each camper working with one piece of regular paper as their object. Without scissors, campers tore the paper and placed it on top of the photographic (light sensitive) paper to create their image. This activity directly associates with the experience of a life-threatening illness and a child's need to regain control over his or her reality. By rearranging the random pieces of paper, the children were making sense out of chaos. They had to be self-determined and motivated; they had to be fully active participants. The result was incredible, the campers showed outstanding creative work specific to their individuality, with full control over the final image. Although a child might be overwhelmed by the creative freedom, being too prescriptive could deny the element of surprise from a successful outcome. Once diagnosed with cancer, a child can often become overprotected, denying the child the typical parameters of childhood. Children learn from trial and error; they need freedom to explore within a safe space for healthy growth, development, and self-esteem. A safe space was achieved by allowing sufficient time for each stage and in creating a nonjudgmental environment to encourage experimentation and intuition.

When presented the activity, campers were asked to become explorers and to trust the process. They were shown how the paper can be cut with a basic example of a rainbow photogram. Showing a simple outcome allows expectations to be realistic. They were then asked to make something out of nothing.

The campers were encouraged to tear the paper spontaneously, using 'finding shapes in the clouds' as a metaphor, to see if any pieces evoked a thought or image (Figure 5.2). When seeing one thing as another, we use our imagination and open possibilities, leading to a change in perspective and seeing things differently: "The imagination is centrally exercised in the encounter with its medium, where the medium itself suggests paths for imagination to follow. The space of the imagination lies between the artist and the medium and connects the two" (Pateman, 1997, p.7).

Figure 5.2 Campers Photograms: 'Making Something out of Nothing'

Creating an atmosphere of creativity, each camper became focused on the process, similar to a meditation, bringing deep relaxation. Becoming receptive and engaged with the material, allowed obstacles and challenges to become new possibilities. When at the enlarger to expose their image onto the photographic paper, the design can be slightly rearranged. At that moment, campers employ choice and control through adjusting the pieces.

The photographic paper is then placed in the tray of chemicals to print out the design. Within seconds, the blank paper starts to suddenly show the image, as if by magic, bringing excitement and surprise to the camper as he or she watches his or her creative choices translate into tangible images. When one creates, one is directly engaged in the act of change, manipulating the material to transform it. Creativity is a nonpassive act that enhances individuality and self-directive choices.

As the light was switched on, all the artwork hanging to dry could be seen and shared. The group processed by reviewing how each started with only one piece of paper but had gone on to create a world. Everyone was surprised by what was created. They were reminded that sometimes when we have less we find possibilities, and that there are many ways to approach things.

This exercise enhanced imagination as the three-dimensional image they created looked quite different on the two-dimensional photographic paper. The fact that they created the image themselves brought them meaning and pride. Everyone made something unique and beautiful, and the activity ended with a round of applause.

Conclusion

The value of the arts as a natural therapeutic process provides insight into the camp's principles, approach, and activities. The photogram illustrates how an activity can be therapeutic while maintaining its recreational approach to optimize a child's healing process.

Art-making reconnects children to their resilience and power, and contributes to the wellness of a child afflicted with a serious illness. Each child orchestrated an image from start to finish, gaining empowerment and perspective. With supported independence, the creative process allows for choices and experimentation.

The photographic activity resulted in individual choices and perspectives and group sharing. Whether a person internalizes or externalizes feelings, art offers a way to explore emotions and themes in a safe space where all perspectives are welcome. The art process is naturally experimental and imaginative. Having given the campers a safe frame and clear boundaries, they were enthusiastic and willing to explore the unfamiliar. As was pointed out in the 2009 Irish National Teachers Organization report, "children need to experience the unpredictable and the uncertain. They need lessons that produce surprise" (Creativity and the Arts in Primary School, 2009, p. 12).

Confronted with a crisis, such as a serious illness, a child's innate curiosity and wonder helps the child to imagine multiple possibilities and inspires a sense of hope. Experiencing a multitude of possibilities cultivates positivity and stimulates deep nurturing. Art-making through TR and EXA is beneficial to the process of dealing with and recovering from life-threatening illness. Art provides a frame within which a child can explore his or her emotions, flexibility, and adaptability while gaining a sense of control. Art can be used as an indirect way to address complex feelings, while generating pleasure and joy, which in turn aids in strengthening a child's confidence and self-esteem.

References

Austin, D. R. (2011). *Lessons learned: An open letter to recreational therapy students and practitioners*. Urbana, IL: Sagamore Publishing LLC.

Barrera, M., Damore-Petingola, S., Fleming, C., & Mayer, J. (2006). Support and intervention groups for adolescents with cancer in two Ontario communities. *Cancer, 107*(7), 1680–1685. doi: 10.1002/cncr.22108

Creativity and the Arts in the Primary School. (2009). *Discussion document and proceeding of the consultative conference on education 2009*. Retrieved from www.into.ie/ROI/Publications/CreativityArtsinthePS.pdf

Groff, D., Battaglini, C., O'Keefe, C., Edwards, C., & Peppercorn, J. (2007). Lessons from survivors: The role of recreation therapy in facilitating spirituality and well-being. *RT and Spirituality, 1*(1), 1–25.

Johnson, D. W., Johnson, R. T., & Holubec, E. J. (1994). *The nuts and bolts of cooperative learning*. Edina, MN: Interaction Book Co.

Knill, P., Levine, E., & Levine, S. (2005). *Principles and practice of expressive arts therapy: Toward a therapeutic aesthetics*. London, UK: Jessica Kingsley Publishers.

Krauss, D. A. (1983). The visual metaphor: Some underlying assumptions of phototherapy. In D. A. Krauss & J. L. Fryrear (Eds.), *Phototherapy in mental health* (pp. 59–71). Springfield, IL: Charles Thomas Publisher, LTD.

Kunstler, R., & Daly, F. S. (2010). *Therapeutic recreation leadership and programming*. Champaign, IL: Human Kinetics.

Pateman, T. (1997). Space for imagination. *The Journal of Aesthetic Education, 31*(1), 1–8. doi: 10.2307/3333476

Perrin, E. C., & Gerrity, P. S. (1981). There's a demon in your belly: Children's understanding of illness. *Pediatrics, 67*(6), 841–849.

Wikström, B. (2005). Communicating via expressive arts: The natural medium of self-expression for hospitalized children. *Pediatric Nursing, 31*(6), 484.

6 Eating Disorders and the Medical Necessity of Collaborative Care

Michelle L. Dean

In the United States, it is estimated that 20 million women and 10 million men suffer from a clinically significant eating disorder, including anorexia nervosa, bulimia nervosa, and binge eating disorder or another specified feeding or eating disorder (OSFED) (Wade, Keski-Rahkonen, & Hudson, 2011). The number of hospitalizations for men and women due to eating disorders that caused anemia, kidney failure, erratic heart rhythms, or other problems rose 18 percent between 1999 and 2006; hospitalizations for children younger than 12 years of age rose most sharply, at 112 percent, followed by a 48 percent increase among patients aged 45 to 64 (Agency for Healthcare Research and Quality, 2014; Zhao & Encinosa, 2009). Eating disorders have the highest mortality rate of all mental health disorders, including those who commit suicide from depression, and it is estimated that 80 percent of people with eating disorders will recover, while the remaining 20 percent will remain chronic or die (Anorexia Nervosa and Related Disorders, 2015; Smink, van Hoeken, & Hoek, 2012). The *Diagnostic and Statistical Manual of Mental Disorders* (5th ed.; *DSM-5*) (American Psychiatric Association, 2013) states that no other mental health disorder is the confluence of medical and psychological issues more lethal than seen in the spectrum of eating disorders.

The development of an eating disorder results from a complex constellation of multifactorial elements that affect the body, mind, and spirit of the individual. The age of onset is typically in adolescence, but may be seen in children as young as 4 years, and can affect men and women across their life span (American Psychological Association, Dancyer, & Fornari, 2014). The treatment of an individual diagnosed with an eating disorder must be collaborative, relying on the expertise of several treatment specialists who can work together. This chapter addresses the need for integrative and collaborative care among medical and mental health professionals.

The emergence of an eating disorder is often a consequence of longstanding issues that express themselves symbolically in behaviors that attempt to cope with underlying problems. Three predispositions for the development of an eating disorder include attachment ruptures, early childhood trauma, and an overly focused external locus of control (Dean, 2006;

McCafferty, Kwak, Dean, & Kane, 2007). These may occur as a result of a loss, temperament differences, as well as trauma or neglect. It has been shown that the earlier the age of abuse or neglect, the more likely self-injurious behaviors, including eating disordered behaviors, may occur (Everill & Waller, 1995; Vanderlinden & Vandereycken, 1993). It has also been shown that childhood trauma is linked to adult disease (Nakazawa, 2016; The Urban Child Institute, 2012).

It has been reported that the immaturity of the central nervous system (CNS) of children who experience early childhood trauma may make them vulnerable to emotional dysregulation (Van der Kolk et al., 2014). This dysregulation makes it difficult to manage painful affect, and thus individuals may turn to destructive, and potentially life-threatening, behaviors such as restricting, bingeing, purging, and other forms of self-harm as a means of numbing or comforting. It has been reported that there is a strong association between eating disorders and histories of sexual abuse, with sexual abuse most strongly correlated to all forms of self-destructive behavior (Schwartz & Cohn, 1996). This supports a need that all treatment providers be educated and trained to deliver a sensitive and trauma-informed response regardless of discipline.

An overly focused external locus of control, just like the eating disorder itself, has a multifactorial etiology that results from a dynamic interplay between biological, psychological, and sociocultural factors that operate along a developmental continuum (American Psychological Association et al., 2014). Looking outside of oneself for acceptance, reassurance, support, and self-confidence can be impaired when the internal scaffolding of self, identity, and esteem is underdeveloped as a result of attachment ruptures or traumatic experiences. Adolescents, in their quest for identity and their developmental process of individuating, are particularly prone to the eruption of an eating disorder. Without a strong sense of self, one may be more susceptible to seeking assurances about value and worth from messages from peers or portrayed in media, such as unrealistic body weight or size aspirations. These three predispositions along with other individual factors, such as comorbid mood disorders and substance abuse, contribute to the need of integrative care from both medical and mental health professionals to address the complexity and lethality of the eating disorder (Anorexia Nervosa and Related Disorders, 2015; Strober, Freeman, & Morrell, 1997; Ulfvebrand, Birgegard, Norring, Hogdahl, & von Hausswolff-Juhlin, 2015).

Types of Treatment Providers

While inpatient and emergency room treatment is, at times, necessary for some individuals who have an eating disorder to avert a medical crisis, suicide, or death, it is imperative that ongoing treatment is provided by an outpatient team. Furthermore, the outpatient treatment team needs to be adept and able to provide long-term, trauma-informed therapy. Short-term treatment is rarely enough to make a lasting and significant change or recovery. Treatment needs to address the eating disordered symptoms in addition to physical, psychological, interpersonal, and cultural factors that contribute to, or maintain, aspects of the disorder. It has been estimated that the average length of treatment is 8 years (BEAT, 2017); therefore, clinicians must be able to maintain psychodynamically informed, long-term relationships with their patients to address the physical and emotional sequela of prior trauma (Kinoy, 2001).

Treatment providers may include an individual therapist who provides a form of *modified psychotherapy* (Bruch, 1973). An art therapist, a uniquely trained psychotherapist, working as a primary therapist, is an ideal candidate for this role, and will need to be knowledgeable about both the psychological and medical needs of the patient, and adept at leading a team in their collaboration. In my experience in outpatient situations, the art therapist leads the team by placing the psychological world at the forefront. By having a skilled art therapist coordinate the care across the various disciplines, it places the significance of the inner psychological and symbolic expressions of the eating disorder in the forefront of underlying issues, attachment ruptures, and previous trauma. Art therapists may also serve as an adjunct therapist to a primary therapist of another discipline, providing opportunities for expression that verbal processing alone cannot always address due to alexithymia, trauma, or processing difficulties that create a disconnect between words and feelings, as is common with survivors of trauma. Part of the team collaboration will include several professionals, who assist the patient in her or his physical, emotional, and spiritual recovery. While the contributing factors to a person's eating disorder are unique, a best practice model is constructed according to the needs of the individual. In addition to the primary therapist, the following treatment providers, with expertise in eating disorder diagnoses, are recommended for a supportive network in which to recover.

A medical doctor is essential to address medical complaints related to eating disorder behaviors. Medical doctors also monitor urine, blood chemistry, and erratic heart rhythms, which may be a result of electrolyte imbalances. These professionals will also prescribe diagnostic tests, such as bone density scans, for short- and long-term health risks (see Appendix 6.A for a list of medical consequences and presentations of eating disorders).

Additionally, excellent dental care is a must. Dental professionals can be among the first medical professionals to identify the need for psychological care, due to the erosion of enamel on the teeth and progressed decay or tooth loss (Ximenes, Couto, & Sougey, 2010). Individuals often avoid professional dental care due to its physical intrusiveness, triggering memories related to prior trauma, and pain. The links between oral health and physical health are well established, and thus support dentists working through a trauma-informed lens.

A nutritionist is necessary to address the unique nutritional needs of the patient. These requirements can include weight restoration, as well as assisting the patient in changing food and weight-related behaviors by sensitively challenging beliefs and values related to preoccupation with food, weight, nutrition, and activity level. A skilled nutritionist assists patients in modifying the quantity and variety of foods, including weekly weigh-ins, while also identifying barriers to change. In this capacity, the nutritionist frees the therapist from tasks related to food and weight so the therapist can focus on the psychological aspects of treatment. Furthermore, the nutritionist can help to identify potential metabolic influences, such as thyroid conditions, when reports of caloric needs and actual intake do not match (Grassi, 2016).

A psychiatrist, as part of the overall treatment team, is also preferred as medication management can be challenging with a low-weight patient whose metabolism may not be functioning as expected, or with a bingeing client whose purging behavior is contraindicated due to side effects with a particular type of medication. Additionally, a skilled psychiatrist may be more aware of underlying addiction risks and prescribe medications with thoughtful consideration.

Lastly, when the patient is a child, an adult residing in the parental home, or is in a significant relationship, the addition of a family therapist can be helpful to address issues within the family dynamic, such as communication and intergenerational, trauma patterns. A family therapist can ensure that the individual therapy remains pure of possible perceived favoritism, splitting, or other subgroupings, which could be destructive to the individual therapeutic alliance. Once well established in individual therapy, the addition of group therapy can be beneficial in addressing interpersonal and social difficulties as well as provide a supportive network of people who have similar experiences. Group therapy can reduce isolation, and can provide the individual with an opportunity to learn new patterns of interpersonal relatedness. Additionally, peer support groups, such as Overeaters Anonymous, can also be helpful as they provide opportunities for connection and friendship. Some support groups also offer 12-step or a spiritual focus.

Each treatment provider is a specialist within his or her discipline, and offers multiple perspectives. The patient not only benefits from the knowledge and expertise of several people, but also in that the team models a 'family' in which the members collaborate, solve problems together, consider input from men and women equally, and acknowledge that the patient has both strengths and weaknesses. The team approach can provide the patient, and family, with increased security and confidence, while undergoing treatment.

A Collaborative Care Approach: Advantages

There are many benefits to the patient and his or her family when working with a team of professionals. The team has a shared responsibility for the treatment of the patient and develops the course of treatment in which the patient is an integral part. The combination of both men and women on the treatment team provides the opportunity for the patient to identify and resolve issues from past relationships and to practice developing healthy, collaborative relationships. The focus of treatment is on multiple and multi-faceted goals versus only one aspect of care, such as refeeding or medication alone. This multiple perspective enables the patient to better understand how food and weight behaviors interface with psychological and medical issues.

A Collaborative Care Approach: Disadvantages

Despite the advantages, there can be some disadvantages as well when working with a treatment team of several people. Some disadvantages may include the logistics of attending to treatment with many providers, especially if the outpatient providers are not in the same office or even in the same town; for example, physical proximity between provider offices may be far and necessitate a large time commitment. There may be inadequate communication among team members if the professionals are not skilled at communicating with one another, or do not value diverse input and perspectives. Degraded communication can lead to poor collaboration among team members, especially when a professional is accustomed to unilateral decision-making, or has difficulty collaborating due to value or judgment differences (McCafferty et al., 2007). Likewise, treatment providers may have difficulty 'sharing' a patient because there is a perceived threat from other providers. For example, when the client has limited financial resources, a choice may need to be made as to whom she or he can see in a particular week; or if insurance is utilized, it may cover some providers but not others. This can create an imposed value as to which provider will be seen and which will not be included in the treatment team.

Competition for financial resources can unfortunately be a real obstacle in the recovery journey of many patients. To get a sense of the staggering costs associated with treatment for an eating disorder, a residential program may cost on average $30,000 a month, with many patients requiring three or more months of treatment (Parker-Pope, 2010). Even after leaving a specialized eating disorder program, patients often require years of follow-up care specialists, such as a psychotherapist, art therapist, psychiatrist, physician, and nutritionist, with costs reaching as much as or more than $100,000 (Alderman, 2010; Parker-Pope, 2010). For many, the expenses of recovery are compatible to the costs associated with a college education from an esteemed private university in the United States. These costs can be difficult to justify or fund, even with insurance, and denial of the seriousness of an eating disorder can minimize the financial investment needed to regain health.

Access to Treatment

Sadly, the majority of individuals diagnosed with an eating disorder do not receive treatment at a specialized medical facility; accessibility, insurance coverages, and gaps in treatment (including perceptions on the need for intensive treatment) all play a factor in individuals not receiving the proper care for their recovery (Kazdin, Fitzsimmons-Craft, & Wilfley, 2017). In addition, limitations on hospital stays have been driven by a lack of understanding and the serious nature of eating disorders, attempts to reduce costs by insurance providers and families, as well as for some, resistance to remain in treatment. It has been shown that only when a person's weight is within 90 to 95 percent of normal range can counseling and medication make a lasting impact, and a patient's relapse rate is as much as 50 percent if her weight is still below 85 percent (Anorexia Nervosa and Related Disorders, 2015).

Recovery

Like many addictions, relapse is a part of the recovery process, especially in the beginning. Recovery for most individuals with an eating disorder constitutes several therapy sessions per week, in addition to weekly or monthly nutritionist and medical doctor visits, with frequency becoming less as medical and psychological progress is made. Signs of physical recovery include the resumption of normal ovulation and menses in post-menarcheal females who may have lost their menses due to low body weight, decreased body dysmorphia and fear of weight gain, and a more normalized eating pattern without significant weight changes for individuals who engage in bulimic tendencies. Psychologically, recovery can include a significant reduction in self-hatred, preoccupation with weight and size, as well as intrusive thoughts. Recovery from the lasting effects of trauma may also include improved intra- and interpersonal relationships, increased self-esteem, a decrease or absence in self-injurious behaviors as well as increases in motivation, cognition, and emotion (Simmen-Janevska, Brandstätter, & Maercker, 2012).

An art therapist working as the primary therapist on an outpatient basis helps moor the treatment team over what can be turbulent waters to recovery. Imagery and art created in the therapeutic session help to give voice to clients' struggles when words are absent or fail to fully describe the complex underlying psychological components of an eating disorder and their potentially grave consequences. The insight and interventions provided by the art therapist help to bridge the unconscious material that may be acted out on a physical level while also charting a course for the expertise of multiple medical professionals to assist in emotional, physical, and spiritual recovery.

For example, many individuals who manifest eating disorders often suffer from alexithymia, which may be defined as having no words for feelings. Due to neurological, psychological, and sociocultural factors, including early childhood trauma, it is common to find alexithymic features among individuals who have eating disorders and other self-injurious behaviors due to their difficulty verbalizing emotions, especially anger—though they may be able to express themselves effectively on other matters (Milia, 2000; Thompson, 2007). The disconnect between words and feelings creates a split that can be addressed through art and images and help bridge emotional states with cognitive and other executive function. In Figures 6.1 and 6.2, a young woman who had transitioned to a day program after an inpatient treatment stay for an eating disorder attempted to capture her feelings before

Figure 6.1 This image was created before a binge-and-purge episode by a woman in her early 20s who had transitioned to a day program for an eating disorder. Due to her alexithymia, she was unable to recognize her distress or put supports in place to prevent acting on her urges. By using art, we were able to process the experience and help her bridge her emotional distress and language in order to gain insight, understanding, and articulation of her symbolic expression of her internal disordered content and experiences

Figure 6.2 This image was created moments after Figure 6.1, immediately following a bingeing-and-purging episode. By processing the image in session at a later time, we were able to identify how the behaviors numbed her and created dissociation, in order to cope with overwhelming affect

and during her urges to purge even though she said she was unaware of the triggers for bingeing and purging and often felt she woke up after such an episode, unaware of what had happened. She discovered the extent of her actions through evidence left behind from consuming large amounts of food. By depicting herself in art, she was able to visually represent her pain and discomfort that she could not describe or had limited awareness of in words. Figure 6.1 shows her distress and helplessness, while Figure 6.2, represents an annihilation or rubbing out (undoing in defense mechanism terms) of her facial features and her identity. Her arms are merged or fused with her body, rendering her in a paralyzed posture, reflecting the extent of her dissociation and disembodiment. These drawings helped her communicate not only with her therapist, and herself, but also helped her to describe her experiences more fully to her treatment team.

Conclusion

Recovery from an eating disorder can be a long, challenging process, but with a team of professionals adept in the medical, psychological, and spiritual aspects of recovery, individuals increase their odds of full recovery. While the medical doctor, dentist, and other specialists address the physical concerns and ramifications, the nutritionist discusses a balanced intake and potential barriers to change as they relate to nourishment, and the art therapist leads the team by placing the psychological world at the forefront. Having a skilled art therapist coordinate the care across the various disciplines highlights the importance of the inner psychological and symbolic expressions of the eating disorder while giving voice to the development of self, which may have been ravished from attachment ruptures and previous trauma. Relationships with self and others can be improved through individual and group therapy, providing opportunities for an increased internal locus of control and a lessening of eating disordered symptoms. Through a cooperative collaborative care model, the various treatment professionals utilize their strengths and skills to mirror a therapeutic process that addresses the multifactorial issues that contributed to the potentially lethal and symbolically charged development of an eating disorder.

References

Alderman, L. (2010, December 3). Treating eating disorders and paying for it. *The New York Times*. Retrieved October 3, 2015, from www.nytimes.com/2010/12/04/health/04patient.html?_r=1&ref=health.

American Psychological Association (APA), Dancyer, I. F., & Fornari, V. M. (Eds.). (2014). *Evidence based treatments for treating disorders: Children, adolescents, and adults* (2nd ed.). New York, NY: Nova Biomedical Science Publishers, Inc.

Agency for Healthcare Research and Quality. (2014, October). *Mental health findings*. US Department of Health & Human Services. Retrieved October 13, 2016, from www.ahrq.gov/research/findings/factsheets/mental/mentalhth/mentalhth3.html.

American Psychiatric Association. (2013). *Diagnostic statistical manual-V* (5th ed.). Washington, DC: American Psychiatric Association.

Anorexia Nervosa and Related Disorders (ANRED). (2015). *Treatment and recovery*. Retrieved October 13, 2015, from www.anred.com/tx.html.

BEAT. (2017). *Eating disorder statistics*. Retrieved September 4, 2017, from www.b-eat.co.uk/about-beat/media-centre/information-and-statistics-about-eating-disorders.

Bruch, H. (1973). *Eating disorders: Obesity, anorexia nervosa and the person within*. New York, NY: Harper Collins.

Dean, M. L. (2006). Preserving the self: Art psychotherapy applications with eating-disordered clients who self-injure. In *The American Art Therapy Association Conference Proceedings* (Vol. 37, p. 27). New Orleans, LA: The American Art Therapy Association.

Everill, J. T., & Waller, G. (1995). Reported sexual abuse and eating disorder pathology: A review of the evidence for a causal link. *International Journal of Eating Disorders, 18*, 1–11.

Grassi, A. (2016, October 20). *Putting a stop to binge eating*. Retrieved September 4, 2017, from www.pcosnutrition.com/putting-stop-binge-eating/.

Kazdin, A. E., Fitzsimmons-Craft, E. E., & Wilfley, D. E. (2017). Addressing critical gaps in the treatment of eating disorders. *International Journal of Eating Disorders, 50*(3), 170–189.

Kinoy, B. P. (2001). *Eating disorders: New directions in treatment and recovery* (2nd ed.). New York, NY: Columbia University Press.

McCafferty, J., Kwak, K., Dean, M. L., & Kane, J. (2007). *Eating disorders: A collaborative approach to treatment*. The 38th Annual American Art Therapy Association Conference, The American Art Therapy Association, Albuquerque, NM, USA.

Milia, D. (2000). *Self-mutilation and art therapy: Violent creation*. Philadelphia, PA: Jessica Kingsley Publishers.

Nakazawa, D. J. (2016). Childhood trauma leads to lifelong chronic illness-so why isn't the medical community helping patients? *Aces Too High News*. Retrieved October 15, 2016, from https://acestoohigh.com/2016/08/10/childhood-trauma-leads-to-lifelong-chronic-illness-so-why-isnt-the-medical-community-helping-patients/.

Parker-Pope, T. (2010, December 3). The cost of an eating disorder, well. *The New York Times*. Retrieved October 3, 2015, from http://well.blogs.nytimes.com/2010/12/03/the-cost-of-an-eating-disorder/?_r=0.

Schwartz, M., & Cohn, L. (Eds). (1996). *Sexual abuse and eating disorders*. New York, NY: Taylor & Francis.

Simmen-Janevska, K., Brandstätter, V., & Maercker, A. (2012). The overlooked relationship between motivational abilities and posttraumatic stress: A review. *European Journal of Psychotraumatology, 3*(1), 18560. doi: 10.3402/ejpt.v3i0.18560.

Smink, F. E., van Hoeken, D., & Hoek, H. W. (2012). Epidemiology of eating disorders: Incidence, prevalence and mortality rates. *Current Psychiatry Reports, 14*(4), 406–414. doi: 10.1007/s11920–012–0282-y

Strober, M., Freeman, R., & Morrell, W. (1997). The long-term course for severe Anorexia Nervosa in adolescents: Survival analysis for recovery, relapse and outcome predictors over 10–15 years on a prospective study. *International Journal of Eating Disorders, 22*, 339–360. doi: 10.1002/(SICI)1098–108X(199712)22:4<339::AID-EAT1>3.0.CO;2-N

The Urban Child Institute. (2012, March). *Early childhood trauma linked to adult disease*. Retrieved October 15, 2016, from www.urbanchildinstitute.org/articles/editorials/early-childhood-trauma-linked-to-adult-disease.

Thompson, J. (2007). *Blocked imagination ~ Emptied speech: A brief account of the Alexithymia concept*. Australia: Soul Books.

Ulfvebrand, S., Birgegard, A., Norring, C., Hogdahl, L., & von Hausswolff-Juhlin, Y. (2015). Psychiatric comorbidity in women and men with eating disorders results from a large clinical database. *Psychiatry Research, 230*(2), 294–299. doi: 10.1016/j.psychres.2015.09.008

Vanderlinden, J., & Vandereycken, W. (1993). Is sexual abuse a risk factor for developing an eating disorder? *Eating Disorders: The Journal of Treatment and Prevention, 1*, 282–286.

Van der Kolk, B., Courtois, C., Steele, K., Waters, F., Kluft, R., Myers, J. E. B., & Lyon, T. (2014). *Trauma & Dissociation in Children* [e-book]. San Francisco, CA: Kanopy Streaming. Retrieved September 4, 2017, from http://0-eds.b.ebscohost.com.catalog.library.uarts.edu/eds/detail/detail?vid=34&sid=1c670195-b934-4864-98cf a3c913edf48c%40sessionmgr101&bdata=JnNpdGU9ZWRzLWxpdmUmc2NvcGU9c2l0ZQ%3d%3d#AN=art.b1438596&db=cat04417a.

Wade, T. D., Keski-Rahkonen, A., & Hudson, J. (2011). Epidemiology of eating disorders. In M. Tsuang & M. Tohen (Eds.), *Textbook in psychiatric epidemiology* (3rd ed., pp. 343–360). New York, NY: Wiley.

Ximenes, R., Couto, G., & Sougey, E. (2010). Eating disorders in adolescents and their repercussions in oral health. *International Journal of Eating Disorders, 43*, 59–64. doi: 10.1002/eat.20660

Zhao, Y., & Encinosa, W. (2009, April). *Hospitalizations for eating disorder from 1999 to 2006* (Statistical Brief # 70). Healthcare Cost and Utilization Project (HCUP). Retrieved October 13, 2016, from www.hcup-us.ahrq.gov/reports/statbriefs/sb70.jsp.

Appendix 6.A

Medical Consequences and Presentations of Eating Disorders

(McCafferty, Kwak, Dean, and Kane, 2007)

- Anemia
- Apathy
- Anergia
- Arrhythmia
- Cardiomyopathies
- Cold intolerance
- Constipation
- Death
- Dehydration
- Dental erosion
- Dependent edema
- Drug abuse
- Elevated liver transaminases
- Hematemesis
- Hyperamylasemia
- Hypoalbuminemia
- Hypocalcemia
- Hypokalemia
- Hypomagnesemia
- Hypophosphatemia
- Hypothyroidism
- Hypoestrogenemia
- Lanugo
- Leukopenia
- Mallory-Weiss
- Mood dysregulation
- Myopathies
- Obsessiveness
- Osteopenia and osteoporosis
- Pancreatitis
- Poor impulse
- Russell's sign
- Sinus bradycardia

7 Visual Narratives as an Art Therapy Treatment in Cancer Care

Jill McNutt

The relationship between art therapy and medicine, in relation to adult cancer, continues to solidify as treatment interventions advance. This chapter will discuss how art therapy can be utilized as a visual narrative to allow an adult to better cope with a cancer diagnosis, supporting his or her emotional state and providing a sense of comfort though art imagery.

History and Background

This chapter is based upon the compilation of 16 years of work within a medical center focused on the psychosocial health of cancer survivors and doctoral research into patients' experience of cancer through the visual narratives process. The visual narratives process was developed at Aurora Health Care in 2009 as a means of facilitating reflection, coping, meaning-making, and altruism for patients diagnosed with cancer and their families facing life changes due to a medical diagnosis. The scope of the visual narratives process will be transcribed and reported in this chapter, with details in the area of personal reflection of experience, media availability, and choice with stages of cancer survivorship. Cancer survivorship has been seen to start at diagnosis (Miller, Merry, & Miller, 2008). This chapter focuses specifically on the cancer patient or survivor, but the visual narratives process may be applicable to patients with alternative life-changing events or to family members navigating the experience alongside patients. The premise of the visual narratives process is to bring some of those learning elements into conscious thought and apply choice as to where creative energies are directed.

As is often the case for the patient, confusion and chaos surround the experience of a cancer diagnosis (Jacobsen & Andrykowski, 2015). The phenomenon can cloud the rational understanding of the event, and the potential struggles are not limited to the initial stages of the cancer experience. During the transitional and extended stages, four potential outcome states have been identified: (1) continued deterioration; (2) return to normal life at a state considered less that previous; (3) return to normal life pattern; and (4) psychological growth as a result of the cancer experience (Andrykowski, Lykins, & Floyd, 2008). Art therapy has the potential to support the psycho-social-spiritual development of cancer survivors and family members as they progress through the seasons of cancer care.

Through many efforts to develop a language, and understanding, with which to share the work of art therapy in oncology care, a perceptual model of care has emerged. This model is a culmination of translated experiences and ideas, creative explorations by persons diagnosed with cancer, and a perspective of the zeitgeist of art therapy in oncology care.

For the cancer survivor, art and art-making has an inherent capacity to aid in the development of meaning, and can relate that meaning to other elements of life, in order to create the narrative to integrate the pre- and post-diagnosis self (Hass-Cohen, Clyde Findlay, Carr, & Vanderlan, 2014). For the patient, learning is ongoing and without predefined variables. Image creation and reflection can expand schemas and challenge heuristics, leading to new meaning for life experiences. Artistic reflections of cancer events have been seen to promote greater self-understanding and a sense of gratitude (McNutt, 2016). The happenstance of being comes with many instances of learning that can distort or enhance the world a person has learned to live in (Krumboltz, 2009).

Four Modes of Art Therapy Intervention

This perceptual model of care includes four major sections related to the art therapy care of cancer survivors. The sections were seen to correspond relatively with previously articulated seasons of survivorship (Miller et al., 2008; Mullan, 1985). The seasons of survivorship start at diagnosis; through diagnosis and treatment, cancer survivors were said to be in the acute season. The next sequential season is transitional, and moves beyond the treatment stage, including fears, adjustments, and loss of the healthcare team. Following the transitional season is extended survivorship, where life is reestablished. The last season is referred to as the permanent season of survivorship (Miller et al., 2008).

Through a thematic analysis of visual narratives, including artist statements and interviews with 15 cancer survivors, eight themes of the cancer experience were found (McNutt, 2016). This analysis revealed four themes that centered on the physical experience of cancer and four themes related to the art therapy experience in regard to cancer care. The themes corresponded to the stages of survivorship, and are represented in the original work as seen in Table 7.1 (McNutt, 2016, p. 61–62).

In alignment with the four modes, art therapists and art practitioners have reported the benefits of art participation and art therapy for cancer survivors, with the earliest reports made from Dreifuss-Kattan (1990) and Predeger (1996). Through her experience as an art therapist with cancer patients, Dreifuss-Kattan (1990) reported that the work allowed patients to transform their perception of the cancer experience and improve quality of life. Predeger (1996) found that through a cooperative experiential art-making inquiry

Table 7.1 Themes and Subthemes of Cancer Survivors Experience with Visual Narratives

Cancer Experience		*Art Therapy Benefit*	
Theme	*Subthemes*	*Theme*	*Sub-themes*
1. Diagnosis and the Onset of the Cancer Journey	Diagnosis Reaction Perception of Control	2. Instilling Hope Through Imagery and Recognizing Strength in Self-Expression	Need for Hope Strength, Encouragement and Possibility Trust
3. Ongoing Treatment and Support	Physical Experience Healthcare Disparities Coping with Treatment Support and Relationships	4. Relaxation and Refocus by Means of Creation, Repetition, and Containment	Expression Catharsis Distraction
5. Transition to Life After Cancer	Ongoing Distress Emotion New Life Freedom	6. Defining Ongoing Survivorship and Reestablishing of Resilience	Self-Learning Metaphor Purpose and Meaning-Making
7. Post-cancer Growth	Gratitude Increased Vitality	8. Refining a Creative Identity and Reimagining the Self	Creative Identity Transformed Image

with breast cancer patients themes of the need for self-expression, elements of control, recognition of changing perspectives, access to a higher level of awareness, connection with the group, increased desire for creativity, and a celebration of the feminine spirit were present.

Luzzatto and Gabriel (1998) made efforts to develop an understanding of art therapy and art psychotherapy, and introduced art therapy as an integral component of the field of psycho-oncology. The two developed *The Creative Journey*, a 10-week group process for cancer survivors for exploring the cancer experience, "strengthening the inner self," and "trusting the environment" (Luzzatto & Gabriel, 2000, p. 265). Luzzatto and Magill (2010, 2015) maintained the inclusion of art therapy in psycho-oncology and reported the five benefits of "(1) reduction in reports of physical pain; (2) cathartic release of emotional issues; (3) improved positive coping strategies; (4) new insight into their own behavior; (5) increased ability to confront existential issues" (Luzzatto & Magill, 2010, p. 423). The identification of these benefits enhances the understanding of the importance of art, creativity, and art therapy in oncology care.

Rockwood-Lane (2005) was a nurse who brought art-making experiences to patients on an inpatient cancer floor; through her qualitative review of the work, she found themes of spiritual growth, discovery and transcendence, enlightening experience, surrender, and connection to the psychic.

Collie, Bottorff, and Long (2006) also interviewed cancer survivors who had engaged in art therapy during cancer treatment; through the analysis of the interviews, themes of the importance of emotional expression, trusting that expression, addressing disempowering self-talk, providing a sense of self-worth, motivation through the aesthetic, and connection with a larger community emerged. Furthermore, Glinzak (2016) found a significant reduction in self-reported distress for cancer survivors who engaged in art therapy in four venues of participation, including bedside in hospital rooms, chairside in infusion clinics, individual art therapy session, and an open studio setting. Participants indicated pre- and post-distress levels, along with a recollection of how the art therapy was beneficial by selecting from the following choices on the feedback form: relaxation and distraction; instillation of hope; introspection and self-learning; and transformation. Glinzak (2016) found that relaxation and distraction was reported more frequently across all venues. During individual sessions, introspection, self-learning, and transformation were more common than among the responses from those participating in other venues like open studio and in infusion clinics.

Visual Narratives

Each of the benefits found by these various authors, as stated above, are available to cancer survivors through participation in the visual narratives process. The process allows cancer survivors to explore the self, both as a composite and as a set of constructs. Through the dually lined relationship, which includes the client and art therapist, as well as the client and the artwork, the art therapist can facilitate the relationship between the cancer survivor and the art process (Luzzatto & Magill, 2015). Attention to the art process and resulting product allows those who have experienced cancer to learn and identify their experience of life pre and post cancer, and recall elements of strength that have not yet come to the surface. Display of the final product along with the artist statement is the culmination of the visual narrative intent. Audiences vary according to artist desire and appropriateness. Visual narrative displays have educated oncology staff on the patient experience, provided hope for new patients, and allowed families a new level of communication.

Visual narrative processes have been offered in individual session, small groups focused specifically on cancer care, and in an open studio format open to the community. Depending on comfort level, participants can choose between the three formats. Both individuals and group formats focus on ways to explore life elements of foundation, texture, composition, color, physical/emotional response, and presentation. The creation of the completed artwork has helped to incorporate these elements into a personal self-concept and artist statement, in order to support the visual narrative and connect the work to the potential viewer. In addition to the format, it is important for the art therapist to survey the art-making space for participants.

Precautions and Safety of Engaging in Art Therapy in Medical Setting

Depending upon the setting and media choice, some projects can get messy. Because art therapy programs often use a shared space within the medical system, it is imperative to protect tables, chairs, walls, and floors. Participants should also be informed of the potentially messy qualities of the artworks and asked to wear casual or worn clothing as they may become stained or worn through work done in this experience.

Some scissors and sharp tools may be used, if viewed as appropriate by the art therapist. The art therapist, having been trained in material use and safety, will observe all cautions to prevent harm. Cautions include lessons on the appropriate use of carving or cutting tools, awareness of potential hidden sharp objects such as pins in a quilt or bookmaking stitches, safe storage, and instruction on placing tools away from table edges to prevent falling. Some medications prevent the blood from clotting and even a small cut can be of great concern.

All materials used in an oncology setting will be nontoxic and approved for use with all ages. Materials must also meet infection control standards, including the criteria that a material needs to be washed and sanitized between uses; therefore, any art material that is unable to be washed, such as clay, should be discarded after one use. Material Safety and Data Sheets should be readily accessible when working on art processes in the medical setting. Participants should also be asked to provide any special precautions or other notifications, including allergies and/or fall risks, prior to engaging in the art therapy session.

Safety of Patient Information

Visual narratives in individual and small group formats are considered a form of art psychotherapy. Informed consent to participate, a general intake and information form, limits of confidentiality, consent to photograph, and consent to display forms should be completed prior to or during the initial session. Session notes taken in and after meetings are stored in a locked file cabinet. Regardless of whether an initial consent to display form was completed, the participating cancer survivor should revisit the topic following the creation of the visual narrative. Visual narratives have been created to benefit a wide range of viewers, and some have been created where a smaller audience is more appropriate. It may be that the cancer survivor and the art therapist are the most appropriate and desired audience; the art therapist and cancer survivor work together to determine the best course of action.

In respect for participants, any photographs taken of cancer survivors and/or visual narratives should be done with a camera that is not connected to the Internet and one that is not transported outside of the medical setting. At no time should the art therapist share or post images of visual narratives onto an online format without explicit written consent regarding the precise Internet site and/or intentions of showing.

Visual Narrative Process

The delineated steps of the visual narrative process below are generalized. Some cancer survivors may use more or less time on certain aspects, and the process should be allowed to emerge on an individualized basis. Goals for visual narrative creation should be established in the early sessions between the cancer survivor and art therapist. Basic goals for the visual narratives are to facilitate reflection on the cancer trajectory and experience, assist clients with self-exploration, including intricacies in recognition of psychological patterns, self-expression, self-definition, and to allow the opportunity for altruism through the intent of final product display.

Beginning Assessment

Two levels of assessment are involved in the beginning stages of visual narrative creation. First, is that of the survivor's cancer story that is to be told; stories can be developmental, situational, or inspirational. Cancer survivors often arrive to the first visual narrative session with a story already in mind, others may have a general idea of where to start, and some do not know what part of the journey to share. Wherever the story begins, due to insights gained during the art-making process, it is most likely to change during the course of visual narrative creation. For finding the starting point of the story, art therapy avenues such as collage, scribble drawings, and use of the bridge drawing assessment have been successful. Many art therapy assessments help to cultivate ideas and important elements for the visual narrative, and some notation of ideas for a basis of the visual narrative are recommended during the early stages as ideas come and go quickly.

The second assessment is in regards to media choice. Material use can be determined by artist preference or by the expected outcome for the narrative. Media exploration can be aligned with the expressive therapies continuum (ETC), depending upon the participant's preference and the desired results in presentation (Hinz, 2009). The ETC correlates media properties such as controllability and dimensionality along a continuum of states of being, ranging from precision of cognitive work through the cathartic energy of the kinesthetic. It should also be noted by the art therapist which media supports comfortable states and/or levels of anxiety during the creation stage.

Media and Theme Exploration

Building a foundation upon which to create the story provides a central focus for art therapy sessions. It also provides a safe and supportive space in which the cancer survivor can tell and retell the stories until they become grounded. The foundational work will help to include insights and developments as they arise in both memory and in real life. Keeping an open mind and awareness, while images arise, will allow the cancer story to evolve and begin to tell itself. The cycle of awareness, identification, and integration can create benefit and growth in the storyteller (Krumboltz, 2009).

Media of choice can be selected, and accompanied by any instruction that needs to take place, at this early stage. The artist/cancer survivor should have enough knowledge to work with media without dictating style. Particularly for survivors in the treatment phase of cancer care, frustration with lack of media control can overshadow the meaning and intent of the art-making process.

Media Fluency and Attuned Space

In order to support the strength and structure of the visual narrative as it develops, the cancer survivor or artist should work with the media to develop a level of fluency. The art therapist supplies basic instruction and provides materials for practice. Cancer survivors are encouraged to engage in a playful manner with the material and to find a relaxed method of interface with it.

During this time, the art therapist continues to develop a therapeutic alliance. The level of therapeutic attunement is accentuated by the engagement in the therapeutic use of art (Kossak, 2009). Safety of space and attunement give way to the survivors' unjudged exploration into the art process and illustration of the visual narrative. The art therapist is also responsible for supporting the relationship of the cancer survivor to the art process and encouraging the triadic communication between art therapist, cancer survivor, and artwork (Luzzatto & Magill, 2010). The cancer survivor will enter this space at a rate of his or her own comfort and readiness.

Also within the attuned space, liminal imagery becomes palpable. Artwork created in this palpable space can be seen as a form of arts-based inquiry and can provide an avenue between conscious and subconscious phenomena. Art-making provides imagery rich with the intermingled psyche of all parties involved (Fish, 2016). In this method, time becomes allusive and imagery arises that may enhance the final images of the visual narrative.

The Working Phase

Following the goals determined in both story and media choice, the working phase may take several sessions and may continue outside of sessions. Identification of the story and presentation will be the focus of determining size, dimensionality, and interface between artist statement and visual work. Discussion regarding boundaries and personal presentation is relevant through the working phase of visual narrative creation. The visual narrative develops through a dynamic communication within the triadic art therapy relationship.

Art creation, when seen as an isomorphic demonstration, brings to the surface glimpses of underlying 'truths' within the self (McNiff, 2004).

Through the process of arts-based inquiry, elements not available in current paradigms can emerge. This phase of art therapy work demonstrates an access to the 'bigger picture.' The original goals for the visual narrative are often transformed through the art-making working phase. The working phase continues as an interface between the evolving visual narrative and decision-making of inclusion of elements that come up and are notated.

Wrapping Up and Presentation Preparation

How one presents one's work to the selected audience is the center of this phase. It can start with the working phase or after the visual narrative is complete. The topics of discussion center on personal presentation along with potential ramifications and social issues regarding outreach and advocacy.

The wrapping up time is also an opportunity for the cancer survivor to reflect on insights gleaned through the visual narrative process. In light of the new material and skills from which to see the cancer experience, and life in general, cancer survivors can experience many emotions. The opportunity exists here to empower and reauthor the metaphoric domains from which life is experienced. Reflection and containment of these experiences can work as a catalyst toward the execution of the artist statement.

Closure and Artist Statement

Many who have experienced cancer have demonstrated growth in light of the experience (Andrykowski et al., 2008). In an art therapy process, such as the visual narrative, one may aid cancer survivors in reacclimating to a post-cancer life accentuated by growth and insight due to the work with art materials and engagement with art therapy imagery.

The writing of the artist statement serves as a summary of the visual narrative process, and an introduction of the artist to the desired audience. The audience selection may include oncology professionals, other cancer survivors, those newly diagnosed with cancer, the general public, or a specific target audience. It remains the right of the cancer survivor artist to decline the public display of the visual narrative. The artist statement also serves as a sort of feedback to the art therapist as the keys to discovering the success of any psychosocial intervention is not how the facilitator performs in sessions, but how the client extends relevant learning seeds from within the session into life at large (Krumboltz, 2009).

Visual Narrative Artwork Example

Natasha Onco Warrior completed her visual narrative during open studio participation. It is currently on display in the entrance corridor of an infusion clinic and is serving as inspiration to patients undergoing chemotherapy and their families. Natasha expressed excitement and joy when she noticed the work was hanging at the most visible location near the entrance door (Figure 7.1).

Figure 7.1 "My Journey"

I walk in the dry and burning Desert of the unknown.
Measuring tools seem to surround me as I must be treated often.
A firm foundation built on Faith and Hope enables me to face the devastation that has torn the fabric of my life. This journey takes me on strange paths, through healing territories that are both beautiful and dangerous. Time is my silent companion while I wait for results, count days since the last procedure, anticipate the next treatment, add up anniversaries, and wonder about the future. I walk. I run. I climb. I tire. I pray. I fall down. I cry. I rest. I get up. I go on. I fall and rise again. I grow in serenity and courage and wisdom. Some tears, like drops of holy water, are left along the way.
The last one falls on this side of the door through which I shall pass into the place of my beautiful ending where all will be well.

Conclusion

Venues for display of the visual narratives have included temporary art exhibitions in public areas of the medical center; traveling exhibits that move between clinical spaces with particular emphasis on sharing with newly diagnosed individuals; displays in specific physician's offices, and installation into an annually rotating artwork display. Reception of the artworks have been positive by patients, families, and oncology healthcare professionals. Art therapy and visual narrative participation has increased hope and strength during cancer treatments, provided relaxation and mindful expression, facilitated introspection and self-awareness, and helped to develop creativity for the cancer survivor.

References

Andrykowski, M. A., Lykins, E., & Floyd, A. (2008). Psychological health in cancer survivors. *Seminars in Oncology Nursing, 24*(3), 193–201. doi: 10.1016/j.soncn.2008.05.007

Collie, K., Bottorff, J. L., & Long, B. C. (2006). A narrative view of art therapy and art making my women with breast cancer. *Journal of Health Psychology, 11*(5), 761–775. doi: 10.1177/1359105306066632

Dreifuss-Kattan, E. (1990). *Cancer stories: Creativity and self-repair.* Hillsdale, NJ: The Analytic Press.

Fish, B. J. (2016). *Arts based supervision: Cultivating therapeutic insight through imagery.* New York, NY: Routledge/Taylor and Francis Group.

Glinzak, L. (2016). Effects of art therapy on distress levels of adults with cancer: A proxy pretest study. *Art Therapy: The Journal of the American Art Therapy Association, 33*(1), 27–34. doi: 10.1080/07421656.2016.1127687

Hass-Cohen, N., Clyde Findlay, J., Carr, R., & Vanderlan, J. (2014). "Check, change what you need to change and/or keep what you want:" An art therapy neurobiological-based trauma protocol. *Art Therapy: Journal of the American Art Therapy Association, 31*(2), 69–78. doi: 10.1080/07421656.2014.903825

Hinz, L. D. (2009). *The expressive therapies continuum: A framework for using art in therapy.* New York, NY: Taylor and Francis Group.

Jacobsen, P. B., & Andrykowski, M. A. (2015). Tertiary prevention in cancer care: Understanding and addressing the psychological dimensions of cancer during the active treatment period. *American Psychologist, 70*(2), 134–145. doi: 10.1037/a0036513

Kossak, M. S. (2009). Therapeutic attunement: A transpersonal view of expressive arts therapy. *Art Psychotherapy, 36*(1), 13–18. doi: 10.1016/j.aip.2008.09.003

Krumboltz, J. D. (2009). The happenstance learning theory. *Journal of Career Assessment, 17*(2), 135–154. doi: 10.1177/1069072708328861

Luzzatto, P. M., & Gabriel, B. (1998). Art therapy. In J. C. Holland (Ed.), *Psycho-oncology* (pp. 653–836). New York, NY: Oxford University Press.

Luzzatto, P. M., & Gabriel, B. (2000). The creative journey: A model for short-term group art therapy with posttreatment cancer patients. *Art Therapy: Journal of the American Art Therapy Association, 17*(4), 265–269. doi: 10.1080/07421656.2000.10129764

Luzzatto, P. M., & Magill, L. (2010). Art therapy and music therapy. In J. C. Holland, W. S. Breitbart, P. B. Jacobsen, M. S. Lederbarg, M. J. Loscalzo, & R. McCorkle (Eds.), *Psycho-oncology* (2nd ed., pp. 422–428). New York, NY: Oxford University Press.

Luzzatto, P. M., & Magill, L. (2015). Art and music therapy. In J. C. Holland, W. S. Breitbart, P. B. Jacobsen, M. J. Loscalzo, R. McCorkle, & P. N. Putow (Eds.), *Psycho-oncology* (3rd ed., pp. 497–502). New York, NY: Oxford University Press.

McNiff, S. (2004). *Art heals: How creativity cures the soul.* Boston, MA: Shambala Press.

McNutt, J. V. (2016). *Art therapy and cancer care: A qualitative analysis of visual oncology narratives.* Doctoral Dissertation. Retrieved from Scholarship at Lesley: http://ir.flo.org/lesley/institutionalPublicationPublicView.action;jsessionid=38610C07DE111FDF9136C01A412743D6?institutionalItemId=2246

Miller, K., Merry, B., & Miller, J. (2008). Seasons of survivorship revisited. *The Cancer Journal, 12*(6), 369–374. doi: 10.1097/PPO.0b013e31818edf60

Mullan, F. (1985). Seasons of survival: Reflections of a physician with cancer. *New England Journal of Medicine, 313,* 270–273. doi: 10.1056/NEJM198507253130421

Predeger, E. (1996). Womanspirit: A journey into healing through art in breast cancer. *Advances in Nursing Science, 18*(3), 48–58.

Rockwood-Lane, M. (2005). Spirit body healing: A hermeneutic phenomenological study examining the lived experience of art and healing. *Cancer Nursing Journal, 28*(4), 285–291.

8 Storytelling with Expressive Arts Therapy

Medical Therapeutic Work with Individuals

Vered Zur and Boaz Zur

We, Vered and Boaz, are a couple who have brought the unique work of expressive arts therapy to Ireland. As we journey through life, we enjoy engaging with people from all over the world, collecting stories and experiencing different cultures. Our personal connections to storytelling has transitioned from listening to stories as children, to telling stories to our own children, to our growth as expressive therapy professionals who now incorporate storytelling into our practice. Our love for traveling around the world has brought us to understand and believe that mankind has been telling stories ever since earliest existence, from the time of the caveman all the way through to our present day. Storytelling is part of culture, and helps people to keep their traditions, find connections, and meaning to life, making the process of storytelling a beneficial component within treatment.

The power of storytelling with those in the medical community can be engaging and healing; allowing the medical patient to actively listen, and/or create their own story, creates a therapeutic platform for emotional, and even physical, processing. Storytelling can help see the world and our life in a different perspective. This chapter will illustrate the therapeutic benefits, and applications, of storytelling within expressive arts therapy within medical communities. As storytelling can become a place where emotions, clarity, and wonder all blend together in the unknown, a medical patient can find a creative channel that can be expressed through the voice, movement, art, and drama of telling a story.

The Connection Between Storytelling and Therapy

The approach of storytelling is composed of three elements: the story, the teller, and the audience (Warren, 2008). Only when the three blend together, as each element intertwines with the others, is the magic of storytelling created. Viewed as an act of healing, storytelling can be therapeutic for individuals, groups, and the community. The Native Americans, for example, told many stories in gatherings, celebrations, and mourning and in the passing of the seasons (Benson, 2015). The whole community was involved in these tales, and the stories and memories have been integrated into the culture.

Storytelling, within a therapeutic approach, allows an individual to lead the characters and storyline, providing a free flow of expression within the process (Angus, 2012). Even though an individual can perform a story, there still needs to be an audience, even if it's an audience of one. A main benefit to storytelling is that it can transform into the environment that the individual chooses: it can be a community experience, where the story is performed for a group, or an individual, more intimate, experience, where the story is performed for the therapist. Whether within a group setting, for a sense of belongingness, or individual, for a deeper level of personal processing, both storytelling experiences bring the essence of the therapeutic work to life—that of empowerment.

Engagement with the audience of choice further adds to the therapeutic value, as a storyteller looks in the eyes of his audience, whether it is a group or the therapist alone, and feels the place where the story being told is having an impact, where it is being processed. There is no learning a story by heart or just reciting from what was prepared. Storytellers let images that they see and feel lead them, allowing the story to appear and come alive. The images are both the anchor and wings in which the storytellers trust to guide them as the story spontaneously develops. Listening to stories happens not only with our ears, but also with our eyes. They come from our imagination: visual, emotional, and physical. Some say a storyteller is like a fisherman with a net, he throws the net into the air and catches stories.

Storytelling in expressive art therapy (EXA) can be viewed as a spiritual path, incorporating the use of one's imagination and creativity to reflect and cope with his or her own personal journey through life. Specifically, within the realm of EXA, storytelling has helped individuals within the medical community to communicate, reflect, and find a safe space to express their fears to the therapist or within a group (Machtinger et al., 2015; Tamagawa et al., 2015). The importance of storytelling in the stage of illness can be seen as a parallel for medical healing; the use of storytelling can happen anywhere, not only within the hospital, and supports the medically ill patient in strengthening the feeling of a supportive community.

The goal of the therapeutic work through storytelling is to support the client so he or she may reach that place of belonging and empowerment. This is especially true with the medically ill client, who many times can feel isolated, anxious, stressed, and fearful when facing a medical diagnosis. Within EXA, we have brought the therapeutic value of storytelling to individuals diagnosed with cancer, brain injuries, and intellectual disabilities, in addition to their caregivers. To build trust between the client and the expressive therapist, there are a few fundamental aspects that must be addressed: a need for expression to be created a safe space, which is nonjudgmental, compassionate, and clear in its boundaries, and a need to be in an environment clear of projections (Rogers, Tudor, Tudor, & Keemar, 2012). Although storytelling can essentially occur in a variety of settings, it is important for the therapist to determine the appropriate environment for the individual to engage in the therapeutic process.

Working with Storytelling in the Therapeutic Session

Although stories have a spontaneity, it is important to help the client in creating a framework for his or her own story. In the therapeutic process, it is the therapist who tells or preforms that first story. This allows the client to sit, listen, and engage with the process in a nonthreatening manner. After the story is complete, the next step is to discuss what the story was about, what could have been changed to assist the story, and finally how the story might be related to the client's, or group's, present situation.

The Hero Path

The art of storytelling consists of six specific components, related to the work of Joseph Campbell, that are incorporated into many stories. Campbell, a Jungian researcher, developed the 'Hero Path' (1990) and found that stories from around the world, no matter from which culture, have a shared commonality or thread. They all share a storyboard of the Hero Path, which consists of six frames that create the overall story (Table 8.1).

In the framework of the Hero Path, the Hero is the main character of the story. The Hero is the one who has the problem or situation that the story focuses on. It is important to state that the Hero does not necessarily have to be a human; it can be an animal, a creature from a fantasy world, or even a being that is half animal and half human. It can also be any age, such as a baby, child, teenager, mature adult, or older person. The second stage is the Problem, which can be anything that concerns the Hero. It can be an actual, created, or an existential problem. In the third stage, the Hero (with their Problem) finds the Helper. The Helper can be a person, animal, tool, or even some type of combination. In the storyboard, the Helper supports the Hero as he or she faces the fourth stage, which is that of Challenge. It can be a singular challenge or a challenge of all sorts, and some obstacles may require the Hero to find resources from within to overcome them. In the fourth stage of Challenge, the Hero has the choice of giving up and not solving the Problem or finding the inner strength to overcome the Challenge. The Hero might even surprise him- or herself in that he or she has managed a way to overcome the Challenge. The Hero then embarks on a Journey, the fifth stage, in search of a resolution to the Problem. On the journey, the Hero, by overcoming the Challenge, enters the sixth stage of Change Process, where there is personal/internal growth. This stage can come in a more complex

Table 8.1 The Hero Path's Six Frames to Creating a Storyboard

Frame/Stage 1: **The Hero**	Frame/Stage 2: **The Problem**
Frame/Stage 3: **The Helper**	Frame/Stage 4: **The Challenge**
Frame/Stage 5: **The Journey**	Frame/Stage 6: **The Change Process**

way; there might be more than one Helper, and/or there might even be two or more main characters. When using storytelling and storyboards in therapy, it is best to start with the basic story development. As the sessions continue, stories can become more in-depth and personalized.

The Application of Storytelling Within the Medical Setting: The Case of Audrey

Audrey was a single woman in her early 60s who was diagnosed with breast cancer. When she arrived at session, she presented as very emotional and appeared stressed. During the intake and rapport building, she was given the opportunity to discuss the things that she believed were important. Audrey spoke about her recent cancer diagnosis, her limited family interactions, and her concerns and fears related to her future. It became clear, as the therapeutic session progressed, that Audrey carried with her emotional deprivation from her childhood. As a child, Audrey's mother struggled with illness. At the time, Audrey took on the role of caregiver and put her childhood aside.

Audrey shared that during this time, she would listen to the radio, dance, and play with her imagination. Audrey says this was a *bit similar to Cinderella's story*. Through her connection to the story of Cinderella, Audrey could discuss her fears related to her medical situation in a more fluid manner and through metaphor. The client identified with the Hero (Cinderella), her Problem, and how Cinderella was able to overcome and move on. Audrey discussed the story with us, as she could connect to it, and was able to identify her concern for her health and future. Since this proved to be both a powerful and beneficial session for Audrey, the next natural step was to incorporate working with storytelling.

At the following session, we used the Architecture of a Session (Knill, 2005, p. 95) as a guideline for the different stages. Every session began with a *checking in*, and continued with *sensitizing* or *bridging* in from daily life. The next stage was going into *decentering* to the artwork, which for Audrey was her life story, through creative writing, drawing, adding photos from her life, and finding relative pictures from magazines. The goal of *decentering* is to actually physically and mentally *decenter*, to move away from one's daily life and open to the surprise that appears in the artwork, which comes in the form as a 'third' between the individual and his or her creative process.

We then introduced Audrey to the storyboard. At this point, she became involved in the artwork to create a six-framed story. Audrey was given paper for her to begin creating her story; it could be her own literal story, or it could be an imaginative story. It was totally up to Audrey. Audrey was able to approach this in a manner she felt most comfortable, by writing, drawing, cutting pictures from magazines, etc.

To enhance her skills as a storyteller, we mentioned that a story is made up of different characters who all have dialogues and monologues. They have emotions that can be happy, sad, love, hate, courageous, fear, and so on. The characters go through various activities and actions, and the story can occur in one or more locations. The story is composed of many details, and there are different rhythms along the occurrence of the plot as it can create different situations. Audrey chose to tell her story using all these techniques.

To encourage, and not overwhelm, we gave Audrey a 'low skill' with 'high sensitivity' activity (Knill, 2005). We recommended that she could draw simple images and not to worry about proper grammar. What was important was that she remained authentic to her own feelings and thoughts. She got totally immersed in her work. In all the following sessions, she would continue from the place she finished from the previous session. We would help her by providing all the materials and by holding the space, by listening to her unfolding life story. She came to me once a week over a period of 3 months.

Over the 3-month period, Audrey told her story in a new way, with new vision and understanding. That brought her to the next stage, which was the 'harvesting' (Knill, 2005, p. 156). This is the place where she harvested the fruits from her story and became the storyteller. There were moments when she danced in the room to express her movement through life. We would create a bridging out from her artwork through reflections to the outside world. At the end of each session, it was ensured that Audrey felt safe enough to leave the therapeutic room and return to her life.

At the end of 12 sessions, Audrey had a scroll that she could open and close to look at and reflect (Figure 8.1). The scroll was filled with drawings, stories, and photos from her life, as well as cutouts from magazines. It began in childhood and moved to present time. She told her life story and acted through the drama and movement scenes from her life. Audrey engaged in many different art modules, but storytelling was her main art medium.

It was important for Audrey to work through her past to this present day. This storyboard reflects a certain period in her life. As she grew up, Audrey was finally allowed to move on and face new challenges and journeys that contributed to a continued change process in herself towards growth. Over time Audrey was able to discuss her present medical situation, recent surgery, upcoming treatments, and her fear and anxiety of the unknown. She identified her own strength and support systems.

Through storytelling, and the application of the Hero, Audrey could identify the Problems she faced, the Helpers in her life, one being herself, and the Challenges she faces as she continues her Journey to arrive and realize the Change Process of moving forward.

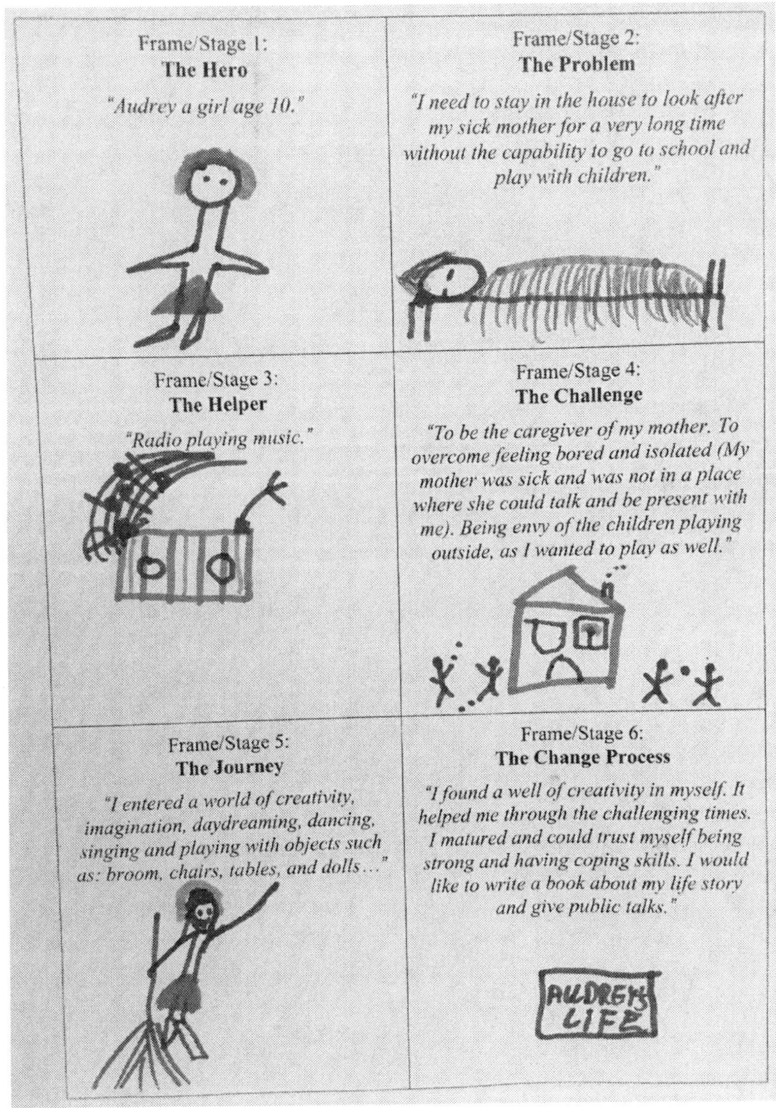

Figure 8.1 The storyboard based on Audrey's personal story

Conclusion

It is amazing to see how people connect to the oral tradition and use it as a tool that can help them reflect. From the case of Audrey, we see how storytelling plays a large role in the process of healing. The tradition of storytelling can allow individuals to face their lives in a nonthreatening way; address challenges, especially related to medical illness; and through the Change Process, lead to a life that is insightful, purposeful, and meaningful.

The creative storytelling process allows the client the opportunity to look around and develop creative ways of looking back at his or her own memories, and present-day challenges; then, an individual can find ways of seeing his or her personal journey to enrich his or her life. People seem to enjoy using the creative work of storytelling. For so many, this process helps them to find ways to grow within a medical diagnosis, and find a belonging to something deep and authentic for themselves. They were courageous to put themselves in to the unknown, into spontaneity and to the surprise. These moments are precious in a new way, with intimacy and openness to a sacred space. Our intention is to keep developing the field of therapeutic storytelling and engaging people with the healing power and beauty. Stories are a precious gift.

References

Angus, L. (2012). Toward an integrative understanding of narrative and emotion processes in emotion-focused therapy of depression: Implications for theory, research, and practice. *Psychotherapy Research, 22*(4), 367–380. doi: 10.1080/10503307.2012.683988

Benson, M. R. (2015). Native American oral texts. In E. S. Nelson (Ed.), *Ethnic American literature: An encyclopedia for students* (pp. 373–375). Santa Barbara, CA: ABC-CLIO.

Campbell, J. (1990). *The Hero's journey: Joseph Campbell on his life and work.* Novato, CA: New World Library.

Knill, P., Levine, E. G., & Levine, S. K. (2005). *Principles and practice of expressive arts therapy: Towards a therapeutic aesthetics.* London, UK and Philadelphia, PA: Jessica Kingsley Publishers.

Machtinger, E. L., Lavin, S. M., Hilliard, S., Jones, R., Haberer, J. E., Capito, K., & Dawson-Rose, C. (2015). An expressive therapy group disclosure intervention for women living with HIV improves social support, self-efficacy, and the safety and quality of relationships: A qualitative analysis. *Journal of the Association of Nurses in AIDS Care, 26*(2), 187–198. doi: 10.1016/j.jana.2014.05.001

Rogers, N., Tudor, K., Tudor, L. E., & Keemar, K. (2012). Person-centered expressive arts therapy: A theoretical encounter. *Person-Centered & Experiential Psychotherapies, 11*(1), 31–47. doi: 10.1080/14779757.2012.656407

Tamagawa, R., Li, Y., Piemme, K. A., DiMiceli, S., Collie, K., & Giese-Davis, J. (2015). Deconstructing therapeutic mechanisms in cancer support groups: Do we express more emotion when we tell stories or talk directly to each other? *Journal of Behavioral* Medicine, *38*(1), 171–182. doi: 10.1007/s10865–014–9589-y

Warren, L. (2008). *The oral tradition today: An introduction to the art of storytelling.* New York, NY: Pearson Learning Solutions.

9 Medical Dance/Movement Therapy for Chronic Conditions

An Overview of Important Outcomes

Sharon W. Goodill and Sabine C. Koch

Medical dance/movement therapy, in the context of this chapter, is a psychosocial support service for patients, their families, and caregivers, and is part of the continuum of integrative healthcare. This discussion is oriented to the needs of adults with chronic medical illnesses, including cancer and pulmonary, cardiac, and neurological conditions. Medical illness has increased its research focus not only in medical dance/movement therapy, but across the creative arts therapies. We discuss the key outcomes: *vitality, mood and emotions, body image, relationship-focused coping, and self-efficacy*, and their measurement with the Heidelberg State Inventory well-being questionnaire, constructed on basis of the identification of the five foci. In addition, this chapter introduces theoretical concepts to support and inform the practice of dance/movement therapy with medically ill people and their loved ones. For the purposes of this discussion, medical illness shall refer to conditions that present initially and primarily as physical (as opposed to psychiatric or behavioral) in nature.

Introduction

Dance/movement therapy (DMT) is a mind–body approach to psychotherapy, and is increasingly offered in the conventional medical arena as a psychosocial service. The basic clinical methods of DMT, originally practiced in mental health settings, are intrinsically suited for adaptation to those with medical conditions, even if the capacity for physical movement is compromised. DMT interventions are directed to the places in human experience where psyche meets soma, where the kinesthetic and the cognitive intersect, and where bodily felt emotions can find motoric expression in the interactive context of a therapeutic relationship. If phenomena and changes in the physical body are a source of pain, distress, anger, or isolation, then a somatically oriented method of psychosocial support and intervention can have meaningful impact.

Research on DMT for medical populations has been proportionally growing since 2000. We observe an increase in research in oncology (Bradt, Shim, & Goodill, 2015; Ho, Fong, Cheung, Yip, & Luk, 2016), neurological disorders and dementia (Karkou & Meekums, 2014), Parkinson's disease (PD) (Hackney & Bennett, 2014), and cardiovascular disease such as chronic heart failure (Gomez Neto, Menezes, & Oliveira Carvalho, 2014). Figure 9.1 shows the increase in publications with a medical DMT title in comparison to other arts therapies from a simplified literature search. For DMT (as seen with the triangle line), two phase changes stand out: Goodill's (2005a) first

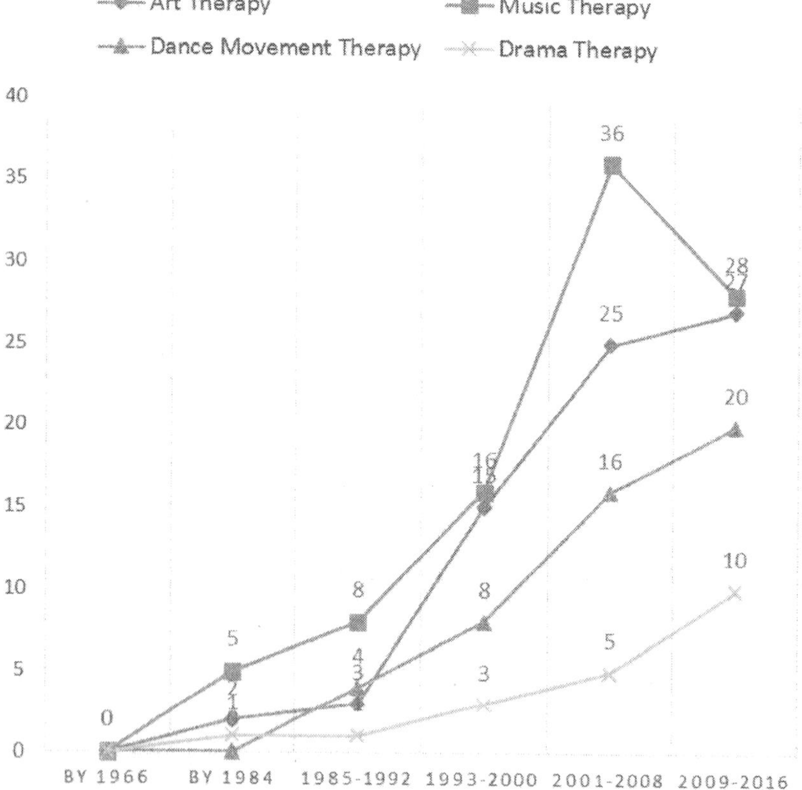

Figure 9.1 A simple Google Scholar search with the four search terms "medical art/music/dance movement/drama therapy," considering the first 10 pages of search results for each discipline (hand selected) yielded the following article numbers for arts therapies in the medical field. A pronounced increase over time is visible for all four major arts therapies

description of the specialty of medical DMT, followed by Hackney and Earhart's (2009) publication on Tango for PD. Today, most medical DMT publications are on PD or dementia, followed by cancer, chronic pain, and chronic heart failure.

This chapter is concerned with the needs of adults living with various chronic medical conditions, salient targeted outcomes for DMT, and their measurement. Chronic illness is a leading cause of death in the world in both developed and developing countries, having eclipsed the threats of both infectious and acute diseases (Hyman, 2005). Comorbidity rates for medical conditions and psychiatric disorders demand our attention and are part of the rationale for integrating mental health services into standard medical care plans. People living with chronic illness are aware of how the medical condition can impact vocational, spiritual, relational, sexual, emotional, and psychological aspects of life. Thus, comprehensive health care should include services that can help patients and their families cope with the many attendant stressors and adjust to the inevitable changes and limitations.

Dance/movement therapists have professionalized as mental health specialists, and are also aligned worldwide with the complementary therapies and arts in healthcare movements. Dance/movement therapists who specialize with patients who are primarily medically ill have completed the requisite education for entry into the field of DMT, and have additional knowledge and expertise particular to the conditions and issues faced by medical patients.

Medical applications of DMT require an integrated theoretical repertoire for the therapist to include constructs developed in health psychology and in the neurosciences. Five core outcomes for medical DMT have been proposed from literature review and clinical experience (Goodill, 2006): vitality, mood and emotions, body image of illness, relationship-focused coping, and self-efficacy (see also Melsom, 1999). In this chapter, these are examined from biopsychosocial perspectives with linkages to existing theory and practice of DMT.

Target Outcomes for Patients with Medical Illness

Vitality

In the DMT literature, vitality has been described as "a positive quality of aliveness. . . " (M. Chace, 1975, cited in Schmais, 1985, p. 24), and vitalization as "an increase of energy which mobilizes the entire body" (Ehrhardt, Hearn, & Novak, 1989, p. 49). For Schmais (1985) vitalization is one of eight therapeutic factors, or healing processes, in DMT as follows:

> In the dance therapy session there is a synergistic effect resulting from the stimulation of being in a group situation and from the activation that is caused by moving . . . freeing the impulse to act and the energy to do so.
>
> (p. 25)

Ehrhardt, Hearn, and Novak (1989) conducted a related study with 66 psychiatric patients who participated in DMT sessions. They used structured interviews, participant responses to videotapes of DMT sessions and participants' ranking of the therapeutic factors. Vitalization was ranked by patients as most important among the healing processes by this sample. The researchers surmised that the clients "valued vitalization most because it affords an antidote to the sedentary patterns of their lives" (p. 54). For people whose illness results in a sedentary life, the vitality offered in DMT can open the door to more invigorated ways of functioning and problem-solving. Ehrhardt and colleagues (1989) noted the conceptual similarity between vitalization and the curative factor *Instillation of Hope*, described by Yalom (1995), and hope can be very important to the medically ill (Folkman & Moskowitz, 2000).

Two subsequent DMT studies focused on vitality (or closely related constructs) as a dependent variable. Over a 14-month period, Bojner-Horwitz, Theorell, and Anderberg (2003) studied women with fibromyalgia who participated in a course of DMT and viewed themselves moving on videotape. Based on the video viewings, participants rated themselves on perceived life energy, mobility, and pain. The treatment group's perception was that of life energy increasing and that of the controls decreasing. The outcome variable, life energy, was defined as how the patients' emotional and physical state was affected by the medical condition.

Coccari and Weiler (2003) reported a pilot study of wellness-seeking individuals who participated in an 8-week program of DMT. Outcomes were measured with self-report and showed statistically significant increases in energy and stamina as well as overall physical vitality. In a description of DMT in cardiac rehabilitation, Seides (1986) observed that "movement gives individuals opportunities to regain a sense of aliveness within the boundaries of their own limitations" (p. 91).

Mood and Emotions

Many psychosocial interventions for medically ill patients attend to emotions. Psychosocial interventions often focus on the complementary goals of decreasing negative emotions (commonly including distress, sadness, fear, and anger) and supporting positive affect and emotions. Emotions typically identified as positive are eagerness, excitement, confidence, happiness, pride, love, hope, and relief; they can occur even during stressful times or in the context of serious health problems (Folkman & Moskowitz, 2000; Lazarus, 2000). Positive emotions are linked to better coping, mastery, and even spiritual transformation in the face of stressful experiences (Folkman & Moskowitz, 2000).

Persistent negative emotions can both accompany and erode health status: "Patients with chronic medical illnesses have higher rates of depression and anxiety and these [. . .] are associated with poor adherence to medical regimens and adverse medical outcomes" (Katon, Unützer, & Simon, 2004,

p. 1153). However, it is also important to give expression to the negative emotions. Numerous studies have been conducted on the health benefits of emotional expression through writing (Smyth & Arigo, 2009). In a study of health status in college students, Krantz and Pennebaker (2007) demonstrated that psychophysical expression about troubling emotions (i.e., a DMT therapy method) decreased negative affect, and when combined with writing, was associated with fewer visits to the health center (Heimes, 2012).

Dibbel-Hope's controlled study (2000) of DMT to assist women in adaptation to breast cancer is an example of how DMT can enhance mood and emotion for people with chronic illness. The 22 women who participated in her 6-week course of group DMT (using the method of authentic movement) showed statistically significant improvements in two components of mood, as measured by the Profile of Mood States (POMS) (McNair, Lorr, & Broppleman, 1981), increased vigor and decreased fatigue. Serlin, Classen, Frances, and Angell (2000) reported similar benefits from 12-week programs of existentially based DMT groups for women with breast cancer. Their data showed significant decreases in fatigue and tension and increases in vigor, as measured also with the POMS.

Body Image of Illness

The body image, as a construct of the subjective perception of the body and body parts, is difficult to measure by self-report because it is in many respects unconscious. Vamos (1993) developed a model for conceptualizing and assessing body image specifically in the context of a chronic physical disability or medical condition, noting that "the advent of physical illness increases its importance in overall self-representation and may therefore have considerable impact on overall self-esteem" (p. 163). It includes four dimensions (Vamos, 1993):

Comfort: pain, tiredness, dyspnea, sleep quality, parasthesias, nausea, enjoyment of food

Competence: cognitive ability, perceptual clarity, mobility, respiratory, nutritional, and sexual function

Appearance: self-evaluated, other-evaluated, visibility of disorder

Predictability: degree of variability, suddenness of change, age-appropriateness of disability

Each medical condition brings its own constellation of challenges to the body image. The body image is an appropriate focus for DMT, first because the health of the body image has implications for other areas of functioning and health:

> Successful psychosocial adaptation to CID [chronic illness and disabilities] is said to reflect the integration of physical and sensory changes

> into a transformed body image and self-perception. Unsuccessful adaptation, in contrast, is evidenced by experiences of physical and psychiatric symptoms such as unmitigated feelings of anxiety and depression, psychogenic pain, chronic fatigue, social withdrawal, and cognitive distortions.
>
> (Livneh & Antonak, 2005, p. 13)

Second, as Kinsbourne (2002) suggested, body image is essentially a "somatosensory background," formed through a coordination of "the somatic senses with intention and action, at times supplemented by vision" (p. 27). Kinsbourne advanced the attentional view of the body image, localizing it not in any part of the brain, but as a repository of information that the body/brain has about itself. According to Kinsbourne (2002), we attend to the body image when necessary, by slowing down, when in injury or pain, or when learning something new. Schilder (1950/1970) provided a strong rationale for dance/movement based rehabilitation of the body image when he described its malleability, as follows:

> Tension and relaxation of muscles, moving the body with and against gravity, with and against centrifugal impulses, may have an enormous influence on the body image. The phenomenon of the dance is therefore a loosening and changing in the body image.
>
> (p. 207)

Seides (1986) described how post-surgical cardiac patients feel as though they were "coming apart" (p. 90), as though the body's integrity had been disrupted, and how DMT supported a sense of integration. Considering Vamos' model in the context of DMT, one can hypothesize that movement interventions would impact body image in the areas of self-evaluation of *Appearance*, aspects of *Comfort* that relate to vitality (e.g., tiredness), and the mobility aspects of *Competence*. Seides' patients were adjusting to the suddenness of change in the body (the *Predictability* component), as surgical patients must do when a body part has been removed or altered, whether or not this entails a change in outward appearance.

Relationship-Focused Coping

The concept of coping (e.g., Lazarus, 2000) has been central to research on psychosocial aspects of medical illness. It seems that how patients and their loved ones both appraise and respond to the stressors associated with illness, and the resources they mobilize (or don't) in these responses, will impact quality of life, and sometimes the medical course of the illness. This is particularly important in chronic conditions, because adherence to self-care regimens is essential for the maintenance of function and control of symptoms. Emotions play a paradoxical role in that prolonged venting of emotions as the primary way of coping turns out not to be effective (Heimes, 2012). Yet, as noted earlier, the expression of emotions is beneficial for one's psychological and physical health.

The concept of relationship-focused coping extends the process of coping with stressors from an individualistic model to one that "considers coping within the interpersonal context of the health care system" (Revenson, 1994, p. 126). Findings by Rohrbaugh and colleagues (2004) focus on relationship-focused coping and the importance of relationships in adaptation to chronic illness. Their study of 191 congestive heart failure (CHF) patients and their spouses investigated both the patients' self-efficacy and the spouses' confidence in the patients and how each predicted patient survival over the ensuing 4 years. Both bode well for patient survival, but when compared, spousal confidence is a statistically stronger predictor than is the patient's own self-efficacy. The researchers concluded that spousal confidence in a CHF patient's ability to recover and survive constitutes a "fundamentally social protective factor" (Rohrbaugh et al., p. 184). Seides (1986) specifically emphasized the importance of including spouses in DMT for cardiac rehabilitation.

In DMT, therapists help their clients generalize from what is learned in sessions to their everyday and intimate relationships. DMT supports the building of relationships through socialization, physical interaction, sharing in creative processes, movement rituals, and nonverbal communication (Baudino, 2015; Serlin, Classen, Frances, & Angell, 2000).

In DMT assessment, elements of the dynamic, expressive movement repertoire are considered coping resources (Bartenieff & Lewis, 1980). From a behavioral standpoint, these observable, patterned building blocks of movement comprise humans' habitual and unique ways of responding to events and experiences, including stressors. For this reason, DMT treatment goals often include expanding the dynamic movement repertoire: increasing the range and mastery of various movement qualities, options for organizing movement in phrases, shaping in the kinesphere and ways of moving through space (Bartenieff & Lewis, 1980). When the expressive movement capacity is enhanced in these ways, an individual has more resources available for coping with stressors and challenges. Shaping in space with directional and three-dimensional movement patterns is associated with how one relates to the physical and social environment, and relationships are built in the process of moving through shared space with attention to oneself and other movers (Kestenberg-Amighi, Loman, Lewis, & Sossin, 1999).

Self-Efficacy

Self-efficacy (SE) has been defined as "the belief that one can successfully perform behaviors to produce a desired outcome" (Bandura, 1977; Berkman, 1995, p. 251) and "the belief that one can do what one has set out to do" (Endler, Kocovski, & Marcrodimitris, 2001, p. 618). A person's perception of one's own capacities is key to assessing SE, which, when strong, is associated with better self-care and adherence to medically prescribed regimens (Farrell, Wicks, & Martin, 2004). Even if SE is low at the point of diagnosis, it can be bolstered through interactive and social processes, particularly interventions, which encourage independent activity on one's own behalf (Berkman, 1995) and can provide empowerment to the patients.

DMT may be particularly suited to the goal of increasing SE and internal health locus of control for medical patients who need intervention in these areas. Consider how in DMT, it is the patient, not the therapist, who usually initiates expressive movement themes, which are then shaped through improvisation into metaphors for problem-solving (Koch, Fuchs, Summa, & Müller, 2012; Sandel, Chaiklin, & Lohn, 1993). Basic features of DMT, patient-initiated physical activity, and responsive attention between the therapist and the patient to the patient's own perceptions of bodily sensations combine to replicate the conditions needed to encourage SE. Bartenieff and Lewis (1980) emphasized the connection between the patients' intent to act and their "independent participation" in recovery through movement (p. 3).

A few DMT studies to date have explored the above notion. A randomized controlled trial (RCT) by Bräuninger (2012) included SE as a moderator variable. Yang (2004) explored the fit between DMT methods and components of SE as outlined by Bandura (1977): (1) enactive mastery experience, brought about through authentic experiences of success; (2) vicarious learning/modeling, attained through observing others' behavior and success; (3) allied social influences that occur through verbal persuasion or support; and (4) judgment of physiological and affective states, meaning how people feel about their physical and emotional states (Bandura, 1977, cf. Yang, 2004). Yang proposed DMT techniques that may facilitate increases in SE (turn-taking, mirroring, using verticality, expanding movement repertoire, stress management methods). Yang's case study of DMT with a woman living with both diabetes and substance abuse problems provided qualitative evidence of the impact on SE and adherence. In her final session, the patient stated: "What I have achieved is that I've learned to take care of myself, exercise, and 'patience' . . . Body and mind are both important for me and I didn't know it before. . . . I am confident. I can take care of my diabetes" (Yang, 2004, pp. 64–66).

In a small RCT of mood and adherence in adults with cystic fibrosis, Goodill (2005b) found that patients who received a brief course of DMT (n = 14) reported better adherence to nutritional self-care regimens 1 month after therapy completion, when compared to the control group (n = 10). SE was not measured, but the link between SE and adherence invites the possibility that a belief in ones' capacity for self-care was involved. Because the DMT intervention included body awareness methods, both active and in stillness, it is possible that learning to pay better attention to one's bodily cues may have led to an appreciation of the body's needs for self-care.

It is hypothesized that good adherence and self-care may be cultivated, perhaps sequentially, through both body awareness and SE. That is, one first must attend to the body's sensory and kinesthetic messages and then draw on a belief in oneself to engage in self-care behaviors. That DMT supports and enhances body self-awareness is well documented (Cruz & Sabers, 1998), and the integration of DMT attributes, with concepts of SE and adherence, constitutes a potent area for future research. Fuchs and Koch (2014) introduced a 10-item self-report measure for body self-efficacy (BSE), containing components of functionality and beauty for use after body-based interventions.

A Well-Being Measure for Patients with Medical Illness

With the Heidelberg State Inventory (HSI) (Koch, Morlinghaus, & Fuchs, 2007), a psychometric self-report measure, was created from the variables Goodill identified as important foci for patients with medical illness (Goodill, 2006; Koch et al., 2007). The five outcomes reported above were each conceptualized as one dimension, and a sixth dimension of 'tension' (fighting vs. indulgent *Effort* movements, an important basic dimension in DMT and Laban movement analysis) was added. Emotion was subdivided into clinical components of positive, depressed, and anxious affect, and body image was dropped because of poor measurability with self-report scales. The dimensions were named *positive affect, vitality, coping, depressed affect, anxious affect,* and *tension* and the scale was found to be reliable in the use with various populations.

The HSI was employed with patients with mental disorders (i.e., depression) (Koch et al., 2007); schizophrenia (Martin, Koch, Hirjak, & Fuchs, 2016); individuals with autism (Koch, Mehl, Sobanski, Sieber, & Fuchs, 2015); male prisoners (Koch, Steinhage, et al., 2015); university students (Koch, 2011); and finally patients with PD (Koch et al., 2016). The six dimensions were relevant to all clinical and nonclinical populations, and the HSI showed significant changes after DMT throughout the studies. The outcomes may thus not be specific to medically ill patients, but may generalize to other populations receiving DMT. Both the HSI and the BSE (body self-efficacy scale) have been extensively tested with various patient and student populations and have been published in open access journals (Fuchs & Koch, 2014; Koch et al., 2016).

Clinical Applications

In sum, research results suggest that DMT can improve affect/mood (e.g., Dibbel-Hope, 2000; Koch et al., 2016), vitality (Bojner Horwitz, Theorell, & Anderberg, 2003; Coccari & Weiler, 2003), body image (e.g., Pylvänäinen & Lappalainen, 2018), self-efficacy (e.g., Koch et al., 2016; Wiedenhofer & Koch, 2017), and coping (Bräuninger, 2012).

Clinically, DMT programming for people with primary medical conditions has been broadly applied. In pediatric populations, this includes oncology, pulmonary, medical rehabilitation, pain conditions, hospice, and NICU. With adult populations, work reported includes medical rehabilitation and neurorehabilitation, oncology, diabetes care, cardiac care, PD, tinnitus, chronic pain conditions, chronic fatigue syndrome, chronic heart failure, hospice, and palliative care. The scope of practice includes inpatient settings, ambulatory or community settings, and home-based care, with individuals and groups, including support services for family members and caregivers.

In clinical practice, DMT interventions can address all five outcomes in an integrated way. As an example of this, note how the following composite description of a typical DMT session from the first author's research study (Goodill, 2005b) involves all five treatment foci [bracketed words], holistically addressed in a single session:

> The warm up is structured with the therapist (SG) and the patient face-to-face, and begins with gentle stretching along with a verbal exchange about the patient's name [a pseudonym] current physical and emotional state, and inquiries about where she is feeling tension, or pain and she is encouraged to stretch in response to her own body's needs and cues [*assessment of own physiological state, a component of self-efficacy*]. I reflect her movement initiations, noticing the small variations that are her own, and encouraging her to amplify or explore them [building *relationship support* and *emotional expression*]. As the movement develops along with verbal exchange, imagery emerges and there is some playful laughter [*vitality*] in the spontaneous movement conversation between us. She is reminded of other conversations outside the hospital, and relates some frustration about how she is seen by others, asserting, "I have CF, I am not CF!" [*body image, emotional expression*] and uses the quality of strength in a movement that involves her full body [*vitality*]. I noted the use of strong, assertive qualities and reinforced that as a *coping* resource. The session ends with guided imagery and relaxation. She emerges from that in a calm state, smiling, and declaring proudly that she could fully relax [*an enactive mastery experience, building self-efficacy*].

The five foci discussed herein are not a complete list of themes and clinical concerns in DMT for adults with medical conditions. Pain relief, spirituality, grief, freedom, meaning, isolation, and other issues (Serlin et al., 2000) can be equally important to individual patients and their loved ones. The described outcomes provide a framework for therapists working with chronically medically ill adults. Holistic interventions, such as DMT, accept that any or all of these issues may seem important on a given day, and that an intervention directed to one problem may well bring some relief or clarity in another area in a systemic way. Numerous works in the psychology literature show the overlap of and relationships between these constructs (e.g., Endler et al., 2001).

Conclusion

The enhanced body awareness achieved in DMT may manifest in better SE and adherence as proposed above, or may bolster the body image. Better mood states may be part of an increase in vitality and may also enable active engagement in supportive relationships. All this would suggest that good psychosocial support will not parse its focus, but rather approach medically ill patients and their loved ones in a holistic way.

References

Bandura, A. (1977). Self-efficacy: Towards a unifying theory of behavioral change. *Psychological Review, 84*(2), 191–215. doi: 10.1037/0033–295X.84.2.191

Bartenieff, I., & Lewis, D. (1980). *Body movement: Coping with the environment*. New York, NY: Gordon and Breach Publishers.

Baudino, L. (2015). Personal communication.

Berkman, L. (1995). The role of social relations in health promotion. *Psychosomatic Medicine, 57*(3), 245–254.

Bojner-Horwitz, E., Theorell, T., & Anderberg, U. M. (2003). Dance/movement therapy and changes in stress-related hormones: A study of fibromyalgia patients with video-interpretation. *The Arts in Psychotherapy, 30*(5), 255–264. doi: 10.1016/j.aip.2003.07.001

Bradt, J., Shim, M., & Goodill, S. W. (2015). Dance/movement therapy for improving psychological and physical outcomes in cancer patients. *Cochrane Database of Systematic Reviews, 1*, 1–4. doi: 10.1002/14651858.CD007103.pub3

Bräuninger, I. (2012). The efficacy of dance movement therapy group on improvement of quality of life: A randomized controlled trial. *The Arts in Psychotherapy, 39*(4), 296–303. doi: 10.1016/j.aip.2012.03.008

Coccari, G., & Weiler, M. (2003). *Exploring the impact of dance/movement therapy on personal vitality in wellness-seeking individuals*. Poster presented at the American Dance Therapy Association 38th Annual Conference, Denver, CO, USA.

Cruz, R., & Sabers, D. (1998). Dance/movement therapy is more effective than previously reported. *The Arts in Psychotherapy, 25*(2), 101–104.

Dibbel-Hope, S. (2000). The use of dance/movement therapy in psychological adaptation to breast cancer. *The Arts in Psychotherapy, 27*(1), 51–68.

Ehrhardt, B. T., Hearn, M. B., & Novak, C. (1989). Outpatient clients' attitudes towards healing processes in dance therapy. *American Journal of Dance Therapy, 11*(1), 39–60. doi: 10.1007/BF00844265

Endler, N. S., Kocovski, N. L., & Marcrodimitris, S. D. (2001). Coping, efficacy, and perceived control in acute vs. chronic illnesses. *Personality and Individual Differences, 30*(4), 617–625. doi: 10.1016/S0191–8869(00)00060-X

Farrell, K., Wicks, M., & Martin, J. (2004). Chronic disease management improved with enhanced self-efficacy. *Clinical Nursing Research, 13*(4), 289–308. doi: 10.1177/1054773804267878

Folkman, S., & Moskowitz, J. T. (2000). Positive affect and the other side of coping. *American Psychologist, 55*(6), 647–654. doi: 10.1037//0003–066X.55.6.647

Fuchs, T., & Koch, S. C. (2014). Embodied affectivity: On moving and being moved. *Frontiers in Psychology, 5*(508), 1–12. doi: 10.3389/fpsyg.2014.00508.

Gomez Neto, M., Menezes, M. A., & Oliveira Carvalho, V. (2014). Dance therapy in patients with chronic heart failure: A systematic review and meta-analysis. *Clinical Rehabilitation, 28*(12), 1172–1179. doi: 10.1177/0269215514534089

Goodill, S. (2005a). *An introduction to medical dance/movement therapy: Health care in motion.* London, UK: Jessica Kingsley Publishers.

Goodill, S. (2005b). Research Letter: Dance/movement therapy for adults with Cystic Fibrosis: Pilot data on mood and adherence. *Alternative Therapies in Health and Medicine, 11*(1), 76–77.

Goodill, S. (2006). Dance/movement therapy for adults with chronic medical illness. In S. Koch & I. Brauninger (Eds.), *Advances in dance/movement therapy: Theoretical perspectives and empirical findings* (pp. 52–60). Berlin: Logos Verlag Berlin.

Hackney, M. E., & Bennett, C. G. (2014). Dance therapy for individuals with Parkinson's disease: Improving quality of life. *Journal of Parkinsonism and Restless Legs Syndrome, 14*(4), 17–25. doi: 10.2147/JPRLS.S40042.

Hackney, M. E., & Earhart, G. M. (2009). Health-related quality of life and alternative forms of exercise in Parkinson disease. *Parkinsonism & Related Disorders, 15*(9), 644–648. doi: 10.1016/j.parkreldis.2009.03.003

Heimes, S. (2012). *Warum Schreiben hilft. Die Wirksamkeitsnachweise zur Poesietherapie [Why writing helps. Efficacy studies in poetry therapy].* Göttingen: Vandenhoeck & Ruprecht.

Ho, R. T. H., Fong, T. C. T., Cheung, I. K. M., Yip, P. S. F., & Luk, M. (2016). Effects of a short-term dance movement therapy program on symptoms and stress in patients with breast cancer undergoing radiotherapy: A randomized, controlled, single-blind trial. *Journal of Pain and Symptom Management, 51*(5), 824–831. doi: 10.1016/j.jpainsymman.2015.12.332

Hyman, M. (2005). Quality in healthcare: Asking the right questions: The next ten years: The role of CAM in the "quality cure." *Alternative Therapies in Health and Medicine, 11*(3), 18–20.

Karkou, V., & Meekums, B. (2014). Dance movement therapy for dementia. *Cochrane Database of Systematic Reviews, 3*(CD011022), 1–17. doi: 10.1002/14651858.CD011022.

Katon, W. J., Unutzer, J., & Simon, G. (2004). Treatment of depression in primary care: Where we are, where we can go. *Medical Care, 42*(12), 1153–1157.

Kestenberg-Amighi, J., Loman, S., Lewis, P., & Sossin, K. M. (1999). *The meaning of movement: Development and clinical perspectives of the Kestenberg movement profile.* New York, NY: Gordon & Breach.

Kinsbourne, M. (2002). The role of imitation in body ownership and mental growth. In A. N. Meltzoff & W. Prinz (Eds.), *The imitative mind: Development, evolution, and brain bases* (pp. 311–330). Cambridge, MA: University Press.

Koch, S. C. (2011). Basic body rhythms and embodied intercorporality: From individual to interpersonal movement feedback. In W. Tschacher & C. Bergomi (Eds.), *The implications of embodiment: Cognition and communication* (pp. 151–171). Exeter: Imprint Academic.

Koch, S. C., Fuchs, T., Summa, M., & Müller, C. (2012). *Body memory, metaphor and movement.* Philadelphia, PA: John Benjamins.

Koch, S. C., Mehl, L., Sobanski, E., Sieber, M., & Fuchs, T. (2015). Fixing the mirrors: A feasibility study of the effects of dance movement therapy on young adults with Autism Spectrum Disorder. *Autism, 19*(3), 338–350. doi: 10.1177/1362361314522353.

Koch, S. C., Mergheim, K., Raeke, J., Machado, C. B., Riegner, E., Nolden, J., ... Hillecke, T. (2016). The embodied self in Parkinson's disease: Feasibility of a single tango intervention for assessing changes in psychological health outcomes and aesthetic experience. *Fronttiers in Neuroscience, 10*(287), 1–13. doi: 10.3389/fnins.2016.00287.

Koch, S. C., Morlinghaus, K., & Fuchs, T. (2007). The joy dance: Specific effects of a single dance intervention on psychiatric patients with depression. *The Arts in Psychotherapy, 34*(4), 340–349. doi: 10.1016/j.aip.2007.07.001

Koch, S. C., Steinhage, A., Haller, K., Kende, P., Ostermann, T., & Chyle, F. (2015). Breaking Barriers: Evaluating and arts-based emotion regulation program in prison. *The Arts in Psychotherapy, 42*, 41–49. doi: 10.1016/j.aip.2014.10.008.

Krantz, A., & Pennebaker, J. W. (2007). Expressive dance, writing, trauma, and health: When words have a body. In I. A. Serlin, J. Sonke-Henderson, R. Brandman, & J. Graham-Pole (Eds.), *Whole person healthcare, Vol. 3: The arts and health* (pp. 201–229). Westport, CT: Praeger Publishers.

Lazarus, R. S. (2000). Toward better research on stress and coping. *American Psychologist, 55*(6), 665–673. doi: 10.1037//0003–006X.55.6.665

Livneh, H., & Antonak, R. F. (2005). Psychosocial adaptation to chronic illness: A primer for counselors. *Journal of Counseling and Development, 83*(1), 12–20. doi: 10.1002/j.1556–6678.2005.tb00575.x

Martin, L., Koch, S. C., Hirjak, D., & Fuchs, T. (2016). Overcoming disembodiment: The effect of movement therapy on negative symptoms in schizophrenia—A multicenter randomized controlled trial. *Frontiers in Psychology*, 7(483), 1–14. doi: 10.3389/fpsyg.2016.00483.

McNair, D. M., Lorr, M., & Broppleman, L. R. (1981). *EITS manual for the profile of mood states*. San Diego, CA: Educational and Industrial Testing Service.

Melsom, A. M. (1999). *Dance/movement therapy for psychosocial aspects of heart disease and cancer: An exploratory literature review*. Unpublished Master's Thesis, MCP Hahnemann University, Philadelphia, PA, USA.

Pylvänäinen, P., & Lappalainen, R. (2018). Change in body image among depressed adult outpatients after a dance movement therapy group treatment. *The arts in Psychotherapy, 59*, 34–45.

Revenson, T. A. (1994). Social support and marital coping with chronic illness. *Annals of Behavioral Medicine, 16*(2), 122–130. doi: 10.1093/abm/16.2.122

Rohrbaugh, M. J., Shoham, V., Coyne, J., Cranford, J. A., Sonnega, J. S., & Nicklas, J. M. (2004). Beyond the "Self" in self-efficacy: Spouse confidence predicts patient survival following heart failure. *Journal of Family Psychology, 18*(1), 184–193.

Sandel, S. L., Chaiklin, S., & Lohn, A. (1993). *Foundations of dance/movement therapy: The life and work of Marian Chace*. Columbia, MD: American Dance Therapy Association.

Seides, M. (1986). Dance/movement therapy as a modality in the treatment of the psychosocial complications of heart disease. *American Journal of Dance Therapy, 9*(1), 83–101. doi: 10.1007/BF02274240

Schilder, P. (1950/1970). *The image and appearance of the human body*. New York, NY: International Universities Press.

Schmais, C. (1985). Healing processes in group dance therapy. *American Journal of Dance Therapy, 8*(1), 17–36. doi: 10.1007/BF02251439

Serlin, I. A., Classen, C., Frances, B., & Angell, K. (2000). Symposium: Support groups for women with breast cancer: Traditional and alternative expressive approaches. *The Arts in Psychotherapy, 27*(2), 123–138.

Smyth, J., & Arigo, D. (2009). Recent evidence supports emotion-regulation interventions for improving health in at-risk and clinical populations. *Current Opinion in Psychiatry, 22*(2), 205–210. doi: 10.1097/YCO.0b013e3283252d6d

Vamos, M. (1993). Body image in chronic illness—A reconceptualization. *The International Journal of Psychiatry in Medicine, 23*(2), 163–178. doi: 10.2190/BLL4-EVAL-49Y3-4G66

Wiedenhofer, S., & Koch, S. (2017). Active factors in dance/movement therapy: Specifying health effects of non-goal-orientation in movement. *Arts in Psychotherapy, 52*, 10–23. doi: 10.2190/BLL4-EVAL-49Y3-4G66

Yalom, I.D. (1995). *The theory and practice of group psychotherapy* (4th ed.). New York: Basic Books.

Yang, H. (2004). *The impact of dance/movement therapy on self-efficacy in adults with diabetes mellitus: A case study*. Unpublished Master's Thesis, Drexel University, Philadelphia, PA, USA.

10 Art Therapy and Tourette Syndrome

Utilizing Guided Imagery and Chakra Exploration

Melanie Biscuiti

This chapter will provide an overview on Tourette syndrome within the medical realm of treatment, and will incorporate alternative therapies with the support of current research. The clinical application of art therapy, from a mindfulness and holistic perspective, will support a detailed experiential using guided imagery meditation and chakra exploration to improve symptom management in Tourette syndrome.

What Is Tourette Syndrome?

Tourette syndrome (TS) is a neurological, involuntary muscular movement disorder typically diagnosed at a young age. Individuals with TS experience a range of physical symptoms, including repetitive movements and verbal unwanted sounds. The sounds, referred to as *copilalia*, and repetitive motor movements, referred to as *tics* or *twitches*, are sudden and continuous until the urge is relieved (Cavanna, Black, Hallett, & Voon, 2017; Chowdhury & Murphy, 2017). In tic disorders, an individual with TS experiences a feeling of energy, or pressure, within their body before a symptom is about to occur. The urge preceding a repetitive behavior is referred to as *premonitory sensations*, and can last until the feeling subsides or until the movement is outwardly expressed (Woods, Piacentini, & Himle, 2007).

Types of motor and sound tics in TS vary from simple to complex: simple motor tics can include eye blinking, nose twitching, and/or jaw and shoulder movements, whereas complex motor tics can include head banging, punching, jumping, and/or exaggerated facial gestures (Chowdhury & Murphy, 2017). Simple vocal tics can include high-pitched sounds, throat clearing, humming, and/or random vowel sounds, whereas complex vocal tics can include repetitive animal sounds, the repeating of sounds heard, and/or inappropriate language (Cavanna et al., 2017).

Additionally, other symptoms and conditions can be linked to the TS diagnosis. For example, a child or adolescent may present with increased impulsivity, hyperactive behavior, and can appear to model constant rituals or obsessions (Chowdhury, 2004). These secondary behavioral elements do not automatically lead to further diagnoses, but if overly prominent, can lead to a dual diagnosis in TS. Conditions associated with TS can include attention deficit hyperactivity disorder (ADHD) and obsessive compulsive disorder (OCD), which can add to the body's overall physical and mental strain, and contribute to the need for treatment (Chowdhury, 2004).

Treatment of Tourette Syndrome

For movement disorders in general, there is a lack of preventive or disease-modifying pharmaceutical treatments. There is no 'cookie cutter' approach to treating TS, and there is currently no single medication prescribed for the medical condition. It should also be noted that not everyone with TS presents with the above symptoms, and many individuals are able to lead a productive life without a pharmaceutical protocol (Chowdhury & Murphy, 2017). Physicians typically prescribe medication to help with tic suppression and treat comorbid illnesses closely linked to TS, such as ADHD and OCD. However, medication cannot fully eliminate the symptoms of TS, but can assist lowering the intensity and frequency of the tics (Kurlan, 2010). For tic suppression and the treatment of secondary conditions, medications that have been known to help with reducing symptoms include antidepressants, antiseizure medications, and dopamine inhibiters (Mayo Clinic, 2016).

Types of therapeutic interventions beneficial to those diagnosed with TS include behavioral therapy, psychotherapy, deep brain stimulation, and relaxation training (Mayo Clinic, 2016). Habit reversal, a common therapeutic intervention in TS, consists of behavioral techniques aimed at increasing tic awareness and supplementing an urge for a more desired behavior (Piacentini & Chang, 2005).

Despite treatment for TS, secondary medical issues can still arise due to the physical and emotional stressors from living with the diagnosis, as well as medication side effects, such as gastrological issues, a lowered immune system, muscle tightness, and muscle pain. This chapter will highlight a holistic mind–body approach to the nonpharmaceutical treatment of TS, and will incorporate mindful meditation and art therapy to aid in the reduction of both primary and secondary symptoms.

A Holistic Approach to the Treatment of Tourette Syndrome

To practice being holistic, one must take into consideration the person as a whole, and not just concentrate on outside influences such as medication, environment, and sociology. For children and adolescents, the typical onset of TS, it is important to first implement the most noninvasive treatment method. A therapist's focus on the natural application of healing techniques, to increase the client's self-exploration and locus of control, is a large component within the holistic approach to treatment (Wilhelm et al., 2012). Attention to the person as an individual, an autonomous goal-directed system, one would consider the importance of balance and healing through the body's total systematic functioning (Csikszentmihalyi, 2014). Utilizing therapeutic modalities to address the individual, and not just the medical illness, can help a client gain control of their diagnosis and improve symptom management.

The Concept of Mindfulness and the Mind–Body Connection

The practice of mindfulness goes back many centuries, and throughout many different cultures and spiritual followers. The implementation of mindfulness itself is secular, rooted in religions such as Buddhism, with an emphasis on self-awareness and self-regulation (Zoogman, Foskolos, & Vousoura, 2017). The medical approach, referred to as mindfulness-based interventions (MBI), is a more recent technique researched and highlighted for physical and mental health treatment by Western medical practitioners (Loizzo, 2017). MBI implements the ability to focus one's breath and energy (the body) to produce a more relaxed psyche. While a challenging creative task, it involves concentrated attention to decrease all other internal or external stimuli. This technique offers an accessible tool to help heighten attention and nurture self-awareness (Loizzo, 2017), linking attention and energy to what is truly valued by the person as their intention or goal (Csikszentmihalyi, 2014). Individuals who are immersed into a challenging activity, such chakras meditation, become able to connect with their higher self to overcome life's challenges to find healing (Muscara, Mengers, & Schlechter, 2017). Utilizing the concept of chakras is a valuable, holistic application to further understanding both mindfulness and the mind–body connection within treatment.

The Concept and Benefits of Chakras

As human beings, our bodies are composed of electromagnetic energy, and within our cells vibrations occur at various frequencies depending on one's unique makeup (Quest, 2016). Throughout the body, there are more than 27 high and low localized energy spots called chakras. There are minor chakras at each organ and joint, as well as at the soles of the feet and palms of hands (Frank & Long-Schuman, 2000). These chakras are a vital element to keeping our physical well-being. Chakras interact with our internal body, helping balance our physical systems, increasing positive energy, and filtering out the negative. Out of the 27 energy points, 7 of those are major central charkas, located at high frequency areas within the body (Quest, 2016). These seven chakras have associated colors innately linked to heighten the internal healing through vibration properties, and are located from the top of our head to the bottom of our spine in alignment with the body (Figure 10.1). Using the chakras, and color areas, during meditation may enhance one's focus and increase the visual intention toward alleviating any pain and discomfort.

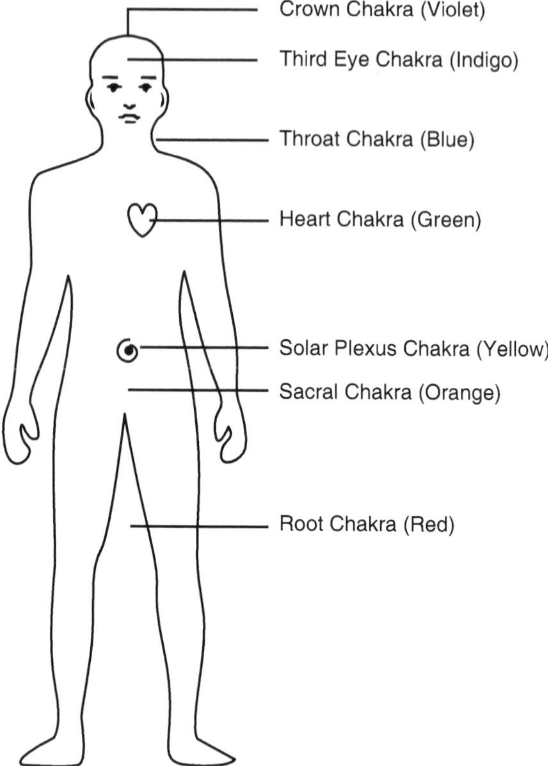

Figure 10.1 The Seven Chakras and Their Associated Color

The use of chakras from a medical standpoint can help one identify an internal pathway to gain healing, when all other medical treatments are not enough. Table 10.1 is adapted from the work of Frank and Long-Schuman (2000), and provides an example of color vibrations within the human body:

Each chakra interconnects with other chakras and is part of the larger picture, linking the flow between what one knows about them self, to what he or she can learn to help heal within a medical condition.

Utilizing Chakras in Symptom Management

By learning how to visualize and recognize a shift in energy within the body, a conscious thought or action may be put in place to help ease and/or manage the output of a primary TS symptom. Learning to be in tune with one's body is essential to healthy living; chakra healing can help clear pathways in our system so that positive energy can pass through the body and nurture the spirit (Mercier, 2007). The process of integrating chakra visualization into practice can help an individual diagnosed with TS gain control over

Table 10.1 Targeted Chakra Points Within the Body

Color Vibration	*Chakra*	*Targeted Area*
Red	Root	Colon, genitals, arms, legs, feet, ovaries, movement
Orange	Sacral	Lower abdomen, pelvic area, hips, bladder, small and large intestine, ovaries, uterus, prostate, colon
Yellow	Solar plexus	Stomach, gastric issues, gallbladder, liver, spleen, pancreas
Green	Heart	Heart, lungs circulation, thymus
Blue	Throat	Esophagus, thyroid, breathing
Indigo	Third eye	Sinuses, headaches, penal and pituitary glands
Violet	Crown	Brain, thoughts, headaches, fear, pineal

their impulse behavior and allow for a smoother transition into symptom management.

An example of this can be seen with an individual experiencing punching tics. It is important to have the individual recognize the physical sensation, or pressure, and connect it to his or her mind, grounding the body with the root chakra and visualizing the red color. Direct the individual's breathing to focus on that particular area, and have him or her visualize his or her arms surrounding the beautiful red color. Incorporating the visualization of a chakra to one's conscious mind can help bring awareness to the physical area in need. It is also important for the individual to utilize the breath to take control of the mind as the body becomes redirected. This process may not work the same on everyone, but the idea is to help an individual gain a higher level of mindfulness between the mind and body, eventually lessening the intensity of the involuntary actions and gaining control.

The use of a holistic approach is a less invasive way to help an individual let go of the tension present in their muscles caused by the physical and emotional tics, as well as the emotional stressors present within a medical diagnosis. The visualization of chakras can be further applied and understood through a specific, guided imagery script that has been developed to refocus and connect one's mind and body to find relief from TS urges.

Guided Imagery Meditation Script with Chakra Exploration

The following guided imagery script can be used as a template for therapists, or can be adapted as needed. After establishing a safe setting for participants, along with body positioning and a steady breathing pattern, begin the guided imagery meditation script:

> *Say to yourself this mantra: To find my inner rainbow, I help heal myself, I take control of my own body, I am mindful of my mind–body connections. The first step is to ground yourself, which is done by bringing your attention to the here and now. When we are grounded, we are more apt to better overcome obstacles and focus on what we can control. Take a moment to scan your body from your head down to your toes. Notice any present pain, twitches, and tics. If you have any urges, don't suppress them. Let them be and bring your focus back to your breathing. Don't fight any thoughts, let them come in and out with your breath. Now visualize a rainbow coming down from a beautiful storm. The clouds start to disappear and a beautiful vibrant rainbow appears. This rainbow is vertically standing tall and long right in front of you. The colors shown are in an ascending order, from the base of your spine and bottom at your feet, to top of your head, beginning with red at your feet: red, orange, yellow, green, blue, indigo, violet. As you sit within the rhythm of your breath, allow the rainbow to make its way toward you, floating as it glides to connect itself within you and your body. Feel your body vibrate with all the colors settling in and lining up from your feet up to your head. Each color represents a different chakra, connecting with the physical elements in our system.*

Begin to focus on the specific chakra colors, their position within the body, and their meaning:

> *Picture the red color of your root chakra. This is located at the base of your spine, from the coccyx bone to the souls of the feet, and is responsible for grounding us, physically and emotionally. When we feel stable, we can function as a whole. Send this area love and light. As we move up our body, be mindful and aware of any present pressure or tics. If you feel urges, don't restrict your movements or sounds. This is where the mind–body connection comes into play with symptom management. Once you become more in tuned to yourself, you will be better prepared to cope with life stressors and keep your energies balanced. Next, visualize the color orange, of the sacral chakra. This is located at the pelvic area, responsible for passion, movement, change and transformation. Feel the flow of energy, sending love and light to this area. Make your way up to the solar plexus chakra, and picture the color yellow. This chakra is located behind the belly button, responsible for our sense of personal power, identity, and will power. Focus on your confidence to transform. Transform your self-perception, your Tourette's syndrome does not define you. You are not your illness, and your illness is not who you really are. Let go of any worry or nerves that attack the stomach. Send this area love and light, surrounding in yellow. The centermost chakra is next; the heart chakra is green in color, located right in the center of the chest. This chakra is responsible for love, love of ourselves and love for another, as well as connecting us to our true essence. Our heart is just as important as our brain. The hard work that it*

> *takes to expel negative energy puts a lot of stress on our heart chakra. Keeping a positive attitude and love in our life, even through hard times, can help us find a way to overcome and be a healthier individual. Getting rid of negativity in our system helps decrease the blocks that cause illness and disease. Feel the flow of energy, sending love and light to this area. Now picture the color blue, of the throat chakra. This is right in the center of the neck and is responsible for communication and expression. Our words are an expression of thoughts, feelings, and actions that describe how we feel. When a tic or twitch occurs, it's our minds way of expressing or satisfying an urge, physically or vocally. Focusing on this area may assist in decreasing the bodies need to express itself in more aggressive ways, and strengthen its ties to a pleasant form of communication and expression. Send love and light to this area. As we make our way up our body, we reach the third eye chakra, which is indigo in color. This chakra is located right in the center of our forehead, in between the eyebrows. This chakra is our minds eye, responsible for self-reflection, intuition, and living in the moment. When one's intention is to find inner healing and control over the body, focusing on this chakra may allow an increase self-exploration and a deep personal meaning. Feel the flow of energy, sending love and light to this chakra. The final chakra, the crown, is located at the top of the head, and is violet in color. This chakra also encompasses all the prism colors. Representing unity and a personal higher power. It brings about balance and unity through all the chakras and our universe. It is our connection to what guides us as humans, and allows us to be open to deeper meaning in our lives. Helping balance our immune system to fight any unwanted aliments.*

Begin to conclude the guided imagery meditation by incorporating all of the chakras:

> *Visualize yourself redirecting an unwanted movement, and explore the colors of the rainbow and how they connect our total body awareness. Take in the waves of light that resonate through the air after a rainbow. Feel the flow of positive energy; picture a spiraling movement of light or colors constantly moving from our feet to our head, clearing the blocks in our system. When blocks are present in our flow of energy, this can hurt our immune system and cause illness or disease, preventing us from truly being healthy. Finding one's balance during a medical illness becomes an essential step to overcoming those obstacles towards healing. Finding what you truly connect to in life is essential to making meaningful changes toward symptom management and taking control of your illness. Focusing that kinetic energy through the chakras can elicit the movement toward balancing one's mind and body. As we learn to be mindful, we gain an understanding over what we can control, and able to let go of what we can't. Our bodies may go against what we want, but if we can direct our thoughts and our breathing, then our bodies will follow.*

End the guided imagery meditation with the client repeating the beginning mantra, and bringing their attention back to the breathing pattern.

To further strengthen the guided imagery meditation process amongst TS individuals, the use of art therapy can be applied to heighten awareness, increase mindfulness, and engage individuals in both a verbal and nonverbal creative outlet.

The Application of Art Therapy to Increase Mindfulness Techniques

Creating art within a therapeutic approach involves a mind–body connection and sensory awareness that does not always happen through verbal therapy alone. Art can form a bridge between the mind and body, eliciting a visceral response when engaged (Malchiodi, 2012). Art therapy can offer an alternative means of communication, aiding to redirect anxiety, pain, and discomfort experienced during a medical condition. When combining a creative modality with focused breathing, chakras, and guided meditation, an avenue for enhancing a higher level of healing and relaxation can emerge. In addition, the visual and sensory application of art media can help individuals relax their muscles to alleviate tension or pain. When individuals do not feel in control of their own mind and body, they tend to focus more on physical symptoms within a diagnosis. Through mindfulness and art-making, individuals with a medical diagnosis can increase their internal sense of control (Malchiodi, 2013).

The idea of control can be foreign when living with a medical condition, specifically one that consists of involuntary movements. Taking back a sense of control, through the art-making process, occurs when an individual lets go of what he or she can't control, and embraces what he or she can control (Hogan, 2016). This can present itself through a chosen chakra, mindfulness breathing, and/or the art-making process.

Providing an art therapy experiential, after the guided imagery meditation on chakras, can enhance mindfulness, and relate to the experience during the guided imagery. It is important for the therapist to choose art materials that are simple and easily applied for mastery. Unstructured materials, such as soft colored pencils, oil/chalk pastels, or paint, such as tempera or acrylic, can allow for a free flow of imagery and personal exploration during the art therapy process.

Art Therapy and Chakra Experiential

Following the meditation, invite participants to visualize the image of the rainbow still aligned vertically within their body. Provide a full body line drawing as a guide, or to be directly used, for participants to connect with their visualization. Instruct participants to create a drawing based on how their rainbow looked or felt, while remaining mindful of their breath. Have participants focus an area and use the specific chakra colors to heal, helping to inspire creativity and let go of the physical and emotion blocks within the body.

After the experiential, encourage participants to remain in a relaxed state. Have them consider the color choice, details, and overall focus of their artwork. The therapist can ask questions such as, *How do you feel in this moment? What blocks were you able to let go of in your body? What physical changes did you experience?*

The inclusion of art therapy is to increase body awareness, steer physical sublimation toward relaxing the muscles, and redirect physical actions. The tools of one's imagination can establish a mind–body connection through the created art. Art therapy creates the opportunity for the unconscious mind to be brought to light through the visual. This could help support an individual with TS to learn to embrace the moment before a behavioral urge and replace negative, unwanted stress, with better control over their body.

Conclusion

With a medical diagnosis, such as TS, the body's immune system becomes weaker and less capable of coping with continued impulses and involuntary movements. Adding mindfulness to one's routine, and finding a positive flow of energy is essential to healthy living and promoting the mind–body connection. The process of engaging in something physical and tangible, such as creating art, provides a chance to reflect, grow, and gain control over TS symptoms through a visual field. Exploring what works for each individual is important in making the connection for a functional symptom management tool. Through repetition and practice, an individual is capable of learning, growing, and overcoming obstacles within a medical diagnosis.

References

Cavanna, A. E., Black, K. J., Hallett, M., & Voon, V. (2017). Neurobiology of the premonitory urge in Tourette's syndrome: Pathophysiology and treatment implications. *The Journal of Neuropsychiatry and Clinical Neurosciences, 29*(2), 95–104. doi: 10.1176/appi.neuropsych.16070141

Chowdhury, U. (2004). *Tics and Tourette syndrome: A handbook for parents and professionals.* Philadelphia, PA: Jessica Kingsley Publishers.

Chowdhury, U., & Murphy, T. (2017). *Tics disorders: A guide for parents and professionals.* Philadelphia, PA: Jessica Kingsley Publishers.

Csikszentmihalyi, M. (2014). *Flow and the foundation of positive psychology: The collected works of Mihaly Csikszentmihalyi.* New York, NY: Springer.

Frank, C., & Long-Schuman, J. (2000). *Reiki I & II introduction to reiki empowerment of the self: The human touch.* Unpublished Training Manual.

Hogan, S. (2016). *Art therapy theories: A critical introduction.* New York, NY: Routledge.

Kurlan, R. (2010). Tourette's syndrome. *New England Journal of Medicine, 363*(24), 2332–2338. doi: 10.1056/NEJMcp1007805

Loizzo, J. (2017). Plasticity and integration: The neuroscience of mindfulness. In E. Zerbo, A. Schlechter, S. Desai, & P. Levounis (Eds.), *Becoming mindful: Integrating mindfulness into your psychiatric practice* (pp. 9–24). Arlington, VA: American Psychiatric Association Publishing.

Malchiodi, C. A. (2012). Art therapy and the brain. In C. A. Malchiodi (Ed.), *The handbook of art therapy* (pp. 17–26). New York, NY: The Guilford Press.

Malchiodi, C. A. (Ed.). (2013). *Art therapy and health care*. New York, NY: The Guilford Press.

Mayo Clinic. (2016). *Symptoms and causes*. Retrieved from www.mayoclinic.org/diseases-conditions/tourette-syndrome/symptoms-causes/dxc-20163624.

Mercier, P. (2007). *The chakra bible: The definitive guide to working with chakras*. New York, NY: Sterling Publishing Company.

Muscara, C., Mengers, A., & Schlechter, A. (2017). Finding wellness through mindfulness and meditation: The growing field of positive psychology and psychiatry. In E. Zerbo, A. Schlechter, S. Desai, & P. Levounis (Eds.), *Becoming mindful: Integrating mindfulness into your psychiatric practice* (pp. 103–120). Arlington, VA: American Psychiatric Association Publishing.

Piacentini, J., & Chang, S. (2005). Habit reversal training for tic disorders in children and adolescents. *Behavior Modification, 29*(6), 803–822. doi: 10.1177/0145445505279385

Quest, P. (2016). *Reiki for life: The complete guide to reiki practice for levels 1, 2 & 3*. New York, NY: Tarcher Perigee.

Wilhelm, S., Peterson, A. L., Piacentini, J., Woods, D. W., Deckersbach, T., Sukhodolsky, D. G., . . . Scahill, L. (2012). Randomized trial of behavior therapy for adults with Tourette syndrome. *Archives of General Psychiatry, 69*(8), 795–803. doi: 10.1001/archgenpsychiatry.2011.1528

Woods, W. D., Piacentini, C. J., & Himle, M. B. (2007). The assessment of tic disorders. In D. W. Wood, J. Piacentini, & J. T. Walkup (Eds.), *Treating Tourette syndrome and tics disorders: A guide for practitioners* (pp. 22–37). New York, NY: The Guilford Press.

Zoogman, S., Foskolos, E., & Vousoura, E. (2017). Mindfulness as an intervention in the treatment of psychopathology. In E. Zerbo, A. Schlechter, S. Desai, & P. Levounis (Eds.), *Becoming mindful: Integrating mindfulness into your psychiatric practice* (pp. 79–102). Arlington, VA: American Psychiatric Association Publishing.

11 Engaging Those with Parkinson's Disease in Group Clay Manipulation Art Therapy

Deborah Elkis-Abuhoff and Morgan Gaydos

I feel like I have a grip on the world. These were the words spoken by a patient diagnosed with Parkinson's disease while engaging in a clay manipulation art therapy group. The power of these words resonated with the therapist because of the emotional and physical struggles that someone with Parkinson's disease faces every day. In visually demonstrating this struggle, another patient illustrated this through the clay by creating a simple box. Upon presenting his creation, and how he related to it: *that's me . . . all boxed in.* He went on to explain that with his diagnosis his mind is sharp but his body doesn't follow. These are just two powerful outcomes that help a patient communicate during the clay manipulation art therapy process. This chapter will discuss the physical, psychological, and neurological symptoms of Parkinson's disease, and the value that an art therapy group process, specifically clay manipulation, has on an individual's ability to cope with progressive symptoms.

Understanding Parkinson's Disease

Parkinson's disease (PD) continues to rank as one of the top neurological disorders within the world, affecting as many as 10 million individuals (Parkinson's Disease Foundation, 2017a). PD is the second most common neurodegenerative diagnosis, following that of Alzheimer's disease, and the risk of being diagnosed increases with age (Lee & Gilbert, 2016). In the Unites States, as many as 60,000 individuals are diagnosed with PD on a yearly basis; however, this number does not account for cases that go undetected (Parkinson's Disease Foundation, 2017a). PD typically affects individuals over the age of 40, with the median onset age of 60, but it is not unlikely that the diagnosis can occur earlier in adulthood (Lee & Gilbert, 2016). Lastly, men are one and a half times more likely to be diagnosed with PD than women (Parkinson's Disease Foundation, 2017a).

The PD diagnosis begins with the onset and recognition of motor symptoms, such as muscle rigidity, freezing and/or shuffling gait, resting tremors, and bradykinesia, which includes a flattened affect (Sveinbjornsdottir, 2016). In addition to motor symptoms, researchers and clinicians have begun to consistently acknowledge the presence of nonmotor, psychological symptoms within the PD diagnosis (Wu, Liscic, Kim, Sorbi, & Yang, 2017). Psychological symptoms, such as depression, obsessive-compulsive thinking, phobic anxiety, and stress, have been reported by PD individuals and contribute to the complex and multifactorial treatment of PD (Elkis-Abuhoff & Gaydos, 2016; Goldblatt, Elkis-Abuhoff, Gaydos, & Napoli, 2010).

The progressive and debilitating motor and nonmotor symptoms are in response to neurological changes within the brain that occur at the onset of the PD diagnosis. To help illustrate the impact of the PD diagnosis, the progression of this disease will be described on a cellular, organism, community, and world level.

Cellular Level

The body was designed for movement; our body's ability to perform an action and react to stimuli begins at a cellular level with the dopaminergic neurons present within the substantia nigra region of the basal ganglia, part of the midbrain (Elkis-Abuhoff & Gaydos, 2016). Dopaminergic neurons produce the chemical dopamine, which allows the body to execute movements and manipulate through its surroundings. Dopaminergic neurons also act as neurotransmitters, which signal communication to other parts of the brain, strengthening their role and need within our neurological makeup. During the onset of PD, dopaminergic neurons within the substantia nigra begin to deplete and the first signs of the diagnosis, that of motor symptoms, begin to develop; as the disease progresses, dopaminergic neurons continue to diminish and the rapid aging process of neurodegeneration intensifies the severity of motor symptoms (Blesa, Trigo-Damas, Quiroga-Varela, & Jackson-Lewis, 2015). Consider dopamine as the motor oil of the body; once it diminishes, the body does not function as smoothly and further complications can arise.

Pharmaceutical medications, such as carbidopa/levodopa, are dopamine promoters commonly used to help dopamine reach the areas of the brain that have become compromised by the PD diagnosis; in addition, dopamine agonists are medications that aim to stimulate parts of the human brain that are affected by dopamine (Parkinson's Disease Foundation, 2017b). Treatment based on dopamine replacement, although seemingly beneficial, may result in adverse effects in long-term use and still requires a great deal of evaluation in scientific trials (Sarrafchi, Bahmani, Shirzad, & Rafieian-Kopaei, 2016).

Organism Level

On an organism level, the brain of a PD individual loses its ability to communicate the execution of movement and relay messages to other parts of the brain, thus compromising the mind–body connection that has allowed the individual to function fluidly and effortlessly. The loss of dopaminergic neurons within the substantia nigra, a basal ganglia structure in the brain, significantly impacts the execution of voluntary movements (Sarrafchi et al., 2016). Furthermore, the basal ganglia is unable to function as part of the whole, thus affecting the overall neurological structure and an individual's ability to control his or her body (Sveinbjornsdottir, 2016).

Deep brain stimulation (DBS) is a surgical brain procedure to help improve motor functioning and control to those diagnosed with PD. DBS is a two-part procedure: (1) the surgeon utilizes an MRI to insert electrodes into targeted areas within the brain, recording the brain cell activity that occurs during the procedure; and (2) an impulse generator implantation is placed within the body, typically under the collarbone or in the abdomen, to provide an electric impulse to areas of the brain responsible for motor movement (Parkinson's Disease Foundation, 2017c). Despite aiding an individual in experiencing a sense of relief from motor symptoms, DBS is invasive in nature and poses many risks, including side effects, such as a worsening of symptoms, and the need for battery replacement implantation surgery (Beudel & Brown, 2016).

Community Level

As the neurological structure continues to degenerate, motor and psychological symptoms progress, and the impact of the PD diagnosis extends into the individual's environment. The increase and severity of PD symptoms can leave an individual with a feeling of loss of control/independence, the inability to cope with changes in lifestyle, and an overall decreased quality of life. The psychological symptoms of depression, obsessive-compulsive thinking, phobic anxiety, and stress can emerge in response to an individual's thoughts and feelings of, and experiences within, the PD diagnosis, and can result in further debilitation (Elkis-Abuhoff & Gaydos, 2016). Although motor symptoms are associated with the loss of dopamine within the brain, damaged dopamine pathways are believed to also contribute to psychological symptoms within the PD diagnosis (Choi et al., 2017). Psychological symptoms, such as obsessive-compulsive thinking, can lead to ruminating thoughts about what the individual is unable to do and can result in social isolation within the community. Similarly, the experience of a stigma or fear of being embarrassed during social interactions can result in phobic anxiety, and can prevent the individual diagnosed with PD from leaving his or her home (Wu et al., 2017). The presence of psychological symptoms, coupled with progressive motor symptoms, impacts the overall quality of life for a PD individual as it can disrupt daily routines, such as running errands, and results in the individual becoming dependent on caregivers to help complete activities of daily living.

In order to provide healthcare services that better address overall symptomology and improve quality of life, the PD community has shifted from physician centered to patient centered (Lageman, Cash, & Mickens, 2014). Although there is still a great need for additional services, organizational events, support groups, and complementary treatment, such as art therapy, are more available within the PD community and offer a more active role to the individual within his or her diagnosis. Despite the limitation that cognition and degeneration can inhibit an individual's decision-making within treatment, a patient-centered approach can help break the stigma of PD and provide supportive therapies that aim to reintegrate individuals back into the community and improve quality of life (Lageman, Cash, & Mickens, 2014).

World Level

When faced with ongoing physical and psychological symptoms, the world of a medical patient drastically changes. For neurodegenerative diseases, the loss of independence, control, and quality of life can decline at a much quicker rate, and an individual diagnosed with PD often loses his or her identity within the diagnosis (Elkis-Abuhoff & Gaydos, 2016). Furthermore, the role of a family member, such as the spouse becoming a 'caregiver,' contributes to the disruption of a PD individual's identity (Leroi, 2017). When individuals lose their identity, they can lose their place in the world. In severely progressive PD symptomology, the inability to speak and/or physically manipulate through their environment further adds to how this diagnosis affects an individual on a worldly, all-encompassing level. In addition, there is no cure for PD, and individuals are left with an ongoing battle as the disease continues to progress. Although pharmaceutical treatment methods can aid in the reduction of symptoms, PD patients can be left with traumatic experiences and psychological symptoms that require the need for supportive therapies (Elkis-Abuhoff & Gaydos, 2016)

Art therapy is a noninvasive, complementary treatment that can target the multifaceted aspects and complex symptom management of PD (Elkis-Abuhoff & Gaydos, 2016, 2018; Elkis-Abuhoff, Goldblatt, Gaydos, & Convery, 2013; Goldblatt et al., 2010; Goldman & Weintraub, 2015; Mirabella, 2015). In a medical model of treatment, the focus lies on identifying and addressing an illness from a curative standpoint; in an art therapy medical model, the focus lies on an individual finding relief from symptoms, strengthening self-worth/identity, and increasing quality of life through the therapeutic process (Elkis-Abuhoff & Gaydos, 2016; Rubin, 2016). With a neurological and degenerative disease, such as PD, the art therapy process begins by stimulating the brain through direct touch and tactile experiences.

Art Therapy and the Parkinson's Diseased Brain

As the need for complementary therapy within the PD community continues to grow, research conducted on the effects of art therapy and art-making within the PD brain continues to gain positive recognition. Art therapy, specifically the creative process, involves multiple interconnected systems within the brain, and can result in improved cognitive flexibility and functioning (King, 2016). The visual, sensory, and metaphorical qualities of an image created during the therapeutic process stimulates a complex system within the brain; with the perception and emotional connection that follows, the image is given personal meaning to the individual (Belkofer & Nolan, 2016). With an individual diagnosed with PD, a sense of meaning through a personal image can help restore a sense of identity. Furthermore, the therapeutic qualities of art therapy allow an individual to have a toolbox of communication skills, whether communication occurs as a result of increased neurological firing within the brain and a relief of symptoms or through the nonverbal properties of the experience (Belkofer & Nolan, 2016; Elkis-Abuhoff & Gaydos, 2016).

Through its expressive and tactile properties, engagement in art therapy has been found to directly stimulate areas of the PD brain that are linked to motor control and cognition (Elkis-Abuhoff & Gaydos, 2016, 2018; Goldman & Holden, 2014). Researchers also believe that art therapy aids in brain plasticity and could even strengthen dopamine pathways within the PD brain by engaging the midbrain, through direct touch of the fingertips and palms of one's hand, that become compromised due to the diagnosis (Elkis-Abuhoff & Gaydos, 2016; Goldman & Holden, 2014; Mirabella, 2015). With this, one can suggest that cellular and organism level needs are being met, and a PD individual's brain is able to form and/or strengthen previously damaged neurological connections during art therapy. The community and world level needs of an individual are addressed through the therapeutic verbal and/or nonverbal processing of the art therapy experience, which can also provide a sense of purpose. Kinesthetic art materials, such as clay, play an essential role in stimulating the brain, through direct touch, and serve as a platform for self-expression and personal meaning, contributing to the therapeutic properties of the art therapy experience.

Clay Manipulation

As a tactile medium, clay requires direct touch and manipulation to transform into a meaningful shape or image. From a psychological standpoint, clay can be used in art therapy to elicit free association, and a safe regression to personal and meaningful memories, making it a valuable medium for neurological disorders (Landgarten, 2013). Clay can be manipulated in many ways, such as pressing down with one's fingertips, stretching and pulling, and squeezing the clay into the palm of a hand. Specifically with PD, its malleable and soft nature accommodates different levels of dexterity, as it can rest in the palm of a hand and be manipulated at an individual's own comfort level and stimulates the nerve endings present in the palm and fingertips through direct touch (Elkis-Abuhoff & Gaydos, 2016; Elkis-Abuhoff et al., 2013; Elkis-Abuhoff, Goldblatt, Gaydos, & Corrato, 2008).

Clay manipulation for individuals diagnosed with PD has been found to stimulate brain activity compromised by the progression of the disease, providing relief from motor symptoms, such as tremors and freezing gate; with this, a PD individual can regain a sense of control within the diagnosis (Elkis-Abuhoff & Gaydos, 2016; Elkis-Abuhoff et al., 2008). Furthermore, clay manipulation has been found to reduce psychological symptoms related to PD, such as depression, obsessive-compulsive thinking, phobic anxiety, and stress, similar to the adult norm (Elkis-Abuhoff et al., 2013; Goldblatt et al., 2010). The neurological and tactile aspects of clay can greatly aid a PD individual in increasing cognition, reestablishing personal connections from the past, and regaining a sense of identity through the relief of symptoms within the diagnosis aspects of treatment that cannot be found in curative, pharmaceutical efforts. As the need for complementary therapies continues to grow in the PD community, so does the need for art therapy to establish its value from a neurological standpoint (Elkis-Abuhoff & Gaydos, 2016, 2018; Mirabella, 2015).

Clay Manipulation Art Therapy: A Group for Those Diagnosed with Parkinson's Disease

In 2013, the work of Elkis-Abuhoff and colleagues transitioned their previous work (2008; Goldblatt, Elkis-Abuhoff, Gaydos, and Napoli 2010) into a clay manipulation art therapy group setting. The group consisted of six males, all diagnosed with PD and new to art therapy treatment. They all arrived apprehensive, and most reported that it was their significant other who talked them into attending. At first, the six men remained quiet and reserved, not really knowing how to express their feelings, but that quickly changed as the group moved forward. Each week the group would focus on a different issue or challenge faced by someone experiencing a PD diagnosis. The weeks were laid out to help assist the patient through the art therapy process, starting off with thoughts, moving to feelings, and ending with moving forward (Week 1: Living with Parkinson's; Week 2: Anxiety and Fears; Week 3: Relationships; Week 4: Getting Older/Aging; Week 5: Emotional/Control; and Week 6: Goal Setting).

Each group session began with a basic check-in and warm-up period. This allowed each participant to have time to share how they were presently feeling, both physically and emotionally, and state what they are bringing to the group based on their present state. This was a time for rapport building, creating group cohesiveness and a safe space for the all group members. This process allowed the group to come together and signified the start of the session.

After the warm-up, the group was introduced to the weekly topic with the therapist saying, *this week we are going to discuss . . .*, and followed up with a statement or two about the topic. Group participants were then asked to make a statement or two about the topic, how they related to it, and what it personally meant to them. This initiated the discussion and prepared the group for the clay directive.

Once everyone had an opportunity to bring meaning to the weekly topic, the clay directive was presented. All clay material, tools, clay mats, water, and hand towels were set on the table for easy access. Each week started with a preparatory exercise: holding a ball of clay in one hand, they were directed to squeeze it 10 times and then do the same with the other hand. Once that was completed, they were asked to pinch the clay into pieces. This was done to warm-up not only the clay but also the gripping and fine motor skills for the participants. Once everyone completed this task, the weekly topic was presented again for participants to engage in the clay manipulation art therapy (i.e., *Now that we are working with the clay, let's think about how we started with discussing the relationships in our lives. Who is important and why, what is our most important relationship? Now take the pieces of clay and work with them to create an object that best represents this relationship.*)

At this point, the patients were given time to individually engage in the clay medium and create an object that directly related to the directive presented. Most times the room would remain quiet with some small side discussions; however, at other times, the verbal processing would start amongst the patients during the clay manipulation. This approach became more natural as the group progressed. Once all patients completed their created clay object, the group came together to discuss and process each piece.

Participants Response to the Group Process

During the first week of the group program, Joe, 67-year-old and married, expressed his journey of living with PD through his created artwork (Figure 11.1). Joe shared that he was very active before his diagnosis and moved through his path in life, and although there were some obstacles, he was able to conquer them. Since his diagnosis, Joe expressed that his path had been blocked, and it became extremely hard for him to move forward. As seen in Figure 11.1, Joe represented his life journey through two paths, both having two small hurdles (as represented by the bridge between the roads). One road had a large mound of clay, which represented his struggle with his day-to-day life as a PD patient. This expression resonated with several others, who also shared how the PD diagnosis had affected their ability to have the life they are used to. The discussion focused on their present abilities, as well as developing and creating a new 'normal.'

Relationships were naturally discussed each week, so when the topic of the week focused on relationships, many of the patients were ready to share. Since the group consisted of all males over age 60, who grew up in an era where the man was the head of the household, several struggled with the shift of being the caretaker to being taken care of. Michael, 76 years old and married, began the session by sharing that he didn't feel like a man, or a good husband, anymore. He continued to discuss how he was the strong

Figure 11.1 Pathway Bridge

one in the relationship, but now felt weak and unable to take care of even basic house repairs.

After the clay manipulation, Michael discussed his artwork (Figure 11.2) by describing it as the pot that his wife of 57 years cooked great meals in. He shared that she has always been a great cook and caregiver, and continued to explain how much *life* they have shared (i.e., their first apartment, house, three children, and all the ups and downs of living). The PD had changed their relationship, but he was able to still identify how he and his wife go through life side by side, and take on the world together. The PD diagnosis was not going to change that aspect of their relationship.

The final week focused on closure and goal setting as the group came to an end. Steve, age 62, had been diagnosed with PD 3 years prior. He created the work shown in Figure 11.3, and shared that the PD diagnosis had brought about a lot of life-altering situations, but not all negative. He continued to state that life is like a book, and he had several chapters that he had *just lived through*. Since the PD diagnosis, he started to look at life differently, and felt blessed for each day. He continued to share that PD turned the page and he entered a new chapter in his life. He did not know what each day would bring, but things constantly change and will be *forever new*. He expressed that he saw life as more of an obstacle course or adventure, rather

Figure 11.2 The Cooking Pot

Figure 11.3 A New Chapter

than an obstacle for living. Finally, he stated that even though he has PD, it will never identify who he is, and he will live each day to the fullest.

This was a strong and positive way to end the 6 weeks of group clay manipulation art therapy. After Steve finished sharing, every patient was able to state that they are ready to move forward and not let the PD diagnosis define who they are.

It is important to note that each week, as the participants came to session, it was quite noticeable that there were resting tremors, shuffled gait, flat affect, and other symptoms related to PD. By the end of a session, participants were smiling, laughing, feeling, and expressing themselves through the application of clay, with an observed decrease in resting tremors. As they left the room and walked out of the building, the group facilitators could see a change in gait, with more readiness and stride. This was interpreted as a direct response to the clay manipulation art therapy directive, in addition to the emotional support provided for by the group process. The 6-week clay manipulation art therapy group allowed the participants to have a safe space to go and share their thoughts and feelings with others experiencing similar struggles. In the end, the group was cohesive and participants felt a strong affiliation to each other. In fact, they all shared their contact information and were discussing meeting the following week for coffee, . . . and maybe some clay.

Conclusion

Engaging in a clay manipulation project, and/or group process, can 'light up' the brain through neurotransmitter firings, and could result in new pathways being developed. Belkofer and Nolan's (2016) use of the qEEG showed that engagement in art has a direct impact on brain waves and function. This notion, in addition to the ability of the group process to strengthen support systems and allow for expression within a safe space, provides a platform for clay manipulation art therapy with those diagnosed with PD to further progress. This form of treatment has been proven to be beneficial, as participants were able to feel a sense of connection and to be understood by a fellow PD individual. In the end, the group clay manipulation art therapy helped each patient to break out of feeling 'boxed in' and get 'a grip on the world.'

References

Belkofer, C. M., & Nolan, E. (2016). Practical applications of neuroscience in art therapy. In J. L. King (Ed.), *Art therapy, trauma, and neuroscience: Theoretical and practical perspectives* (pp. 157–172). New York, NY: Routledge.

Beudel, M., & Brown, P. (2016). Adaptive deep brain stimulation in Parkinson's disease. *Parkinsonism & Related Disorders, 22*, S123–S126. doi: 10.1016/j.parkreldis.2015.09.028

Blesa, J., Trigo-Damas, I., Quiroga-Varela, A., & Jackson-Lewis, V. R. (2015). Oxidative stress and Parkinson's disease. *Frontiers in Neuroanatomy, 9*(91), 1–9. doi: 10.3389/fnana.2015.00091

Choi, W. S., Kim, H. W., Tronche, F., Palmiter, R. D., Storm, D. R., & Xia, Z. (2017). Conditional deletion of Ndufs4 in dopaminergic neurons promotes Parkinson's disease-like non-motor symptoms without loss of dopamine neurons. *Scientific Reports*, 7(44989), 1–14. doi: 10.1038/srep44989

Elkis-Abuhoff, D., & Gaydos, M. (2016). Medical art therapy applied to the trauma experienced by those diagnosed with Parkinson's disease. In J. L. King (Ed.), *Art therapy, trauma, and neuroscience: Theoretical and practical perspectives* (pp. 195–210). New York, NY: Routledge.

Elkis-Abuhoff, D., & Gaydos, M. (2018). Medical art therapy research moves forward: A review of clay manipulation with Parkinson's disease. *Art Therapy: Journal of the American Art Therapy Association, 35*(2). In press. doi: 10.1080/07421656.2018.1483162

Elkis-Abuhoff, D. L., Goldblatt, R. B., Gaydos, M., & Convery, C. (2013). A pilot study to determine the psychological effects of manipulation of therapeutic art forms among patients with Parkinson's disease. *International Journal of Art Therapy, 18*(3), 113–121. doi: 10.1080/17454832.2013.797481

Elkis-Abuhoff, D. L., Goldblatt, R. B., Gaydos, M., & Corrato, S. (2008). Effects of clay manipulation on somatic dysfunction and emotional distress in patients with Parkinson's disease. *Art Therapy: Journal of the American Art Therapy Association, 25*(3), 122–128. doi: 10.1080/07421656.2008.10129596

Goldblatt, R., Elkis-Abuhoff, D., Gaydos, M., & Napoli, A. (2010). Understanding clinical benefits of modeling clay exploration with patients diagnosed with Parkinson's disease. *Arts & Health, 2*(2), 140–148. doi: 10.1080/17533010903495405

Goldman, J. G., & Holden, S. (2014). Treatment of psychosis and dementia in Parkinson's disease. *Current Treatment Options in Neurology, 16*(3), 281–306. doi: 10.1007/s11940-013-0281-2

Goldman, J. G., & Weintraub, D. (2015). Advances in the treatment of cognitive impairment in Parkinson's disease. *Movement Disorders, 30*(11), 1471–1489. doi: 10.1002/mds.26352

King, J. L. (2016). Introduction. In J. L. King (Ed.), *Art therapy, trauma, and neuroscience: Theoretical and practical perspectives* (pp. 1–10). New York, NY: Routledge.

Lageman, S. K., Cash, T. V., & Mickens, M. N. (2014). Patient-reported needs, non-motor symptoms, and quality of life in essential tremor and Parkinson's disease. *Tremor and Other Hyperkinetic Movements, 4*, 240–251.

Landgarten, H. B. (2013). *Clinical art therapy: A comprehensive guide*. New York, NY: Routledge.

Lee, A., & Gilbert, R. M. (2016). Epidemiology of Parkinson disease. *Neurologic Clinics, 34*(4), 955–965. doi: 10.1016/j.ncl.2016.06.012

Leroi, I. (2017). Disrupted identities: Movement, mind, and memory in Parkinson's disease. *International Psychogeriatrics, 29*(6), 879–881. doi: 10.1017/S1041610217000370

Mirabella, G. (2015). Is art therapy a reliable tool for rehabilitating people suffering from brain/mental diseases? *The Journal of Alternative and Complementary Medicine, 21*(4), 196–199. doi: 10.1089/acm.2014.0374

Parkinson's Disease Foundation. (2017a). *Statistics on Parkinson's disease*. Retrieved from www.pdf.org/parkinson_statistics.

Parkinson's Disease Foundation. (2017b). *Prescription medications*. Retrieved from www.pdf.org/parkinson_prescription_meds#dopamine.

Parkinson's Disease Foundation. (2017c). *Surgical treatments*. Retrieved from www.pdf.org/surgical_treatments.

Rubin, J. A. (Ed.). (2016). *Approaches to art therapy: Theory and technique*. New York, NY: Routledge.

Sarrafchi, A., Bahmani, M., Shirzad, H., & Rafieian-Kopaei, M. (2016). Oxidative stress and Parkinson's disease: New hopes in treatment with herbal antioxidants. *Current Pharmaceutical Design*, *22*(2), 238–246.

Sveinbjornsdottir, S. (2016). The clinical symptoms of Parkinson's disease. *Journal of Neurochemistry*, *139*(S1), 318–324. doi: 10.1111/jnc.13691

Wu, S. L., Liscic, R. M., Kim, S., Sorbi, S., & Yang, Y. H. (2017). Nonmotor symptoms of Parkinson's disease [Editorial]. *Parkinson's Disease*, 1–2. doi: 10.1155/2017/4382518

12 Art Therapy and Amyotrophic Lateral Sclerosis

Juliet L. King and Robert M. Pascuzzi

Amyotrophic lateral sclerosis is a devastating neurological disease that impacts physical and psychic function at initial diagnosis and throughout the course of the illness. Amyotrophic lateral sclerosis is characterized by multiple direct and indirect stressors that affect sense of well-being, mood, anxiety, fear, cognition, and existential equilibrium. Patients experience a creeping progressive paralysis that traps them in their physical bodies. Research on the etiology of the illness is necessary, along with substantial inquiry into its emotional impact. Currently, there is no documented evidence-based psychological intervention for treating people with amyotrophic lateral sclerosis or their caregivers, and no specific psychological method of treatment that addresses coping skills or the consequent development of psychological conditions, such as depression and anxiety (Kurt, Nijboer, Matuz, & Kübler, 2007). While the latter symptomatology may very well be a healthy response to being diagnosed with a neurodegenerative disease, adapting a whole-person perspective to the illness is essential for optimal treatment. Issues of coping, helplessness, and end-of-life concerns likely affect longevity (Averill, Kasarskis, & Segerstrom, 2007), along with having an impact on the relationships of those involved in care and the capacity to tolerate and process questions of meaning and purpose. This chapter serves as an attempt to educate the public of the physical and psychological impact of amyotrophic lateral sclerosis and offer suggestions for how art therapy practice and research can influence contemporary medical care for people with amyotrophic lateral sclerosis and their caregivers.

Introduction to Amyotrophic Lateral Sclerosis

The terms amyotrophic lateral sclerosis (ALS), Lou Gehrig's disease, and motor neuron disease are all used interchangeably when describing what essentially is 'the neurologists' disease.' The Father of Neurology, Jean-Martin Charcot, originally studied ALS in the 1860s and formally reported the diagnosis in 1874. The subsequent 140 years have consisted of neurologists obtaining a thorough history and conducting a classic bedside examination to reveal the localization of asymmetrical upper and lower motor neuron deficits with an indolent progressive clinical course best described as a 'creeping paralysis.' The original clinical description and diagnosis have minimally evolved considering the broad strides in improved understanding of pathogenesis and biological behavior of motor neurons (Goetz, 2000). Perhaps no other disease over such an expanse of time has generated similarly strong reactions, fears, and existential questions as ALS. Even physicians who experience occasional muscle twitches, referred to as fasciculations, lie awake at night contemplating this diagnosis. Charcot combined clinical observations with work on the pathophysiology that established ALS as a specific clinical disorder, specifically the pathological changes in the lateral corticospinal tract (causing stiffness and contractures; i.e., upper motor neuron signs) and degeneration of the anterior horn of the spinal cord associated with atrophy and lower motor neuron weakness. He correctly surmised that the clinical symptomatology of ALS represented two distinctive motor systems.

The most common motor presentation in ALS involves gradual and progressive painless loss of strength and function involving one hand. The second most common motor presentation is characterized by a slowly progressive and painless foot-drop. In addition, about 25 percent of patients have their symptoms begin with slurring of speech and impaired swallowing, called bulbar onset ALS (Al-Chalabi & Hardiman, 2013). Regardless of where ALS begins, it gradually spreads over time to involve other areas of the body. The spread is generally regional, suggesting a component of cell-to-cell influence over progression. The rate of progression varies among patients and is difficult to predict early on. Some patients have a rapidly progressive clinical course and do not survive for 1 year after the onset of the initial symptoms. Other patients have a very slow clinical course, with a gentle slope of loss of function, and survive for 20 or 30 years or more.

Other than muscle cramps, which are fairly common and treatable, ALS tends to not cause pain until weakness becomes more severe, at which point immobility can produce a variety of comfort and self-care challenges that affect a person's quality of life. Although ALS does not typically affect thinking or memory, which is important when considering self-perception and awareness of the disease and its impact on the quality of life of individuals diagnosed, there is a large subgroup of patients who demonstrate cognitive impairment secondary to the diagnosis.

Cognitive Impairments in ALS

As cognition and sensory processing is typically normal, patients diagnosed with ALS see and contemplate their relentless loss of function and independence on both conscious and unconscious levels. Patients often lose the ability to effectively communicate, owing to involvement of the muscles of speech, and are faced with an inability to swallow and the decisions surrounding placement of feeding tubes. Patients develop weakness of respiratory muscles and can contemplate mortality and decisions of long-term mechanical ventilation. Patients worry about their burden on caregivers and family, and families worry about the patient. Sleep deprivation, stress, exhaustion, financial challenges, and the totality of a life-altering illness pervade many households and families. Burnout, loss of identity, and loss of autonomy are common concerns. The genetic potential for affected children and siblings generates major worries for the patients and their relatives. Those patients who have associated dementia and more subtle cognitive abnormalities (up to 50 percent) further complicate the psychological and emotional equilibrium for patient and family well-being (Giordana et al., 2011). While most ALS patients have preserved cognition and memory, some degree of cognitive impairment is demonstrated with detailed testing in up to 50 percent (most of these patients have relatively mild abnormalities that may not be apparent to the casual observer). Frontotemporal dementia occurs in 5 to 15 percent of ALS patients, and the onset usually parallels the development of weakness. The implications for study of pathogenesis, as well as practical decision-making, are substantial. The potential for cognitive impairment represents a major source of stress and concern for patients and families and a challenge for counseling and intervention (Giordana et al., 2011).

Depression and anxiety are common in ALS patients and caregivers (Pagnini, 2013). The incidence of depression in ALS was reported by Roos et al. (2016) with a case-control study of 1,752 patients diagnosed from July 2005 to December 2010 and 8,760 controls. Prior to ALS diagnosis, patients were at higher risk of receiving a clinical diagnosis of depression compared to controls, with the highest risk noted during the year before diagnosis. Patients with ALS also had a highly increased risk of depression within the first year after diagnosis. Antidepressant use was more common in patients with ALS than in controls, especially during the year before and the year after diagnosis (Roos et al., 2016).

Rabkin, Goetz, Murphy, Factor-Litvak, and Mitsumoto (2016) studied cognitive impairment, behavioral impairment, depression, as well as the wish to die in the ALS population and found that, with some, the wish to die was not associated with a depressive or cognitive impairment. The authors emphasized that there needs to be more research in the development of targeted interventions for patients and their families as they both have significantly more risk for comorbid depression, stress, and poor quality of life. Chen et al. (2015) studied 93 ALS patients, along with their 93 caregivers, and found strong correlations between depression and anxiety among patients and their caregivers. Depression and anxiety in ALS patients and their caregivers were closely associated with each other, but not with physical disability or disease duration. Studies have suggested that emotion perception deficits commonly occur in patients diagnosed with ALS, and that behavioral changes such as disinhibition and impulsivity have a greater impact on caregiver burden than the level and pattern of physical disability (Lillo, Mioshi, & Hodges, 2012; Oh, Oh, Kim, Park, & Kim, 2016). Furthermore, caregivers of patients with moderate to severe behavior change reported significantly heavier developmental burden, physical burden, and total burden than those with no behavioral change (Cui et al., 2015) Thus, existential well-being, as well as spirituality issues, perceived by patients diagnosed with ALS were directly related to quality of life, severity of mood disturbance, and burden experienced by their caregivers (Pagnini et al., 2011). Trail, Nelson, Van, Appel, and Lai (2003) indicated a need to explore factors contributing to quality of life, depression, and attitudes toward treatment options with patients and caregivers throughout the course of the illness. The specific needs and goals of the two groups may differ, and the study demonstrates the need for education and discussion, followed by referrals and interventions, appropriate to the needs of the patients and caregivers.

Treatment Interventions and Modalities from a Conventional Perspective

Psychotherapy and counseling, psychological intervention, and related modalities are underutilized and in need of expansion. Given the frequency with which patients diagnosed with ALS have impaired verbal communication, it behooves the healthcare profession to engage, develop, research, and implement programs of art therapy as a fundamental discipline integrated into the armamentarium of approaches to management of patients and their caregivers. The treatment of ALS involves multidisciplinary care by a team skilled in recognizing and managing the broad array of symptoms. One specific medication, riluzole, has been proven to aid in the overall treatment of ALS by slowing down the rate of progression by about 10 percent (Bensimon, Lacomblez, & Meininger, 1994). In addition to the physical and cognitive symptoms common in ALS, there is a range of social, emotional, and behavioral challenges for patient and caregiver that extend beyond the scope of contemporary medical treatment and intervention. The use of integrative and supportive modalities in the management of ALS, including art therapy and other creative arts therapies, is minimal even though patients and families are seeking such (Pan et al., 2013). Evidence of art psychotherapy interventions and research in the treatment of ALS are almost nonexistent.

It is true that the history of conventional medicine is replete with assumptions, beliefs, and clinical management, which have lacked proof and when studied methodically have shown to be incorrect and in some cases detrimental. For those who champion art and creativity, the world of belief, imagination, and tradition is proper and desirable. However, in a profession focused on evaluating and treating patients with serious health problems, clinicians and healthcare practitioners have a responsibility to work in the universe of truth, science, and proof. The artist-therapist should utilize his or her talent in creative approaches to patient care, novel beliefs, and observational skills to develop clear hypotheses and then commit to testing those ideas in formal prospective controlled clinical trials. Ultimately the value, support, acknowledgment, and utilization of the art therapy profession depends on this critical shift in emphasis to embed the profession in contemporary medical care.

Conventional medicine is so large and expansive that it has become obvious that a scientific method to managing patients is essential. Without science, even the brightest and best-motivated individuals will practice with biases. Like art therapists, medical professionals have historically believed in their methods and impact without evidence, which exacerbates subjectivity and impacts patient bias. For example, it has been proven that if a physician knows a patient is getting an active drug, and not a placebo, he or she will rate the patient as improved compared with an unbiased evaluation conducted by a blinded evaluator who is unaware of whether the patient is on a real drug or a placebo; if an unblinded evaluator knows a patient is on a placebo, then he or she will rate the patient worse than he or she really is as compared with the blinded physician (Noseworthy et al., 1994).

A classic example of the problems when healthcare practitioners, in this case a physician, shortchanges the scientific method is the case of Lou Gehrig. Lou Gehrig was 36 years old when he began to struggle with baseball, and his diagnosis was made in the summer of 1939 at the Mayo Clinic. Told of this prognosis, he sought out experimental therapy in New York and entered a clinical trial of high-dose vitamin E conducted by Israel Wechsler, a famous and respected neurologist. Wechsler treated Mr. Gehrig and 19 other ALS patients and reported their results in the *American Journal of Medical Sciences* in 1940. The results indicated that vitamin E therapy "definitely arrested and somewhat improved" Lou Gehrig's ALS and that the majority of the patients benefitted significantly according to the published report (Wechsler, 1940, p. 766).

In reality, Lou Gehrig and others did not benefit from the intervention. The observed and reported benefits were the result of Dr. Wechsler's performing a nonblinded trial in which there were no controls. Wechsler knew that patients were engaged in an intervention that he believed in; the patients liked their doctor and wanted the drug to work (Wechsler, 1940). The relationship instilled hope, and thus the clinician and patients saw and reported what they wanted to; what they believed in. Had there been a control group and a blinded evaluator, this study would have shown that vitamin E was not effective. From the days of bloodletting to remove evil humors, the health professions have been peppered with opinions, beliefs, and well-intended experts who teach and influence others, but have also unfortunately done the wrong thing due to the lack of science and methodology, otherwise known as the scientific method (Beecher, 1955; Pascuzzi, 1998).

Integrating Art Therapy with Contemporary Medical Treatment

Beliefs and biases are ever present, but art therapy cannot remain submerged in an abyss of well-intentioned artist-practitioners who claim successful treatment because it is observed, intuited, and believed in. Art therapy is centered on a knowledge base, dedicated clinical skills, pattern recognition and deductive reasoning, clinical diagnosis, and ultimately the treatment of patients. Although great strides toward progress have been made, the field needs systematic definition and standards for measuring and maintaining competence that is grounded in scientific inquiry. It is true that the primary element that makes the profession so meaningful is paradoxical and makes it difficult to define; that is the art. Art and art-making are understood in so many ways; from the Aristotelian catharsis of grand manner painters to mice that respond with increased immunity when shown beautiful things. The maturity of art therapy into its rightful place in the mainstream of health science requires a commitment to shift from the artistic-subjective in design to one that wears the science-based lens of objectivity. In order to embed the profession in contemporary medical practice, the effects of art therapy need to be quantified; we need to establish which parts of the intervention are responsible for the effects and which yield the best results. After this, we need to focus on amplifying the processes so that they can be generalized and applied in the efforts of having a more meaningful impact on patients, deploying treatment across the broader population.

It would be myopic to believe that engaging in scientific inquiry only includes quantitative analysis. The collection of valuable scientific data expands beyond numerical interpretation and is generated from methodologies that include qualitative, mixed-methods, and arts-based inquiry. The call for evidence generated from a range of methodologies will serve to standardize the educational curriculum, skill sets, and best practices, which would then position art therapy in the same realm as allied health professionals that receive consistent reimbursement for services provided. It is necessary to cultivate a way of thinking about the profession and conduct research that remains true to its foundations in artistic imagery, creative processing, and most important, the therapeutic relationship. It is possible for art therapy to be an emerging discipline in science and medicine, and we are at an historical inflection point, poised to enter the mainstream of scientific inquiry when built from a foundation and understanding of neuroscience. This chapter proposes these philosophies when expanding the multidisciplinary treatment team for ALS and other neuromuscular disorders to include art therapy assessment and intervention.

Tenets of Art Therapy

While it is beyond the scope of this chapter to provide a comprehensive literature review on the subject, the field of art therapy has intuited the connections between artistic expression and brain processes with the identification of three primary tenets, all of which can be underscored with neuroscience principles: (1) the bilateral and multidirectional process of creativity is healing and life enhancing; (2) the materials and methods utilized affect self-expression, assist in self-regulation, and are applied in specialized ways; and (3) the art-making process and the artwork itself are integral components of treatment that help to understand and elicit verbal and nonverbal communication within an attuned therapeutic relationship (King, 2016).

These tenets underscore and support the use of art therapy intervention with patients who have ALS and their caregivers. Essentially, the tenets underscore the use of art therapy with any population, and considering art therapy practice and intervention within the context of neuroscience benefits all involved, from patient to clinician, treatment team, administration, healthcare reimbursement entity, legislative bodies, so on and so forth.

If we apply the cognitive, behavioral, and emotional needs of patients with ALS within the context of art therapy theory, we can easily see how the interventions we intuit and have practiced will be of great use to the population. The use of nonverbal, sensory-based, and expressive therapies may provide opportunity to understand more clearly the lived experience of those affected with ALS and their caregivers. As there is little research on the subject of ALS and art therapy, it may be useful to understand how evidence from other patient groups, such as those with mobility challenges, might inform potential treatment goals and provide suggestions for comprehensive care. In particular, art therapists might help patients understand and symbolically express elements of their psychic functioning so that cognitive processing of personal experiences is less threatening, more objective and thus easier to identify and understand. Making art in the presence of another, and in an attuned therapeutic relationship, allows for mental processes to be distributed across different areas of the brain, an understanding of which is becoming clarified through research in neuroaesthetics that seeks to identify structures and functions responsible for aesthetic experiences (Skov & Vartanian, 2009).

The use of different art materials affects self-expression, a theory of which is elucidated through the expressive therapies continuum (ETC) (Kagin & Lusebrink, 1978; Lusebrink, 1990). The ETC, fairly considered the most scientifically cogent theory of intervention known to the field thus far, is a conceptual and hierarchal model based on the layered nature of visual expression and information processing that parallels the complexity of artistic production (Lusebrink & Hinz, 2016). The ETC is described in three levels: sensory/kinesthetic, perceptual/affective, and cognitive/symbolic. It is hypothesized that the regions and the functions of the brain are associated with the characteristics found on each level, all of which are influenced through the use of art materials (Lusebrink & Hinz, 2016). How the therapist considers media properties when determining interventions is foundational to art therapist training. For example, when working with those who have limited mobility, utilizing a malleable material such as clay may be successful due to its sensory and kinesthetic properties and the stimulation of areas of the brain responsible for sensory processing. Studies have shown that clay manipulation leads to increases in relaxation, capacity for self-reflection, and the ability to explore and express emotions, along with decreases in the symptoms of depression, obsessive-compulsive thinking, and phobic anxiety related to Parkinson's Disease (Elkis-Abuhoff, Goldblatt, Gaydos, & Convery, 2013; Goldblatt, Elkis-Abuhoff, Gaydos, Napoli, 2010; Strand & Waller, 2010). These findings also demonstrate the value of engaging patients in creative expression to enhance the quality of life gained through aesthetic experiences.

The art therapist guides the patient throughout the creative process, which spans the ETC. It is understood that verbal reflection and written responses to the artwork made in sessions engage cognitive functions that allow for a verbal articulation of one's feelings and thoughts. Art therapy has helped patients with muscular dystrophy communicate their subjective experiences and reorganize scattered thoughts into more concrete and detailed narrative (Ullmann, 2013; Viscardi, 1994). In multiple case studies conducted with those diagnosed with ALS, Whalen (2004) found that making written associations to magazine collage and imagery already produced helped to work through resistance and afford patients with a necessary sense of control in the process of developing a context to discuss grief and loss. The experimentation afforded through the art materials, and various projects offered, allowed for the discussion of legacy and life review, common treatment goals for those in palliative care. Creative arts therapies in-services for staff and healthcare professionals helped to facilitate one's own mortality review and reflect upon the impact that listening to the stories of those dying has on the psyche of the individual who is helping them through the process. Art therapy has also shown to reduce burnout and increase social support in hospice staff caregivers (Salzano, Lindemann, & Tronsky, 2013).

Despite the growing awareness for staff and caregiver support, there is much work to be done, as caregiving creates great stress on multiple levels. Although the majority of art therapy research on caregiving focuses on cancer patients and the aging population, many of the goals and interventions would likely be appropriate for those affected by ALS. Art therapy has shown to be effective in stress reduction and anxiety, along with helping caregivers accept the reality of cognitive decline by careful introduction to artwork that quickly shows degeneration through the imagery created (Sezaki & Bloomgarden, 2000; Walsh, Martin, & Schmidt, 2004).

Conclusion

As medical research continues to produce information on the environmental and genetic etiology of ALS, more opportunity is afforded to learn about the psychological aspects of the disease and how to treat it. Utilizing psychotherapeutic interventions such as art therapy, in combination with other pharmacological interventions, has potential to provide relief for patients and their caregivers. Art therapy also provides opportunities to learn more about the mind and psyche of the individual through thoughtful examination of what is created and the narrative that accompanies it, ultimately providing increased opportunity for self-reflection and the exploration of meaning in one's life.

While the profession of art therapy continues to work hard generating valuable data that speaks to its efficacy, we are simultaneously coauthoring a new and essential chapter in neuroscience. The opportunities to learn about the psyche through the methods and materials used in art therapy provide the treatment team with insight otherwise not obtained through verbal description and patient-caregiver testimony alone. It is through the participation in research and involvement as members of the contemporary medical treatment teams that art therapy will be taken seriously as a sound clinical intervention.

Art therapist practitioner-researchers have a responsibility to provide insight and education to our healthcare colleagues about the values of our important work, especially as we seek to learn more about how to help with people who are in great need such as those with ALS. The ongoing transition to a scientific level of the study of the brain and behavior as it relates to aesthetics, the creative process, and the helping professions helps us define and communicate the universal language of expression and connectedness devoid of all the baggage that seems to separate us as siloed practitioners. It is with this intention and spirit that we can all work together in lending a hand of healing and support for those in need.

References

Al-Chalabi, A., & Hardiman, O. (2013). The epidemiology of ALS: A conspiracy of genes, environment and time. *Nature Reviews Neurology*, *9*(11), 617–628. doi: 10.1038/nrneurol.2013.203

Averill, A. J., Kasarskis, E. J., & Segerstrom, S. C. (2007). Psychological health in patients with amyotrophic lateral sclerosis. *Amyotrophic Lateral Sclerosis*, *8*(4), 243–254. doi: 10.1080/17482960701374643.

Beecher, H. K. (1955). The powerful placebo. *Journal of the American Medical Association*, *159*(17), 1602–1606.

Bensimon, G., Lacomblez, L., & Meininger, V. F. (1994). A controlled trial of riluzole in amyotrophic lateral sclerosis. *New England Journal of Medicine*, *330*(9), 585–591.

Chen, D., Guo, X., Zheng, Z., Wei, Q., Song, W., Cao, B., . . . Shang, H. (2015). Depression and anxiety in amyotrophic lateral sclerosis: Correlations between the distress of patients and caregivers. *Muscle & Nerve*, *51*(3), 353–357. doi: 10.1002/mus.24325

Cui, B., Cui, L.Y., Liu, M. S., Li, X. G., Ma, J. F., Fang, J., & Ding, Q.Y. (2015). Behavioral symptoms in motor neuron disease and their negative impact on caregiver burden. *Chinese Medical Journal*, *128*(17), 2295–3000. doi: 10.4103/0366-6999.163393.

Elkis-Abuhoff, D. L., Goldblatt, R. B., Gaydos, M., & Convery, C. (2013). A pilot study to determine the psychological effects of manipulation of therapeutic art forms among patients with Parkinson's disease. *International Journal of Art Therapy*, *18*(3), 113–121.

Giordana, M. T., Ferrero, P., Grifoni, S., Pellerino, A., Naldi, A., & Montuschi, A. (2011). Dementia and cognitive impairment in amyotrophic lateral sclerosis: A review. *Neurological Sciences*, *32*(1), 9–16. doi: 10.1007/s10072-010-0439-6.

Goetz, C. G. (2000). Amyotrophic lateral sclerosis: Early contributions of Jean-Martin Charcot. *Muscle & Nerve*, *23*(3), 336–343. doi: 10.1002/(SICI)1097-4598(200003)23:3<336::AID-MUS4>3.0.CO;2-.

Goldblatt, R., Elkis-Abuhoff, D., Gaydos, M., & Napoli, A. (2010). Understanding clinical benefits of modeling clay exploration with patients diagnosed with Parkinson's disease. *Arts & Health: International Journal for Research, Policy & Practice*, *2*(2), 140–148. doi: 10.1080/17533010903495405.

Kagin, S. L., & Lusebrink, V. B. (1978). The expressive therapies continuum. *Art Psychotherapy*, *5*(4), 171–180. doi: 10.1016/0090–9092(78)90031–5.

King, J. L. (Ed.). (2016). *Art Therapy, trauma and neuroscience: Theoretical and practical perspectives*. New York, NY: Routledge.

Kurt, A., Nijboer, F., Matuz, T., & Kübler, A. (2007). Depression and anxiety in individuals with amyotrophic lateral sclerosis: Epidemiology and management. *CNS Drugs*, *21*(4), 279–291.

Lillo, P., Mioshi, E., & Hodges, J. R. (2012). Caregiver burden in amyotrophic lateral sclerosis is more dependent on patients' behavioral changes than physical disability: A comparative study. *BMC Neurology*, *12*(1), 156. doi: 10.1186/1471-2377-12-156.

Lusebrink, V. B. (1990). *Imagery and visual expression in therapy*. New York, NY: Plenum Press.

Lusebrink, V. B., & Hinz, L. D. (2016). The expressive therapies continuum as a framework in the treatment of trauma. In J. L. King (Ed.), *Art therapy, trauma, and neuroscience: Theoretical and practical perspectives* (pp. 42–66). New York, NY: Routledge

Noseworthy, J. H., Ebers, G. C., Vandervoort, M. K., Farquhar, R. E., Yetisir, E., & Roberts, R. (1994). The impact of blinding on the results of a randomized, placebo- controlled multiple sclerosis clinical trial. *Neurology*, *44*(1), 16–20.

Oh, S. I., Oh, K. W., Kim, H. J., Park, J. S., & Kim, S. H. (2016). Impaired perception of emotional expression in Amyotrophic Lateral Sclerosis. *Journal of Clinical Neurology*, *12*(3), 295–300. doi: 10.3988/jcn.2016.12.3.295.

Pagnini, F. (2013). Psychological wellbeing and quality of life in amyotrophic lateral sclerosis: A review. *International Journal of Psychology*, *48*(3), 194–205. doi: 10.1080/00207594.2012.691977

Pagnini, F., Lunetta, C., Rossi, G., Banfi, P., Gorni, K., Cellotto, N., . . . Corbo, M. (2011). Existential well-being and spirituality of individuals with amyotrophic lateral sclerosis is related to psychological well-being of their caregivers. *Amyotrophic Lateral Sclerosis*, *12*(2), 105–108. doi: 10.3109/17482968.2010.502941.

Pan, W., Chen, X., Bao, J., Bai, Y., Lu, H., Wang, Q., . . . Liu, J. (2013). The use of integrative therapies in patients with amyotrophic lateral sclerosis in Shanghai, China. *Evidence-Based Complementary and Alternative Medicine*, *2013*, 1–5. doi: 10.1155/2013/613596.

Pascuzzi, R. M. (1998). Blinded and seeing the light, (John Noseworthy, Lou Gehrig and other tales of enlightenment). *Seminars in Neurology*, *18*(3), 415–418.

Rabkin, J., Goetz, R., Murphy, J. M., Factor-Litvak, P., & Mitsumoto, H. (2016). Cognitive impairment, behavioral impairment, depression, and wish to die in an ALS cohort. *Neurology, 87*(13), 1320–1328. doi: 10.1212/WNL.0000000000003035.

Roos, E., Mariosa, D., Ingre, C., Lundholm, C., Wirdefeldt, K., Roos, P. M., & Fang, F. (2016). Depression in Amyotrophic Lateral Sclerosis. *Neurology*, *86*(24), 2271–2277. doi: 10.1212/WNL.0000000000002671.

Salzano, A. T., Lindemann, E., & Tronsky, L. N. (2013). The effectiveness of a collaborative art-making task on reducing stress in hospice caregivers. *The Arts in Psychotherapy*, *40*(1), 45–52. doi: 10.1016/j.aip.2012.09.008.

Sezaki, S., & Bloomgarden, J. (2000). Home-based art therapy for older adults. *Art Therapy: Journal of the American Art Therapy Association, 17*(4), 283–290. doi: 10.1080/07421656.2000.10129756.

Skov, M., & Vartanian, O. (Eds.). (2009). Introduction: What is neuroaesthetics? In M. Skov & O.Vartanian (Eds.), *Foundations and frontiers in aesthetics: Neuroaesthetics* (pp. 1–7). Amityville, NY: Baywood Publishing Co.

Strand, S., & Waller, D. (2010). The experience of Parkinson's: Words and images through art therapy—A pilot research study. *International Journal of Art Therapy, 15*(2), 84–93. doi: 10.1080/17454832.2010.524890.

Trail, M., Nelson, N. D., Van, J. N., Appel, S. H., & Lai, E. C. (2003). A study comparing patients with amyotrophic lateral sclerosis and their caregivers on measures of quality of life, depression, and their attitudes toward treatment options. *Journal of the Neurological Sciences, 209*(1), 79–85. doi: 10.1016/S0022-510X(03)00003-0.

Ullmann, P. (2013). Adaptive art therapy with children who have physical challenges and chronic medical issues. In C. A. Malchiodi (Ed.), *Art therapy and health care* (pp. 17–32). New York, NY: Guilford Press.

Viscardi, N. (1994). Art therapy as a support group for adolescents with muscular dystrophy. *Art Therapy: Journal of the American Art Therapy Association, 32*(3), 66–68.

Walsh, S. M., Martin, S. C., & Schmidt, L. A. (2004). Testing the efficacy of a creative-arts intervention with family caregivers of patients with cancer. *Journal of Nursing Scholarship, 36*(3), 214–219. doi: 10.1111/j.1547-5069.2004.04040.x.

Wechsler, I. S. (1940). The treatment of amyotrophic lateral sclerosis with vitamin E. *The American Journal of the Medical Sciences, 200*, 765–778.

Whalen, D. (2004). Meeting your metaphor: The use of the arts and the imagination with dying persons. In R. P. Magniant (Ed.), *Art therapy with older adults: A sourcebook* (pp. 101–121). Springfield, IL: Charles Thomas Publisher, LTD.

13 Recovery from Grief and Pain

Results from an Art Therapy Relational Neuroscience Four-Drawing Art Therapy Trauma and Resiliency Protocol

Noah Hass-Cohen and Joanna Clyde Findlay

Introduction

How people find resiliency, adapt to, or grow from interpersonal loss and pain is of great interest to art therapists (Hass-Cohen, 2016). Resilience is a reiterative growth process involving actual and perceived physical safety, interpersonal relationships, and a balanced stress-and-reward system function (Rutten et al., 2013). Internal resilience can be both learned and strengthened, and it is likely that it is mediated by creativity (Prescott, Sekendur, Bailey, & Hoshino, 2008; Wu et al., 2013). Loss-mediating resiliency factors include repressive coping, attachment and social relationships, view of self and identity, worldview, and positive emotions (Mancini & Bonanno, 2009); significant resilience-mediating responses to pain are likely a combination of positive emotions and lowered pain-catastrophizing (Ong, Zautra, & Carrington, 2010). For grief and pain, drawings and measures suggest that resiliency was likely supported by achieving allostasis, establishing a new balance between distancing from the grief experience and opening up to the pain experience, leading to increased creative resources and expression of positive feelings (Lynch, Sloane, Sinclair, & Bassett, 2013). This chapter will discuss art therapy relational neuroscience (ATR-N) principles and protocols, specifically the four-drawings resiliency protocol (4DRAW-RP), in order to guide therapists in these allostatic-supporting practices (Hass-Cohen, 2008; Hass-Cohen & Clyde Findlay, 2015). Two 4DRAW-RP protocols are presented. Both were drawn by the same participant; in the first protocol she focused on her grief, and the second on her pain.

Art Therapy Relational Neuroscience Principles

The ATR-N principles are: Creative Embodiment, Relational Resonating, Expressive Communicating, Adaptive Responding, Transformative Integration, and Empathizing and Compassion, which form the acronym CREATE (Hass-Cohen & Clyde Findlay, 2015). Creative embodiment highlights the resiliency role of arts-based movement, observation, and imitation, whereas relational resonating highlights therapeutic, familial, and social relationships and earned secure attachment. Expressive communicating and adaptive responding are a focus of the 4DRAW-RP. The former showcases the dynamic interface of imagination, emotion, cognition, and creativity; the later underscores the advantages of expressive arts for safely reducing the fear-inducing effects of memories and events and increasing rewarding creative experiences. Adaptive responding and relational resonating constructs combine to create the 4DRAW-RP drawing request, which promotes safety and social connectivity. Finally, the Transformative Integrating and Empathizing and Compassion principles point to the integrated effects of the first four principles in praxis (Hass-Cohen & Clyde Findlay, 2015).

The Four-Drawing Resiliency Protocol

A pain study conducted by Hass-Cohen and Clyde Findlay (2009) established 4DRAW-RP requests: (1) *If you were to draw the problem, what would it look like?* (2) *Draw an image of yourself,* (3) *Draw the internal and external resources that help with the problem,* and (4) *Draw yourself now.* The first drawing request supports therapeutic attunement and facilitates identifying which aspect of the traumatic event creates stress and what kind of stress it is. The second drawing request elicits a representation of the relationship between the problem and the self. As the first drawing stirs up stress, the second drawing often includes clues to the client's attachment style, as distress and a negative self-view stimulate attachment insecurity (Muller, Sicoli, & Lemieux, 2000). The third request invites the identification and exploration of resilient personal characteristics, behavioral actions, and social resources (Joseph & Linley, 2008). The final, fourth drawing, a repeated self-portrait, when compared with the previous self-drawing, may measure change as it is drawn after the person is reminded of their resources (Bridgham & Hass-Cohen, 2008; Hass-Cohen, 2008).

The clinical 4DRAW-RP incorporates four directives and pre- and post-drawing resiliency resources checklist (RRCs, Appendix 13.A). The research version of Hass-Cohen, Bokoch, Clyde Findlay, and Banford (2018) includes adapted global attachment subscales previously used by Hudson, Fraley, Chopick, and Hefferman (2015). Furthermore, Post-Traumatic Growth Inventory (PTGI) (Tedeschi & Calhoun, 1996) and creativity submeasures (Williams et al., 2013) are also included in the clinical 4DRAW-RP.

The Neuroscience of Fear

Stress Responses to Loss and Pain

Short- and long-term stress responses are frequently activated in individuals experiencing pain and grief, and are not mutually exclusive. Short-term stress responses to stressors are mobilizing and will typically self-resolve, whereas long-term responses, which support endurance, resolve slowly. When there is a lack of sufficient resources, mobilizing- and endurance-based stress responses become chronic and damaging to bodily functions.

Stress responses can be conceptualized as on a continuum of in control, striving for mastery and control, turning to others achieving control, repressive coping, loss of control, and potentially freeze responses (Henry & Wang, 1999; Mancini & Bonanno, 2009; Taylor, 2006).

The short-term stress, sympathetic adrenal medulla (SAM) axis response is activated by interactions between the fear center (the amygdala) and memory functions (facilitated by the hippocampus). SAM acts to release epinephrine (E) and norepinephrine (NE). These combine to motivate the flight-or-fight response and to balance bodily reactions through activation of the parasympathetic nervous system restorative relaxation response (Sapolsky, 2004). As E and NE are released, the brain's reward system works in tandem with SAM. NE also activates the brain's self-center, the ventral-medial prefrontal cortex (vmPFC), resulting in increased motivation, enhanced memory functions, and decreased fear (Figure 13.1).

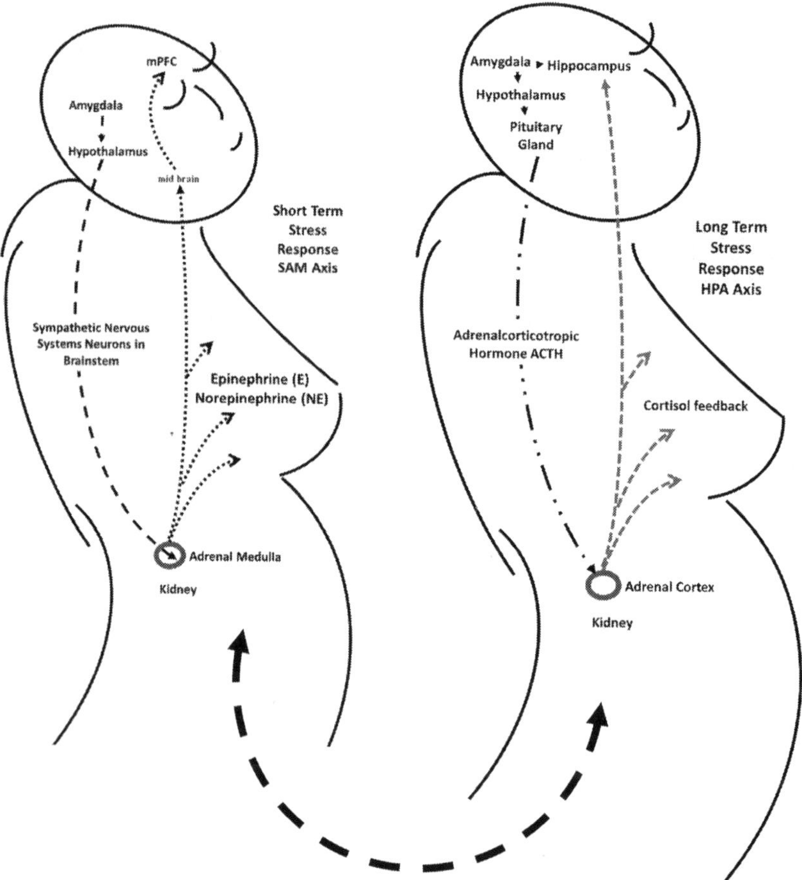

Figure 13.1 SAM and HPA. SAM Axis Stress Response and the Long-term Hypotha lamic-Pituitary-Adrenal (HPA) Axis Response, Hass-Cohen

The hypothalamic-pituitary-adrenal (HPA) axis is an endocrine response that is designed to react to events perceived as uncontrollable, such as loss. In this case, the amygdala and the hippocampus first signal the hypothalamus, which is a hormone regulator. Connected to the limbic structures, which are associated with emotive functions, the hypothalamus responds to bottom-up sensory and emotive neural cues and top-down cortical information. It responds with hormonal messaging, which initiates the activation of complex neurochemical feedback loops that control allostatic-balancing functions of cortisol that is discharged by the adrenal. When balanced, cortisol signals the pituitary gland and hypothalamus to turn off the long-term stress response (Sapolsky, 2004) (Figure 13.2).

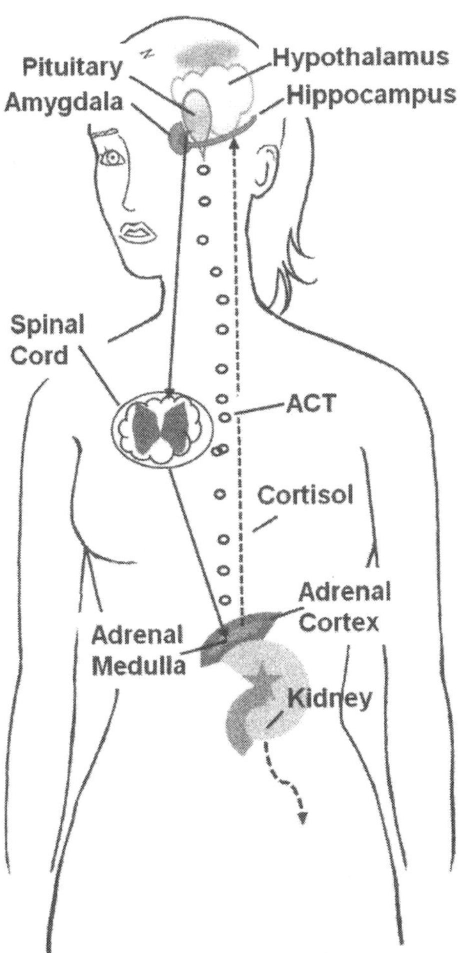

Figure 13.2 The Hypothalamic-Pituitary-Adrenal (HPA) Axis

The Neuroscience of Pain

Short- and long-term stress responses to pain act in tandem and are influenced by the perception of pain, the pain dimensions, as well as personal life history. The bottom-up sensory transmission of pain and emotional reaction to the pain can be mediated by cognitive top-down modulation of the experience (Woo, Roy, Buhle, & Wager, 2015). Sensory pain sensations are transmitted to the spinal cord and from there to the thalamus (the sensory gateway), the sensory cortices (body map), and the insular lobe (mind–body center) by nociceptors, which release the excitatory neurotransmitter glutamate (McMahon & Koltzenburg, 2004). The pain message activates the emotional and cognitive neuropathways to act in tandem. The limbic system (emotion center) and the anterior cingulate cortex (ACC, an anxiety regulator) convey the pain experience (mind–body connector) to the vmPFC (self-center), and the nucleus accumbens (within the reward system) (Woo et al., 2015).

The Neuroscience of Attachment

The neuroscience of attachment involves a widespread subcortical and cortical matrix, yet research supports findings that the neuroscience of fear and motivation described above is at the center of attachment experiences throughout the life cycle (Beckes & Coan, 2015). While most theories of attachment have emphasized cognitive aspects of theory of mind, a neurologically informed perspective suggests that the attachment neuro-circuitry is mostly embodied in nonverbal and bodily connections between the insular cortex, the anterior insular cortex, the ACC, and the vmPFC (Beckes & Coan, 2015).

The Price of Stress: Cognitive, Emotional, and Physiological Impacts

Stress contributes to structural and neurochemical changes in the nervous and endocrine systems that negatively affect cognitive, emotional, and relational coping, as well as immune system functioning (Sapolsky, 2004).

High levels of E, NE, and cortisol contribute to dendritic shortening in the medial prefrontal cortex (mPFC), which impairs top-down cognitive regulation of the amygdala. At the same time, dendritic growth in the amygdala neurons and in memory centers of the brain (hippocampus and orbital frontal cortex) increases bottom-up influences of fear on cognitions (McEwen, Eiland, Hunter, & Miller, 2011). Thus, the combination of a hypoactive mPFC and hyperactive amygdala reduce the person's ability to process, extinguish, and regulate fear-based negative emotions and increase vulnerability to confusion and forgetfulness. In loss and grief, a long-term stress response has been associated with loneliness, depression, isolation, and changes in attachment security (Parkes, 1998). Negative self-emotions associated with excessive NE and decreased serotonin contributes indirectly to immune dysregulation by increasing proinflammatory cytokine production (Miller & Raison, 2016). Dysregulated levels of long-term cortisol damage the immune system, potentially resulting in reduced levels of infection-fighting cells (lymphocytes) and increased inflammatory problems contributing to the exacerbation of existing medical conditions (Buckley et al., 2012). With this, it seems as if cortisol tricks the immune system into attacking normal parts of the body as if they were invaders.

The Neuroscience of Resilient Protective Responses

Resiliency and distress neuropathways may overlap. For example, the mPFC sensitive to fearful reactions is also thought to be involved in differentiating the self from others and self-reflection (Passingham, Bengtsson, & Lau, 2010), implicit and explicit evaluations, immediate and intuitive meaning-making (Seitz, Franz, & Azari, 2009), and in social impacts (McEwen, 2012). Thus, experience-driven resilience is a complex cognitive-emotive and social process involving the progressive learning of coping responses (Reivich, Seligman, & McBride, 2011).

The mPFC plays a major role in the acquisition of stress resilience, which is expressed as long-lasting, protein neuronal synthesis. For example, during uncontrollable stress, recalling the memory of a prior controllable experience elicits mPFC activation, mimicking control. Some mPFC-mediated resiliency can also result from repeated suppression of activity in the amygdala (Myers-Schulz & Koenigs, 2012). Amygdala-to-mPFC interactions are an opportunity for adaptive cortisol responses, which have been found to also mediate growth hormones, promoting neuroplasticity, learning, and memory function. This may explain why moderate amounts of stress support resiliency and sometimes spontaneous post-traumatic growth (McEwen, 2012).

The amygdala generally activates in response to a variety of novel and emotionally salient information, generating fear, motivation, and surprise. It does so through its connections to the reward system's locus coeruleus, which reacts to physiological stress and to sensory inputs. The brain's reward system helps regulate the fear and stress response, contributing to feelings of pleasure and joy (Rutten et al., 2013). The reward system is connected to the mPFC, the cognitive-frontal lobe, and the emotive-limbic system and functions through the release of 'good feeling' neurochemicals, E, NE, dopamine (DA) and serotonin, which strengthen the connections between cues and their associated rewarding outcomes. When optimized, NE helps regulate stress, excitation, and inhibition through its influences on glutamate and gamma aminobutyric acid (GABA), both of which are needed for the weakening of conditioned fear responses (Rutten et al., 2013). DA is implicated in many motivation-inducing activities, including negative (such as stress, substance use, and anger), and positive (such as touch and creativity) ones (Beckes & Coan, 2015). Serotonin projections also play an important role in the regulation of PFC, amygdala, hippocampus, and NE functions (Vasterling & Brewin, 2005). Finally, natural brain opiates and the GABA system in the reward system's ventral striatum are involved in processing sensory pleasure, such as pleasurable touch. Touch releases natural brain opiates (Berridge & Robinson, 2003), such as oxytocin, which is involved in creating social bonds and is initiated by pleasurable social contact.

It is from these ATR-N perspectives that the 4DRAW-RP examines self-representation (drawing 2) and self-enhancement (drawing 3) in the context of emotive fearful reactions (drawing 1), cognitive and social resources (drawing 3), and transformative integration (drawing 4). Engaging with art-making likely activates 'good feelings' neurochemicals that contribute to allostasis.

Grief and Pain 4DRAW-RP

The death of Etta's 80-year-old mother was a shock to the family. Etta's mother, who had a heart condition, passed away within a matter of hours after being released from the hospital. Etta had suddenly lost her mother. About a month later, Etta, a 50-year-old Middle Eastern woman, experienced acute and disabling pain from inflammation in her joints. Her images and narratives highlight the potential contribution of 4DRAW-RP and creativity to resilient balanced stress and reward system coping.

Drawing 1: If You Were to Draw the Problem, What Would It Look Like?

Etta said that she experienced a cycle of anger, numbness, forgetfulness, and pain whilst taking care of her family. She completed the 4DRAW-PR twice. In "Death," Etta depicts family and friends attending the graveside (Figure 13.3–1a).

Etta's figure in a green dress is closest to the grave. While her father and sister hold flowers, she is empty-handed. None of the figures have faces or hands, and the scenery is schematically represented as green grass, four fluffy green trees, and a bright sun and clouds.

Etta said that her pain made her angry and embarrassed, as she could not move, walk, take care of her family or do any household tasks. In "Pain," Etta drew a suffering face, which she said was *me*. She has closed eyes with large blue tears and red and black bursts of color above her head expressing her anguish: *I wanted to show my pain, anger, and confusion* (Figure 13.3–1b).

According to the ATR-N Expressive Communicating principle, "Death" represents an organized and controlled repressed coping—the drawing could be mistaken for a drawing of a day in the park. Grief frequently permeates every aspect of daily life. Not confined to time, space, or location, grief activates a long-term stress repressive and distancing coping response. Accordingly, "Death" shows a distanced bird's-eye view, whereas "Pain" is a close-up emotive image.

Figure 13.3–1a "Death." Draw the Problem, Light Blue Background (Grief 4DRAW-RP)

Figure 13.3–1b "Pain." Draw the Problem, Blue Background (Pain 4DRAW-RP)

The comparison of her problem drawings ("Death" and "Pain"), which were drawn within a month period, possibly suggest that "Pain" expresses the arousal of the sympathetic SAM response. The activation of SAM helps the person feel in control, especially if she can remove, mitigate, or move away from the pain trigger. The release of endogenous pain inhibitors, E and NE, further contributes to control the degree of pain (Ossipov, Dussor, & Porreca, 2010). A SAM stress response can help reveal emotions and thoughts (McEwen, 2012). It is likely that a complex interplay between the expression of repressive, positive, and negative emotions positively affects physical well-being (Hershfield, Scheibe, Sims, & Carstensen, 2013). Thus, Etta's expression of pain likely helped her cope not only with the physical pain, but also with the emotional pain of her grief.

Arousal is helpful when it helps coping with stressors and when it is balanced with protective responses of the parasympathetic nervous system such as those associated with relaxation, which Etta engaged with. This relaxation response assists in establishing allostatic balance, therefore representing positive adjustments to adversity (Sapolsky, 2004).

Drawing 2: Draw an Image of Yourself

"Etta" is represented as a smiling, schematic figure with black eyes and brown stylized hair and a pale blue, buttoned dress (Figure 13.3–2a). Her limbs, drawn in a light skin tone, blend into the white background of the paper and are difficult to see. As in "Death," "Etta's" hands extend downward, possibly representing attachment insecurity (Fury, Carlson, & Sroufe, 1997; Hass-Cohen, 2008). Although "Etta" seems to be looking forward, her left eye is looking to the left. This may be a clue to some confusion that the otherwise composed figure conveys and may reflect a dominant right-hemispheric reaction typical for people experiencing trauma (Chapman, 2014). Etta said that she needed to hold everything together for everyone in her family and take care of them: *I had sad feelings, but I tried to show myself with a smile on my face . . . I had to put a mask on my face.*

In contrast, "Sickness" reveals a vivid image of a woman wearing a red shirt and blue skirt. Here the pale lines depicting her swollen limbs and hands are clearly visible against the blue background (Figure 13.3–2b). The downward gaze suggests introspection; *it shows me in pain with a swollen knee, arms, and fingers and my anger and a fat Etta.* She added that she had chosen the blue background paper to be *dark as a symbol of pressure, hopelessness, and pain.* Again, it seems that Etta's physical pain was perceived as a legitimate opportunity to acknowledge suffering, whereas her invisible grief remained hidden, masked by a social smiling face.

Shame, self-blame, and identity loss are common reactions amongst the bereaved and those suffering from pain (Parkes, 1998). It seems that when Etta was reminded of her stressors (loss and pain), an insecure internal working model (IWM) was represented. In "Sickness" the IWM is described as a negative, shameful, and fat self-image, and in "Etta" a younger self,

Figure 13.3–2a "Etta." Draw yourself, White Background (Grief 4DRAW-RP)

symbolized by the schematic drawing characteristics and split gaze, was represented. Not only did Etta lose a beloved attachment figure, but her own body also seemed to have also betrayed her.

According to the CREATE principle of relational resonating, it is also possible that as the therapeutic relationship developed between Etta and the second author, some of her personal and cultural prohibitions against self-expression dissolved. This interpersonal connection likely allowed for the beginning expression of right-hemispheric negative implicit emotions, which add to long-term stress, cortisol, and inflammation. From an emotive nonverbal perspective, the coping functions of the amygdala's basolateral region are of tremendous interest to art therapists; it is sensitive to both sensory information and higher-order auditory and visual processing

Figure 13.3–2b "Sickness." Draw yourself, Blue Background (Pain 4DRAW-RP)

information via its connections with the tactile and sound centers of the brain (temporal lobes). These connections create opportunities for explicit processing of visual and auditory inputs, which can mitigate the fear response and play a critical role in developing resiliency (LeDoux, 2000). Recognizing this range of supportive resources opens up possibilities for divergent adaptive responding and post-traumatic growth.

Drawing 3: Draw the Internal and External Resources That Help with the Problem

In "Hope," a cluster of smiling family and friends' faces represent Etta's social resources (Figure 13.3–3a). Nature, an external resource, is depicted as a

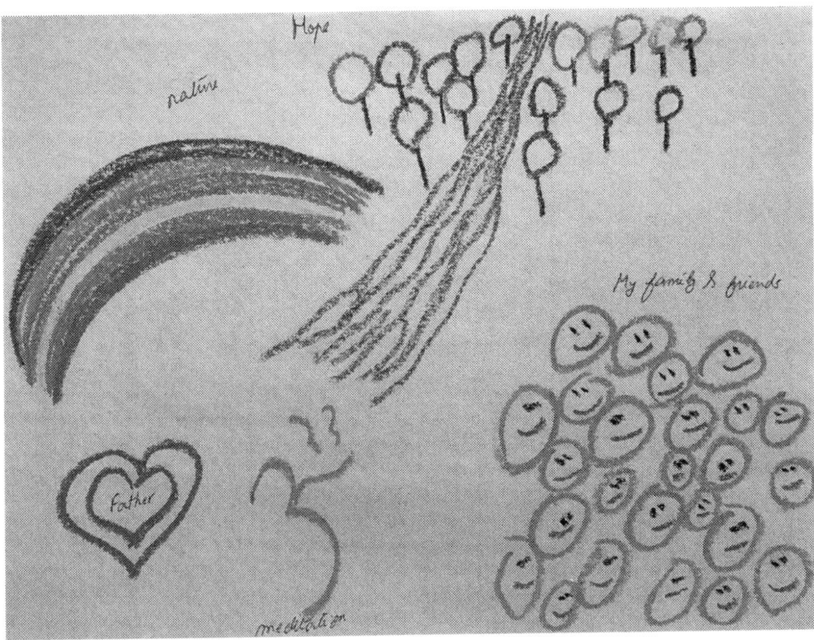

Figure 13.3–3a "Hope." Draw the Internal and External Resources that Help with the Problem, Yellow Background (Grief 4DRAW-RP)

bright rainbow, blue river, and a group of light and dark green schematic trees. Two concentric red hearts represent Etta's love for her deceased and living parents and a faint OM symbol represents inner meditation resources.

Etta said that the love of her family and friends was the most crucial internal and external resource. This was *because they had the same pain, they understood 100 percent.* Yet when Etta experienced pain, her husband and sons actively showed their support when they *cooked, cleaned up, did the laundry, and did everything*. In the context of a traditional Middle Eastern family, this was a significant remedy and source of support. Aid gave Etta the inner peace needed for her meditation and studies, which are symbolized by a candle and a book. Both "Hope" and "Love and Hope" are drawn on a *sunny* yellow background. In contrast with "Hope," "Love and Hope" shows full stick figures, and each figure is depicted in his unique colors (Figure 13.3–3b). Here the green OM symbol is vibrant and the red heart is a solid form. Etta added that her most important internal resource was meditation and her spiritual belief that *every person has a time in which they are destined to leave this earth*. Etta said that pain made her pay attention to the inflammation, which she perceived as her bodily reaction to stress. She asked her body *why are you stressed?* and responded, *hey, this is Etta—what are you doing? Why are you angry? We are not enemies!* She took prescribed medication, altered her diet,

Figure 13.3–3b "Love and Hope." Draw the Internal and External Resources that Help with the Problem, Yellow Background (Pain 4DRAW-RP)

and dedicated herself to meditation and self-care. The inflammation and pain passed away after 3 months. Item analysis of the pre- and post-PTGI also showed that the largest ranges of change were on items of spirituality, compassion, and agency (3- to 4-point changes).

From an adaptive responding perspective within CREATE, the third protocol request asks clients to intentionally identify and represent their active coping skills. It elicits the perceived experience of control and change. When comparing "Hope" and "Hope and Love," the shift to include "Love" in the title, as well increased detail and vivid expression in both drawing characteristic and narratives, provides compelling evidence for evolving explicit awareness of self and resources. Drawing their resources likely assists clients in the explicit examination appraisal strategies that might be helpful in increasing positive emotions or decreasing negative emotions and to assist with reinterpretation, which requires meaning-making and narration. Positive feelings, thoughts, and attitudes, as well as availability of spiritual resources, were associated with better health, altered autonomic activity, and immune function (Daruna, 2004). Narration of the events and impacts also significantly influences positive self-development and the generation of helpful implicit emotional responses (Cohen, Mannarino, & Deblinger, 2006). To enhance this effect, clients are asked to talk about their resources in detail. This contrasts with the first two drawings where the therapist does not elicit a conversation.

The explicit articulation of disturbing emotions or thoughts is expressed in the nervous system by descending, top-down frontal cortex modulating projections, and this cerebral cortex activity alters the experience of pain (Woo et al., 2015). Positive expectations about decreased pain have also been shown to produce a reduction in perceived pain similar to the effects of an analgesic dose of morphine (Ossipov et al., 2010). Amygdala fear responses are frequently conditioned, and thus cognitive interventions need to be supplemented by means such as meditation, which reduces negative reactivity and may increase the capacity for alternative reactions (Segal, Williams, & Teasdale, 2001). Meditation evokes the parasympathetic relaxation response, which is known to curtail and rebalance the expression of cortisol and NE and help reduce weight and inflammation (Sapolsky, 2004).

Allostatic adjustment is for the most part interpersonally and socially mediated (Schulkin, 2011). In this context, 'interpersonal' refers to dyadic interactions, whereas 'social' refers to a broadening circle of traditional and nontraditional familial, work, educational, and community networks. Social support factors are linked to improved changes in psychological and biological pathways of disease and distress. One of the most robust findings is the positive impact of personal relationships on immune and endocrine regulation (Kiecolt-Glaser, McGuire, Robles, & Glaser, 2002).

For Etta, results from the RRC showed a 15 percent increase in resources across the two 4DRAW-RP protocols, with specific increases in the number of social and emotional resources after completing the Pain 4DRAW-RP.

Drawing 4: Draw Yourself Now

The fourth drawing, which is a second drawing of the self, comes after the resource drawing and discussion. "Graduation" shows Etta holding her diploma with a blue graduation gown, cap, and glasses (Figure 13.3–4a). Etta explained that her graduation was a gift to her mother and *while drawing the regalia and cap my heart was full of joy, and I can see the power of drawings.*

Both "Graduation" and "Etta" were drawn with similar drawing characteristics. However, in "Graduation," the figure is endowed with items that can be considered resilient resources. The hat may be understood as a positive status symbol as well as protective garment from the weather, glasses are

Figure 13.3–4a "Graduation." Draw Yourself as You See Yourself Now, White Background (Grief 4DRAW-RP)

also protective shields, which symbolize better vision and perhaps insight, and the figure has something to hold, show, and share as opposed to "Etta" and "Death," where the figure has empty hands. Although both drawings are drawn schematically, "Graduation" seems to subjectively impress the viewer as an older, larger Etta. Etta also said that *working helped me to forget my pain, acceptance came—I accepted it as part of life*. However, in both drawings, the position of Etta's hands are down, at a 45-degree angle to her body, suggesting continued attachment insecurity. In both drawings, the limbs of the

Figure 13.3–4b "Happiness." Draw Yourself as You See Yourself Now, Green Background (Pain 4DRAW-RP)

figure are drawn in pale colors, possibly suggesting an implicit yet powerful ignoring of the pain that she experienced in her limbs shortly after her mother's passing.

"Happiness," the fourth drawing in the "Pain" series, is in sharp contrast to the others (Figure 13.3–4b). Etta wears dark blue pants, a green top, and is not hiding her body behind a gown. Most important, she stands with her arms raised and without stretched fingers. The drawing is a clear and robust symbol of self-esteem and attachment security (Hass-Cohen, 2008). This impression is also supported by results from an attachment subscale. On an item that asked her to rate: *I don't feel comfortable opening up to others*, her response shifted from a rating that was *low* agreement before the drawing activity to a *high* agreement. This finding suggests heightened self-awareness of her familial and cultural prohibitions; in a follow-up communication, Etta shared that women in her culture will often keep emotions to themselves, especially negative ones.

In "Happiness," the neck, arms, and hands with expressive fingers stand out vibrantly against the green paper. Etta said, *I can see myself as a happy, skinnier, woman, this is helpful, good motivation for me. I did it!* She added that she intentionally chose a green background to show 'healing.' The figure in "Happiness" is larger than in "Sickness." The figure in "Sickness" has a downturned mouth, whereas in "Happiness," she has a broad smile and looks straight out of the page. Her limbs are no longer swollen and drawn with scratchy lines but bold strokes. Etta added, *The first one is me with pain—swollen knee, arms, and fingers, anger and a 'fat' Etta. In the fourth drawing, I can see a happy Etta—I lost 35 pounds after the beginning of my illness. It was a huge accomplishment—now I feel very healthy and safe and sound.* From a resiliency perspective in CREATE, 'healing' was with her even in the first drawing of the protocol, depicted as the color of her dress.

Happiness is associated with functions of the reward system, which favors goal-directed and motivated behaviors, decisions, positive actions, emotions, and optimism (Feder, Nestler, & Charney, 2009). Optimism bias, such as that exhibited by Etta in her last drawing, is a resilient tendency to expect future events to be positive. Happiness was associated with higher activation in the rostral ACC, which modulates amygdala arousal, and was positively correlated with dispositional optimism (Pizzagalli et al., 2009).

It is possible that the rewarding, pleasurable experience induced by art-making can increase DA production without increased NE and cortisol responses. In addition, an attuned therapeutic relationship can support the emergence of optimism and hope. With repetition, a supportive relationship and rewarding activities can potentially balance the ill effects of grief and pain on the reward system. Thus, the reward system and associated therapeutic work show promise for reductions in the pathophysiology of stress-related psychiatric disorders and the development of resiliency.

Summary

Etta's 4DRAW-RP seemed to enhance cognitive appraisal, relaxation, and emotive-psychosocial adjustments that promoted allostasis. Her Grief and Pain 4DRAW-RPs show an amalgam of negative emotions with strong positive emotions and illustrate how art therapy interventions can help mitigate the increase of stress-induced cortisol and catecholamines. There also seems to be a trend of increased vivid and organized expression, as all of the pain protocol drawings have a colorful background and they are all drawn upright (portrait). In this case study, the CREATE principle of transformative integrating illustrated an integrated and balanced relationship between the stress and reward systems. This is a sequence of autonomic and endocrine efforts at control and mastery, which, if successful, not only revert to parasympathetic relaxed responding but also mitigate the long-term effects of chronic stress (de Kloet et al., 2006). The sequential visual expressions of sensory, emotional, and cognitive pain likely assisted in revealing coping skills and the potential for symptom reduction. These claims are supported by our impressions from the drawings and narratives and self-report measures. Excitingly, and a venue for future research, item analysis of Etta's RRC-Personal category showed an overall increase in endorsed items with three new items endorsed (creativity, curiosity, and decorating).

In summary, the ATR-N framework links art therapy practices with clinical neuroscience research and suggests that the shared neuro-circuitry of distressed reactions and creative responding provide a window of opportunity for arts-based intervention. We also suggest that creativity is both a protective factor for coping with distressing events and that it enhances other resiliency-promoting resources.

References

Beckes, L., & Coan, J. A. (2015). Relationship neuroscience. In J. Simpson & J. Dovidio (Eds.), *APA handbook of personality and social psychology, Vol. 3: Interpersonal relations* (pp. 119–149). Washington, DC: APA Press.

Berridge, K. C., & Robinson, T. E. (2003). Parsing reward. *Trends in Neurosciences, 26*(9), 507–513. doi: 10.1016/S0166–2236(03)00233–9.

Bridgham, T., & Hass-Cohen, N. (2008). Art therapy and acquired immune deficiency syndrome. In N. Hass-Cohen & R. Carr (Eds.), *Art therapy and clinical neuroscience* (pp. 283–309). New York, NY: Jessica Kingsley Publishers.

Buckley, T., Sunari, D., Marshall, A., Bartrop, R., McKinley, S., & Tofler, G. (2012). Physiological correlates of bereavement and the impact of bereavement interventions. *Dialogues in Clinical Neuroscience, 14*(2), 129–139.

Chapman, L. (2014). *Neurobiologically informed trauma therapy with children and adolescents: Understanding mechanisms of change* (Norton Series on Interpersonal Neurobiology). New York, NY: W. W. Norton & Company.

Cohen, J. A., Mannarino, A. P., & Deblinger, E. (2006). *Treating trauma and traumatic grief in children and adolescents*. New York, NY: The Guilford Press.

Daruna, J. H. (2004). Book review: The Rorschach Test Challenges Science with the complexity of imagination. *Journal of Psychopathology and Behavioral Assessment, 26*(2), 147–149. doi: 10.1023/B:JOBA.0000013662.74610.ea.

de Kloet, C. S., Vermetten, E. E., Geuze, E. E., Kavelaars, A. A., Heijnen, C. J., & Westenberg, H. M. (2006). Assessment of HPA-axis function in posttraumatic stress disorder: Pharmacological and non-pharmacological challenge tests, a review. *Journal of Psychiatric Research, 40*(6), 550–567.

Feder, A., Nestler, E. J., & Charney, D. S. (2009). Psychobiology and molecular genetics of resilience. *Nature Reviews Neuroscience, 10*(6), 446–457. doi: 10.1038/nrn2649.

Fury, G., Carlson, E. A., & Sroufe, L. A. (1997). Children's representations of attachment relationships in family drawings. *Child Development, 68*(6), 1154–1164. doi: 10.1111/j.1467–8624.1997.tb01991.x.

Hass-Cohen, N. (2008). CREATE art therapy relational neuroscience principles (ATR-N). In N. Hass-Cohen & R. Carr (Eds.), *Art therapy and clinical neuroscience* (pp. 283–309). New York, NY: Jessica Kingsley Publishers.

Hass-Cohen, N. (2016). Review of the neuroscience of chronic trauma and adaptive resilient responding. In J. King (Ed.), *Art therapy, trauma and neuroscience: Theoretical and practical perspectives* (pp. 100–138). New York, NY: Routledge.

Hass-Cohen, N., Bokoch, R., Clyde Findlay, J., & Banford, W. A. (2018). A four-drawing art therapy trauma and resiliency protocol study. *The Arts in Psychotherapy*. https://doi.org/10.1016/j.aip.2018.02.003.

Hass-Cohen, N., & Findlay, J. C. (2009). Pain, attachment, and meaning making: Report on an art therapy relational neuroscience assessment protocol. *The Arts in Psychotherapy, 36*(4), 175–184. doi: 10.1016/j.aip.2009.02.003.

Hass-Cohen, N., & Clyde Findlay, J. (2015). *Art therapy & the neuroscience of relationships, creativity, and resiliency*. The Interpersonal Neurobiology Series. New York, NY: W. W. Norton & Company.

Henry, J. P., & Wang, S. (1999). Effects of early stress on adult affiliative behavior. *Psycho-Neuroendocrinology, 23*(8), 863–875.

Hershfield, H. E., Scheibe, S., Sims, T. L., & Carstensen, L. L. (2013). When feeling bad can be good: Mixed emotions benefit physical health across adulthood. *Social Psychological Personal Science, 4*(1), 54–61. doi: 10.1177/1948550612444616.

Hudson, N. W., Fraley, C. R., Chopick, W. J., & Hefferman, M. (2015). Not all attachment relationships develop alike: Normative cross-sectional age trajectories in attachment to romantic partners, best friends, and parents. *Journal of Research in Personality, 59*, 44–55. doi: 10.1016/j.jrp.2015.10.001.

Joseph, S., & Linley, P. A. (2008). Psychological assessment of growth following adversity: A review. In S. Joseph & P. A. Linley (Eds.), *Trauma, recovery, and growth: Positive psychological perspectives on posttraumatic stress* (pp. 21–38). Hoboken, NJ: John Wiley & Sons.

Kiecolt-Glaser, J. K., McGuire, L., Robles, T. F., & Glaser, R. (2002). Psychoneuroimmumology; Psychological influences on immune function and health. *Journal of Consulting and Clinical Psychology, 70*(3), 537–547.

LeDoux, J. E. (2000). Emotion circuits in the brain. *Annual Review of Neuroscience, 23*, 155–184. doi: 10.1146/annurev.neuro.23.1.155.

Lynch, M., Sloane, G., Sinclair, C., & Bassett, R. (2013). Resilience and art in chronic pain. *Arts & Health: International Journal for Research, Policy & Practice, 5*(1), 51–67. doi: 10.1080/17533015.2012.693937.

Mancini, A. D., & Bonanno, G. A. (2009). Predictors and parameters of resilience to loss: Toward an individual differences model. *Journal of Personality*, (6), 1805–1832. doi: 10.1111/j.1467-6494.2009.00601.x.

McEwen, B. S. (2012). Brain on stress: How the social environment gets under the skin. *Proceedings of the National Academy of Sciences*, 17180–17185. doi: 10.1073/pnas.1121254109.

McEwen, B. S., Eiland, S., Hunter, R. G., & Miller, M. M. (2011). Stress and anxiety: Structural plasticity and epigenetic regulation as a consequence of stress. *Neuropharmacology, 62*(1), 3–12. doi: 10.1016/j.neuropharm.2011.07.014.

McMahon, S. B. & Koltzenburg, M. (2004). *Wall & Melzack's Textbook of Pain*, 5th edition. Philadelphia, PA: Elsevier Health Sciences.

Miller, A. H., & Raison, C. L. (2016). The role of inflammation in depression: From evolutionary imperative to modern treatment target. *Nature Reviews Immunology, 16*, 22–34. doi: 10.1038/nri.2015.5.

Muller, R. T., Sicoli, L. A., & Lemieux, K. E. (2000). Relationship between attachment style and posttraumatic stress symptomatology among adults who report the experience of childhood abuse. *Journal of Traumatic Stress: Official Publication of The International Society for Traumatic Stress Studies, 13*(2), 321–332. doi: 10.1023/A:1007752719557.

Myers-Schulz, B. B., & Koenigs, M. M. (2012). Functional anatomy of ventromedial prefrontal cortex: Implications for mood and anxiety disorders. *Molecular Psychiatry, 17*(2), 132–141. doi: 10.1038/mp.2011.88.

Ong, A. D., Zautra, A. J., & Reid, M. C. (2010). Psychological resilience predicts decreases in pain catastrophizing through positive emotions. *Psychological Aging, 25*(3), 516–523. doi: 10.1037/a0019384.

Ossipov, M. H., Dussor, G. O., & Porreca, F. (2010). Central modulation of pain. *Journal of Clinical Investigation, 120*(11), 3779–3787. doi: 10.1172/JCI43766.

Parkes, C. M. (1998). Bereavement in adult life. *BMJ Learning, 316*(7134), 856–859. Retrieved from www.ncbi.nlm.nih.gov/pmc/articles/PMC1112778/

Passingham, R. E., Bengtsson, S. L., & Lau, H. C. (2010). Medial frontal cortex: From self-generated action to reflection on one's own performance. *Trends in Cognitive Science, 14*(1), 16–21. doi: 10.1016/j.tics.2009.11.001.

Pizzagalli, D. A., Holmes, A. J., Dillon, D. G., Goetz, E. L., Birk, J. L., Bogdan, R., . . . Fava, M. (2009). Reduced caudate and nucleus accumbens response to rewards in unmedicated individuals with major depressive disorder. *American Journal of Psychiatry, 166*(6), 702–710. doi: 10.1176/appi.ajp.2008.08081201.

Prescott, V., M., Sekendur, B., Bailey, B., & Hoshino, J. (2008). Art making as a component and facilitator of resiliency with homeless youth. *Art Therapy: Journal of the American Art Therapy Association, 25*(4), 156–163. doi: 10.1080/07421656.2008.10129549.

Reivich, K. J., Seligman, M. E. P., & McBride, S. (2011). Master resilience training in the U.S. Army. *American Psychologist, 66*, 25–34. doi: 10.1037/a0021897.

Rutten, B. P. F., Hammels, C., Geschwind, N., Menne-Lothmann, C., Pishva, E., Schruers, K., . . . Wichers, M. (2013). Resilience in mental health: Linking psychological and neurobiological perspectives. *Acta Psychiatrica Scandinavica, 128*(1), 3–20. doi: 10.1111/acps.12095.

Sapolsky, R. M. (2004). *Physiological correlates of bereavement and the impact of bereavement interventions*. New York, NY: W. H. Freeman & Co.

Schulkin, J. (2011). Social allostasis: Anticipatory regulation of the internal milieu. *Frontiers in Evolutionary Neuroscience, 2*(111), 1–15. doi: 10.3389/fnevo.2010.00111.

Segal, Z. V., Williams, J. M. G., & Teasdale, J. D. (2001). *Mindfulness-based cognitive therapy for depression: A new approach to preventing relapse*. New York, NY: The Guilford Press.

Seitz, R. J., Franz, M., & Azari, N. P. (2009). Value judgments and self-control of action: The role of the medial frontal cortex. *Brain Research Reviews, 60*(2), 368–378. doi: 10.1016/j.brainresrev.2009.02.003.

Taylor, S. E. (2006). Tend and befriend biobehavioral bases of affiliation under stress. *Current Directions in Psychological Science, 5*(6), 273–277. doi: 10.1111/j.1467–8721.2006.00451.

Tedeschi, R. G., & Calhoun, L. G. (1996). The posttraumatic growth inventory: Measuring the positive legacy of trauma. *Journal of Traumatic Stress, 9*(3), 455–471. doi: 10.1007/BF02103658.

Vasterling, J. J., & Brewin, C. R. (2005). *Neuropsychology of PTSD: Biological, cognitive, and clinical perspectives*. New York, NY: The Guilford Press.

Williams, T., Hill, E., Gomez, E., Milliken, T., Goff, J., & Gregory, N. (2013). The resiliency and attitudes skills profile: An assessment of factor structure. *Illuminare, 11*. Retrieved from https://scholarworks.iu.edu/journals/index.php/illuminare/article/view/3179.

Woo, C. W., Roy, M., Buhle, J. T., & Wager, T. D. (2015). Distinct brain systems mediate the effects of nociceptive input and self-regulation on pain. *PLos Biology*, *13*(1). doi: 10.1371/journal.pbio.1002036.

Wu, G., Feder, A., Cohen, H., Kim, J. J., Calderon, S., Charney, D. S., & Mathé, A. A. (2013). Understanding resilience. *Frontiers in Behavioral Neuroscience*, 7(10). doi: 10.3389/fnbeh.2013.00010.

Appendix 13.A

Beliefs

1. Sticking to my goals
2. Believing in myself
3. Reminding myself of my values
4. Drawing on religion and/or on spirituality
5. Discovering what is important in life
6. Finding benefit in what happened
7. Looking up to a role model
8. Fighting spirit, trying hard
9. Being optimistic
10. Believing in fate

Emotions and Feelings

1. Expressing emotions
2. Crying on the inside
3. Crying on the outside
4. Taking risks
5. Expressing gratitude and thankfulness to others
6. Feeling empathy/compassion for self
7. Avoiding anything to do with what happened
8. Laughing, have fun, joyfulness

Thinking and Cognitions

1. Seeing things from another person's perspective
2. Prioritizing and taking a step at a time
3. Thinking about/understanding what happened/getting information
4. Accepting what happened
5. Accepting responsibilities
6. Telling myself that it was not my fault
7. Increased awareness and mindfulness
8. Trusting past experiences
9. Experiencing and practicing mastery and control
10. Preparing myself for the worse and being careful

Social and Cultural

1. Practicing my cultural/community tradition
2. Practicing my families' traditions
3. Getting help from family
4. Getting help from others or my community
5. Caring, helping others or advocacy
6. Convincing others to change their opinion
7. Engaging in social activities
8. Getting professional help
9. Finding a new partner/friend/spouse
10. Having pets, animals

Taking Care of Self

1. General self-care
2. Meditation
3. Relaxation
4. Eating and sleeping
5. Keeping busy, working at work or at home
6. Coffee, nicotine, substances, medical prescriptions
7. Exercising
8. Moving away-another neighborhood, city, country
9. Task oriented
10. Working or looking for work

Personal Interests

1. Creativity
2. Beauty
3. Discovering new things or experiences
4. Imagination
5. Curiosity
6. Decorating
7. Gardening
8. Generating many solutions or finding one solution
9. Creating art/visiting art shows/listening/creating music (circle)
10. Cooking

Resiliency resources checklist

Hass-Cohen & Clyde Findlay, 2015

14 Exploring the Impact of Art Therapy with Stroke Recovery

Morgan Gaydos and Melanie Biscuiti

Stroke continues to be a leading cause of medical illness within the United States and affects many individuals on multiple levels. The process of recovery differs from person to person, but typically requires medical rehabilitation and ongoing therapy to regain what the body has lost. This chapter will provide a thorough overview of the physical and emotional effects of a stroke and how art therapy can be utilized as a complementary treatment method within the medical model of recovery.

Understanding the Warning Signs and Pathology of a Stroke

Approximately 800,000 Americans experience a stroke each year, with an estimated 6.5 million individuals affected by and living with the diagnosis (Zweifler, 2017). Stroke has remained the fifth leading cause of death in the country and is one of the main causes of physical disability (American Stroke Association, 2018a). The occurrence of a stroke does not discriminate by age, and can affect anyone, from infants to the elderly.

A stroke occurs when the body's blood flow to the brain becomes compromised, either through a blood clot or vessel bleed, and results in a debilitation of the body. Risk factors, such as high blood pressure, obesity, and hypertension, have been known to contribute to the prevalence of a stroke diagnosis, as well as risk markers such as ethnicity, race, and age (Boehme, Esenwa, & Elkind, 2017). To better understand what happens to the body and brain during a stroke, it is important to examine the three types of stroke that occur: ischemic, hemorrhagic, and transient ischemic attack (TIA), all of which differ from a pathological standpoint (American Stroke Association, 2018b).

Types of Stroke

Ischemic strokes are the most common, specifically in older adults, and are primarily caused by an obstruction, or blood clot, within a blood vessel (Yamada, Ozark, & Ovbiagele, 2016). An ischemic stroke begins when the obstruction prevents the body's blood flow from reaching the brain, resulting in the brain's breakdown of functioning and the body's physical response. Fatty deposits known as cerebral thrombosis and cerebral embolism are the main reason for blood vessel blockage (American Stroke Association, 2018b). Research has shown that approximately 80 percent of strokes are ischemic, with hypertension as the most identified risk factor (Boehme et al., 2017).

Hemorrhagic strokes, although not as common, are more severe than ischemic strokes and are characterized by a bleeding event, such as a blood vessel rupture, within the brain (Flügel et al., 2016). Hemorrhagic strokes occur in approximately 13 percent of stroke cases and result in a mass bleeding that compresses the affected tissue area of the brain (American Stroke Association, 2018b). Hemorrhagic strokes contain four subcategories: intracerebral hemorrhage, subarachnoid hemorrhage, arteriovenous malformations, and cerebral amyloid angiopathy. Despite a difference in hemorrhagic epidemiologies, hypertension remains a main risk factor for this type of stroke, in addition to age (Flügel et al., 2016).

Lastly, a transient ischemic attack (TIA), also known as a 'mini stroke,' occurs when there is a temporary blockage of blood to the brain (American Stroke Association, 2018b). TIAs are crucial to identify because they are considered a major warning sign of an impending stroke; however, the symptoms often recede by the time the patient seeks medical attention, which can make it difficult for practitioners to identify the cause (Yamada et al., 2016).

Symptoms of a Stroke

Whether ischemic, hemorrhage, or TIA, it is important to gain awareness into the visible signs of a stroke. Warning signs can present quickly, and if not properly identified can delay or even complicate medical interventions, which can lead to a patient's ineligibility for acute treatment procedures (Mellon, Doyle, Rohde, Williams, & Hickey, 2015). As both a preventative measure and a community awareness action, health organizations worldwide have implemented the FAST campaign, an acronym for recognizing the most common initial signs of a stroke: F (Face, changes in one's facial appearance such as drooping), A (Arm, weakening or paralysis of an arm), S (Speech, difficulty speaking or a slower speech pattern), and T (Time, seek medical attention immediately) (American Stroke Association, 2018c). Despite the awareness that FAST can help better ensure timely treatment interventions and reduce the severity of residual symptoms stemming from a stroke, individuals can still experience a loss of control within their neurological, cognitive, and physical capabilities after onset.

Given that the onset of a stroke compromises neurological functioning, other symptoms can include loss of function in the legs, sudden confusion or increased difficulty in understanding, blurry vision, change in gait and/or dizziness, and headaches (Mao et al., 2016). Early assessment of risk factors, increasingly effective screening tools, and community education resources have been implemented by practicing physicians to aid individuals in recognizing all signs of a stroke. However, the nature and severity of stroke symptoms differ from person to person; post-stroke symptoms also differ on an individual basis, and changes in neurological, cognitive, and physical functioning can range from mild to severe.

Post-Stroke Symptoms

Due to the trauma that the brain experiences during a stroke, many individuals experience post-stroke neurological deficits that can include a loss of functioning in a limb, difficulty walking, decreased fine motor skills, and impaired speech (Clark, Bennett, Ward, & Jones, 2016). Cognitive deficits, such as increased confusion and a delayed thought process, are also considered to be a residual symptom; however, depending on the age of the individual, cognitive deficits can be difficult to distinguish from the general aging process (de Graaf et al., 2018). Changes in quality of life, day-to-day functioning, and degree of independence have been found to contribute to psychological distress such as depression, anxiety, social isolation, loneliness, and stress (Clark et al., 2016).

The degree of post-stroke treatment, ranging from surgery, medical procedures, pharmaceutical interventions, rehabilitation, and complementary therapies, can assist individuals during their recovery. However, with the presence and overlap of neurological, cognitive, and psychological post-stroke symptoms, individuals can perceive their stroke recovery as an uphill battle. Specifically, many individuals can experience a lack of continuity in treatment with the difficulty in adjusting to life with limitations and/or residual symptoms while at home, whether recently discharged from medical care or years after the stroke diagnosis (Clark et al., 2016). The incorporation of complementary therapies, such as art therapy, can help enhance the recovery process by helping to alleviate neurological, cognitive, physical, and psychological symptoms that remain residual through the overall art-making process.

The Benefits of Art Therapy with Individuals Who Experienced a Stroke

Nonpharmaceutical interventions have continued to remain on the forefront of research trends within the field of medicine, with an emphasis on improving symptom management and quality of life. As seen in individuals who suffer a stroke, lingering neurological, cognitive, and physical deficits can make the recovery process increasingly difficult. In addition, treatment interventions such as medication and physical therapy, although beneficial in rehabilitation, do not address the emotional response to a medical diagnosis. Art therapy has been clinically found to be an effective treatment for providing relief from physical symptomology, improving neurological/cognitive deficits, and instilling emotional support for psychological distress (Elkis-Abuhoff & Gaydos, 2018; Mahendran et al., 2017).

Enhancing Neurological and Cognitive Deficits

As art therapy continues to make its presence known in the field of medicine, clinicians are increasing their understanding on the benefits of art therapy through a neuroscience lens. Art-making has always been innately viewed as having a direct and positive effect on the brain; however, recent collaborative efforts in the field of neuroscience have strengthened this concept. Clinical evidence has emerged that supports the impact of art therapy to stimulate, and activate, areas of the brain that have become compromised with a neurological diagnosis (Elkis-Abuhoff & Gaydos, 2018; Hass-Cohen & Clyde Findlay, 2015; King, 2016). Brain stimulation during the process of art therapy begins with direct physical touch and allows for the mind–body connection to strengthen within an individual.

Our bodies have countless nerve endings and pressure points for stimulation, many of which are located within the palms of the hands and fingertips. During art therapy, stimulation points become triggered when physically manipulating an art material; this engagement sends messages to the brain for increased activity (Finger, 2001). Even if the individual has limited arm/hand movement or functioning, typical in severe strokes, adaptations can be made by choosing kinesthetic and sensory art materials for optimum brain stimulation such as clay forms or textured paper and/or fabric. In addition, engagement in art therapy materials has been found to improve brain plasticity; that is, the brain's ability to change/adapt during developmental growth or recover from a traumatic event (Hass-Cohen & Clyde Findlay, 2015; King, 2016). Specifically with stroke, neurological damage to the brain can create a chain reaction that results in cognitive, physical, and emotional complications—identifying a greater need to target brain stimulation and plasticity during treatment.

Understanding art therapy's ability to address neurological deficits leads clinicians to also explore art-making's effect on cognition with stroke individuals. From a cognitive standpoint, art therapy has been found to improve overall cognition and results in the ability of individuals to better process and express their thoughts and feelings (Kongkasuwan et al., 2016; Mahendran et al., 2017). The role of visual imagery in art therapy can improve cognition by allowing an individual to consider the 'whole picture,' gaining new perceptions into challenges and obstacles (Solomon, 2016). Visual imagery can be utilized as a nonverbal outlet for exploration and expression, allowing an individual with cognitive deficits to retrieve emotional material without fully relying on verbal communication (Czamanski-Cohen & Weihs, 2016).

Creating a tangible piece of art can evoke reminiscing, sensory reliving, and increased emotional processing (Solomon, 2016), an area of cognition that can easily be hindered by the overwhelming effect of a stroke. Individuals engaged in art therapy can use their creation to better externalize emotional and cognitive material, allowing them to participate in a therapeutic, reflective process (Czamanski-Cohen & Weihs, 2016). The creation of a piece of art can also evoke a sense of accomplishment and mastery, which can lead to a shift in thought processing and overall perception for improved cognition. Improved cognition, specifically in stroke, can help individuals work toward establishing a sense of control over their diagnosis by changing their perception and ability to tap into emotional responses.

Improving Physical and Emotional Symptomology

Physical debilitation, considered the most noticeable effect of a stroke, can make it increasingly difficult for individuals to manipulate and engage in the world around them (American Stroke Association, 2018a). When faced with physical disability post-stroke, art therapy offers adaptive materials and techniques that can accommodate loss of functioning within a limb. During the art therapy process, individuals are provided the opportunity to work past limitations with fine motor skills or limited range of movement and can use their level of physical functioning to create a piece of art (Eum & Yim, 2015). In addition, research has also reported that during ongoing art therapy sessions, individuals have been able to increase the use of their stroke-affected limb when engaging with the art materials (Reynolds, 2012). By adapting and embracing physical limitations, post-stroke individuals can work toward regaining a sense on control over their body and reestablishing their sense of identity within their diagnosis. This effect can also be attributed to the art's effect on the neurological and cognitive functioning of the brain; as brain stimulation improves, individuals may experience a relief in physical symptomology when engaging in the art-making process, specifically with that of sensory materials (Elkis-Abuhoff & Gaydos, 2018).

Art therapy sensory and/or kinesthetic materials provide a great sense of mastery for those limited in physical functioning, while simultaneously allowing for the creative process to freely emerge. Sensory art materials, specifically applied to traumatic medical conditions, require intimate physical manipulation that allows individuals to create a symbolic representation of their thoughts and feelings relating to their diagnosis and/or recovery (Huss & Sarid, 2013). Materials such as clay forms or thickened paint with adaptive brushes can provide sensory stimulation without relying on fine motor movements, providing an increased sense of comfort and relaxation to the body (Elkis-Abuhoff & Gaydos, 2018; Eum & Yim, 2015). In addition, sensory and kinesthetic materials may be more inviting to individuals who experience physical limitations post stroke, as the worry of how to hold an art material or how to draw in detail is eliminated. This phenomenon can result in a greater focus on a stroke individual's recovery, including that of emotional wellness.

When an individual experiences negative physical change, the loss of functioning, control, and independence can lead to emotional distress within his or her life. Research has shown that the application of art therapy has had a positive effect on depression, anxiety, and fear for those recovering from a stroke (Eum & Yim, 2015; Kongkasuwan et al., 2016; Reynolds, 2012). Kongkasuwan et al. (2016) found that stroke individuals engaged in art therapy reported an increase in their ability to cope with emotional psychological responses, which helped to improve their overall level of confidence and quality of life. As both a verbal and nonverbal outlet for self-expression, art therapy naturally allows for increased engagement and communication between the therapist and client, providing them with the opportunity to gain insight and understanding into their emotional state (Eum & Yim, 2015).

Whether practiced in or out of medical settings, the creative process of art therapy is life enhancing and emotionally healing for an individual recovering from a diagnosis (Huss & Sarid, 2013). Increased emotional expression, in conjunction with the satisfaction of creating a meaningful piece of artwork, can provide stroke individuals with increased control within their recovery, as they take the focus from their limitations to their capabilities and creativity. Improving one's emotional state through art therapy can also help individuals gain an increased ability to cope with residual symptoms and change their self-perception relating to a diagnosis.

The Application of Art Therapy: A Case Study

JL is a 38-year-old Caucasian female, separated from her husband. She is currently unemployed due to some complications with her disability, resulting from a stroke, and has been creating handmade fashion products with her one hand to help make ends meet. The stroke occurred in the right hemisphere of her brain and contributed to dystonia, a neuromuscular disorder, which left her with partial paralysis, muscles spasms, and involuntary movements on the left side of her body. JL is mobile; however, the partial functioning on her left side has caused her to overcompensate on her right side. JL has received occupational and physical therapy to help assist her in regaining some functioning, but she ultimately learned to adapt to her physical limitations.

JL reported that she always found herself gravitating toward being creative, and began to cross-stitch during her free time. JL used the wooden fabric rings to hold a piece of fabric canvas tight and straight, and could use the needle and thread with her right hand. JL then received her first sewing machine and began to explore a new type of art form which encompassed quilting, embroidery, and accessory making. JL spoke about how creating items for people, such as gifts, made her feel good. She also stated that her creations were product based; however, she innately recognized that there was some type of therapeutic value to her creativity.

JL entered into the art therapy session with excitement, as she had never engaged in this type of therapy before. The materials chosen were both familiar and accessible: 18″ × 24″ white drawing paper, a variety of scraps of colored fabric (solid and patterned), glue strip roller, cutting board, and a fabric blade. Having used these items, JL was able to manipulate these tools with one hand. These materials allowed for a smooth application with minimal physical manipulation required. When JL saw the materials, she stated that although she has been working with fabric for over 10 years she had never used the medium to create a piece quite like this before.

JL was invited to reflect on her personal journey, and to focus on her creativity as a coping skill for medical experience. Using fabric scraps, JL was encouraged to create a collage of the fabric pieces to tell her story. JL was also prompted to physically sort through the fabric pieces to activate her engagement with the medium, and was offered the fabric cutter to create her own shapes. She primarily used her right hand, but would occasionally use her left hand with a closed fist to help guide the materials across the page or hold the fabric down on the paper as she used the fabric cutter. When doing so, it took JL a few moments to shift her left arm into a position where she could use it, but did so in a manner that reflected the adaptation to her left-side limitations.

As she thoughtfully sorted through the fabric pieces, JL chose colors that she connected with, and put them to the side. JL began to lay pieces of fabric across the page in a quiltlike composition, figuring out the layout before applying glue, and became silent during this time. She then proceeded to brush off the fabric from the page and started gluing the pieces in the middle the paper with her right hand (Figure 14.1). She worked very quietly and focused, with an occasional statement of *oh, I like this*. JL continued to work on her own, fully engaged with both the art medium and directive, until she decided that her artwork was complete.

JL began to process her piece of artwork, as she smiled and visually connected with picture (Figure 14.2). When asked about her experience using this approach with fabric, JL stated that the process was *freeing* with *no restrictions*, and that this type of application was like an applique technique in sewing—something that she previously viewed as being too challenging with her physical limitation. When asked about the composition of her artwork, JL explained that her depiction of a house represented her inner being. The house is positioned in the middle of the page, colorful and patterned, with a black box encompassing it. JL stated that the heavy black border represented a wall of obstacles, including all her ongoing medical issues, stress, and the chaos she feels is going on around her. JL added that the floating pieces around the house, also inside the box, represented the good things in her life, one being a positive change in her health and relationships.

Outside the black box are two floating pieces of fabric on either side, which she identified as her *creative space*. JL expressed that she knows there are more good things to come, but she must overcome her obstacles to get

Figure 14.1 JL Creating her Artwork with One Hand

Figure 14.2 JL's Artwork Reflecting her Post-stroke Journey

there, *my art and creativity will help me.* The left side piece of fabric has a butterfly on it, which she identified as freedom from her limitations and struggles relating to her stroke. Lastly, JL spoke about the long piece of fabric at the bottom, which represented the positive and productive road she wants to get back on when she gets back on her feet. JL could connect the personal meaning of her artwork to her post-stroke journey, and organically allowed the art process to tell her story and embrace her obstacles in a therapeutic manner. Furthermore, JL recognized the art-making process as a coping skill for both emotional expression and relief from stress, stating that *if I'm in pain, and can't go out, it's a perfect escape . . . I can keep my mind focused, and some anxieties or tension will be alleviated.*

Conclusion

Through the understanding of stroke onset, pathology, and residual symptoms, there is a clear need for complementary therapies, such as art therapy, to address and support complex symptom management. The application of art therapy, through carefully chosen materials and directives, can aid stroke individuals in finding relief from physical limitations and improving their emotional well-being by focusing on their capabilities through creative engagement.

References

American Stroke Association. (2018a). *About stroke.* Retrieved from www.stroke association.org/ STROKEORG/AboutStroke/About-Stroke_UCM_308529_SubHomePage.jsp.

American Stroke Association. (2018b). *Types of stroke.* Retrieved from www.strokeassociation.org/STROKEORG/AboutStroke/TypesofStroke/Types-of-Stroke_UCM_308531_SubHomePage.jsp.

American Stroke Association. (2018c). *Warning signs.* Retrieved from www.strokeassociation.org/STROKEORG/WarningSigns/Stroke-Warning-Signs-and-Symptoms_UCM_308528_SubHomePage.jsp.

Boehme, A. K., Esenwa, C., & Elkind, M. S. (2017). Stroke risk factors, genetics, and prevention. *Circulation Research, 120*(3), 472–495. doi: 10.1161/CIRCRESAHA.116.308398.

Clark, E., Bennett, K., Ward, N., & Jones, F. (2016). One size does not fit all—Stroke survivor's views on group self-management interventions. *Disability and Rehabilitation, 40*(5), 569–576. doi: 10.1080/09638288.2016.1268653.

Czamanski-Cohen, J., & Weihs, K. L. (2016). The bodymind model: A platform for studying the mechanisms of change induced by art therapy. *The Arts in Psychotherapy, 51*, 63–71. doi: 10.1016/j.aip.2016.08.006.

de Graaf, J. A., van Mierlo, M. L., Post, M. W., Achterberg, W. P., Kappelle, L. J., & Visser-Meily, J. M. (2018). Long-term restrictions in participation in stroke survivors under and over 70 years of age. *Disability and Rehabilitation, 40*(6), 637–645. doi: 10.1080/09638288.2016.1271466.

Elkis-Abuhoff, D., & Gaydos, M. (2018). Medical art therapy research moves forward: A review of clay manipulation with Parkinson's disease. *Art Therapy: Journal of the American Art Therapy Association, 35*(2). In press. doi: 10.1080/07421656.2018.1483162.

Eum, Y., & Yim, J. (2015). Literature and art therapy in post-stroke psychological Disorders. *The Tohoku Journal of Experimental Medicine, 235*(1), 17–23. doi: 10.1620/tjem.235.17.

Finger, S. (2001). *Origins of neuroscience: A history of explorations into brain function*. New York, NY: Oxford University Press.

Flügel, A. K., Steiner, T., Schill, J., Jahangir, N., Chughtai, M., Qureshi, M. H., & Qureshi, A. I. (2016). Hemorrhagic strokes. In R. P. Lisak, D. D. Truong, W. M. Carroll, & R. Bhidayasiri (Eds.), *International neurology* (2nd ed., pp. 28–36). Hoboken, NJ: John Wiley & Sons.

Hass-Cohen, N., & Clyde Findlay, J. (2015). *Art therapy and the neuroscience of relationships, creativity, and resiliency: Skills and practices*. New York, NY: W.W. Norton & Company.

Huss, E., & Sarid, O. (2013). Using imagery to address physical and psychological trauma. In C. A. Malchiodi (Ed.), *Art therapy and healthcare* (pp. 136–145). New York, NY: The Gilford Press.

King, J. L. (Ed.). (2016). *Art therapy, trauma, and neuroscience: Theoretical and practical perspectives*. New York, NY: Routledge.

Kongkasuwan, R., Voraakhom, K., Pisolayabutra, P., Maneechai, P., Boonin, J., & Kuptniratsaikul, V. (2016). Creative art therapy to enhance rehabilitation for stroke patients: A randomized controlled trial. *Clinical Rehabilitation, 30*(10), 1016–1023. doi: 10.1177/0269215515607072.

Mahendran, R., Rawtaer, I., Fam, J., Wong, J., Kumar, A. P., Gandhi, M., . . . Kua, E. H. (2017). Art therapy and music reminiscence activity in the prevention of cognitive decline: Study protocol for a randomized controlled trial. *Trials, 18*(1), 324. doi: 10.1186/s13063-017-2080-7.

Mao, H., Lin, P., Mo, J., Li, Y., Chen, X., Rainer, T. H., & Jiang, H. (2016). Development of a new stroke scale in an emergency setting. *BMC Neurology, 16*(1), 168–177. doi: 10.1186/s12883–016–0695-z.

Mellon, L., Doyle, F., Rohde, D., Williams, D., & Hickey, A. (2015). Stroke warning campaigns: Delivering better patient outcomes? A systematic review. *Patient Related Outcome Measures, 6*, 61–73. doi: 10.2147/PROM.SS4087.

Reynolds, F. (2012). Art therapy after stroke: Evidence and a need for further research. *The Arts in Psychotherapy, 39*(4), 239–244. doi: 10.1016/j.aip.2012.03.006.

Solomon, G. (2016). Evidence for the use of imagery in time-limited art psychotherapy, emotional chance and cognitive restructuring. In R. Hughs (Ed.), *Time-limited art psychotherapy: Developments in theory and practice* (pp. 153–179). New York, NY: Routledge.

Yamada, L., Ozark, S., & Ovbiagele, B. (2016). Ischemic stroke and transient events, TIA. In R. P. Lisak, D. D. Truong, W. M. Carroll, & R. Bhidayasiri (Eds.), *International neurology* (2nd ed., pp. 3–4). Hoboken, NJ: John Wiley & Sons.

Zweifler, R. M. (2017). Initial assessment and triage of the stroke patient. *Progress in Cardiovascular Diseases, 59*(6), 527–533.

15 Art Therapy in the Detoxification Phase of Treatment of Substance Use Disorders

Holly Feen-Calligan and Wendy Case

Accounts of art therapy in the treatment of substance use disorders appeared in publication as early as the 1950s (Moore, 1983). The therapeutic qualities and benefits of art therapy in treating substance use disorders (e.g., helping recovering persons access and express feelings; developing greater awareness of factors contributing to addiction; and facilitating emotional, physiological, and spiritual recovery) have been well documented over the last 60+ years; the intrinsic value of art therapy as a treatment modality has greatly expanded with what is now known about the process of addiction in the brain. A more recent summary of this literature suggests a primary role for art therapy in addiction treatment within the framework of the expressive therapies continuum (Hinz, 2009b).

The focus of our chapter further advances a model of addiction treatment using the expressive therapies continuum, with an emphasis on the role of trauma in the diagnosis and treatment substance use disorders. Recent developments in the neuroscience of trauma, such as the polyvagal theory (Porges, 2011) and the work of trauma expert Dr. Bessel van der Kolk (2015), offer supporting evidence regarding the efficacy of art therapy in creating a stable and viable framework in the treatment of SUD. Our chapter is drawn from scholarly literature of contemporary detoxification protocols relative to art therapy, input from art therapists working in the field, and features the experiences of Wendy Case, a psychotherapist, art therapist, and addiction specialist.

Substance Use Disorders and Modern Detox Protocol

Substance use disorders (SUD) are newly defined by the *Diagnostic and Statistical Manual of Mental Disorders* (5th ed.; DSM-5), by level of severity and determined by the number of diagnostic criteria met by an individual (American Psychiatric Association, 2013).

SUD occur when the recurrent use of alcohol and/or drugs causes clinically and functionally significant impairment, such as health problems, disability, and failure to meet major responsibilities at work, school, or home. According to the DSM-5, a diagnosis of SUD is based on evidence of impaired control, social impairment, risky use, and pharmacological criteria (American Psychiatric Association, 2013).

Treatment for SUD begins with detoxification, or the process of removing toxins from the body, readjusting normal functions in the absence of the drug (Miller, Forcehimes, & Zweben, 2011), and establishing a continuum of care (Adedoyin, Burns, Jackson, & Franklin, 2014). Initiating a kinesthetic behavioral therapy while clients are in the early stages of inpatient detox can be challenging, as they can often be stressed by the new environment and present with physical pain, fluctuating body temperatures, anxiety, and other somatic and psychiatric issues related to withdrawal. Clients may also endure a radical shift in pharmacology, as the medications made available to stabilize them are largely non-narcotic, and don't bring the relief of their preferred substance. This can cause sleep disturbance, mood swings, fatigue, poor focus, and feelings of hopelessness. These issues are often compounded by guilt, shame, and anxiety related to the events preceding the client's choice to enter treatment.

To understand the nature of 'detox' treatment in the modern era, advanced pharmacological stabilization has replaced the traditional, longer-term 'detox' level of care. Given the strictures of healthcare coverage and the trend toward outpatient treatment for SUD, the symptoms previously described are likely to be ongoing throughout a client's inpatient treatment stay and, possibly after discharge. Brighton Center for Recovery's Chief Medical Officer Dr. David Yanga, stresses that, due to the ongoing changes related to provider coverage, the conventional definition of detox has become somewhat obsolete:

> Detox is medical slang for the treatment of severe early withdrawal symptoms, but the physiological withdrawal takes weeks. An adequate stay in terms of stabilization of symptoms would be north of 14 days, but the majority of these days are not afforded in the modern healthcare system.
>
> (D. Yanga, personal communication, January 21, 2017)

Detox basically means transitioning from the highest level of withdrawal management preceding a move into active programming. Historically, this used to take a week or more; acute withdrawals are now usually stabilized within 1 to 3 days, which means clients are continuing to detox throughout a typical 5- to 30-day inpatient treatment stay. Thus, detox is often integrated into formal treatment programming.

Despite the short-term treatment strategies prevalent today, reaching people at vulnerable states, such as during early detoxification, presents an opportunity to cultivate motivation for recovery and willingness for treatment (Vickers, 2004). Motivation is believed to be critical for recovery (Miller et al., 2011), as evidenced by the stages of change model (Miller & Rollnick, 2002), which is fast becoming a standard of assessment and outcome measurement in SUD treatment. Motivation can be enhanced when psychosocial interventions (such as group therapy, 12-step meetings, and expressive modalities like art therapy) are offered concurrently with medically supervised withdrawal and treatment programming (Aletraris, Paino, Edmond, Roman, & Bride, 2014).

Substance Use Disorders and Addiction

All known addictive drugs impact reward centers in the brain, creating unnatural surges of dopamine that distort cues for pleasure and affect associative learning and memory function (Volkow, Koob, & McLellan, 2016). Addiction is a biopsychosocial phenomenon that is believed to follow a typical disease model, as evidenced by its genetic heritability and neurobiological factors (American Society of Addiction Medicine, 2011). Conceptualized as a disease for many years (e.g., Jellinek, 1960), addiction is known to be a "primary, chronic disease of brain reward, motivation, memory and related circuitry" (American Society of Addiction Medicine, 2011, para. 1).

McCauley (2009) explains addiction as a disease of the brain, resulting in a failure to correctly assess decisions or make choices; the defect lies in the area responsible for guiding behavior—the midbrain. The midbrain is the organ responsible for survival, informing the individual to eat, drink, defend against harm, etc. Such survival can be experienced as a "gut feeling." To ensure that we do the routine things needed for survival, the brain makes these things pleasurable. However, in active addiction a disruption occurs in the brain's ability to perceive pleasure accurately (Robinson & Berridge, 2003).

All humans have hedonic (pleasure) systems that can put us at risk for addiction, but the interface of genetic predisposition, organic stressors, and environmental challenges can make some individuals more vulnerable to developing SUD than others. Multiple factors contribute to the onset of addiction, including genetics, reward systems, developmental experiences, memory, stress, and choice (McCauley, 2009).

The earliest part of a pleasurable experience is the release of dopamine in the brain. Dopamine functions on the reward center of the brain, informing it when the reward is satisfying, better, or less than expected. The dopamine hypothesis theorizes that the addict is conditioned into thinking the drug is better than expected, associating the drug with an anticipated outcome (such as stress relief); hence, the substance becomes an indicator of physical and emotional survival. When an addict's brain is confronted with stress, the substance becomes the primary means to tolerate it. Once the brain has reinforced that something is good for survival, it locks this in memory with glutamate. This cue, locked in memory, can reemerge, making the person susceptible to craving when separated from the drug of choice or exposed to the internalized cue. This can occur even after years of continuous abstinence (McCauley, 2009).

The Role of Trauma

It is important to consider that physicians and mental health professionals also treat SUD clients for trauma (Morrison, Berenz, & Coffey, 2014). As evidenced in twin studies, addiction has a strong genetic component (Bierut et al., 1998), which means that those seeking SUD treatment are likely to have grown up with active addiction in the home or with a primary caregiver who was impacted by substance use in his or her family of origin.

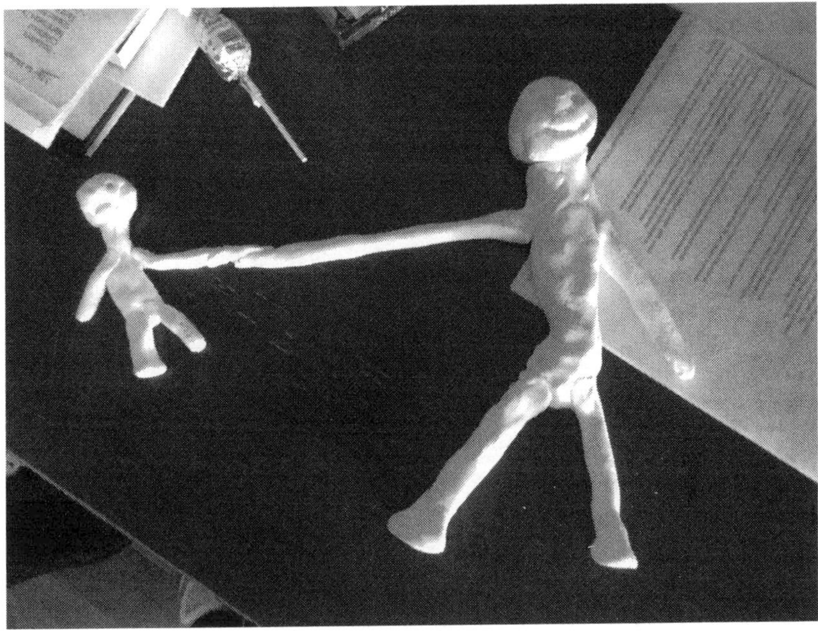

Figure 15.1 Spontaneous Clay Figures Created by an Alcohol-dependent Female with a History of Long-term Child Sexual Abuse (CSA) by an Older Brother

Even if a client did not come from a genetic legacy of SUD, the lifestyles involved in procuring and sustaining one's drug of choice can be trauma inducing. Myriad consequences can also be overwhelming to individuals' physical and emotional well-being, their ability to care for basic needs, provide for their families, or exercise domain over their choices. Developmental trauma; physical, sexual, and emotional abuse (Figure 15.1); social functioning; and attachment issues also play a pivotal role in screening for SUD, as clients often adopt substance use as a means of coping with overwhelming anxiety and trauma-induced psychopathology.

Though trauma is largely concomitant with addiction; clients entering treatment for SUD are not always adequately screened for post-traumatic stress disorder (PTSD) (Najavits, Sullivan, Schmitz, Weiss, & Lee, 2004), even though those with SUD are three times more likely to have a PTSD co-occurring diagnosis (Gielen, Havermans, Tekelenburg, & Jansen, 2012). SUD can also co-occur with other psychiatric disorders (Mauro, Furr-Holden, Strain, Crum, & Motjabai, 2016), including depression and anxiety (Simmons & Suarez, 2016). People with SUD may also have life-threatening medical illnesses such as cirrhosis, pancreatitis, hypertension, or seizures (Shu, Lin, & Chang, 2015). Addressing the array of problems involved in SUD is critical for positive treatment outcomes (Figure 15.2).

Figure 15.2 Self-Portrait of Female IV Heroin User

Art Therapy as a Primary Modality in the Treatment of Substance Use Disorders

Art therapy facilitates the goals of detoxification through helping people process the stress of withdrawal and stimulating motivation for treatment (Feen-Calligan, 2007). This is accomplished through establishing an environment that is safe and conducive to recovery, where people are introduced to the purpose and goals of art therapy, the protocol of the groups is explained, and the artworks and participants are treated with respect. Such a practice promotes an environment of 'gaman,' a Japanese concept that translates to 'enduring with dignity' (Case, 2016).

With the high-level co-occurrence of trauma with SUD, studies have found that SUD and PTSD have similar psychosocial and neurochemical features (Matto, 2005). Trauma is stored in the brain as imagery (Pifalo, 2007); art therapy, therefore, offers an image-based means to explore difficult or emergent material (e.g., Figure 15.2) in a way that accurately reflects the personal narrative of the individual's experience (Matto, Corcoran, & Fassler, 2003). Art therapy also allows clients to tell their own stories in their own way, helping them to shape goals and ambitions that are unique to them (Prescott, Sekendur, Bailey, & Hoshino, 2008).

The expressive therapies continuum (ETC) offers a particularly detailed platform for approaching SUD and co-occurring disorders from an art therapy standpoint. A procedural theory rooted in neuroscience, ETC integrates bilateral stimulation of the brain with a developmental hierarchy of global functioning designed to optimize kinesthetic and sensory, perceptual and affective, and ultimately cognitive and symbolic understanding of the client's internal and external experience. This allows clients to gain perspective on the issues that inform their emotional world and well as their life, relationships, and choices. Emphasis on the 'emergent function' occurs when the client can understand or perceive an important aspect of his or her experience, which advances the individual into a more sophisticated means of processing (Hinz, 2009a). The advantage of using art therapy in this way is that it can meet the individual at his or her place of need. For example, alexithymia, or the inability to access words to describe emotional experiences, can be a byproduct of trauma and SUD (Gantt & Tinnin, 2009). Kinesthetic processing, such as the pounding of clay, can release feelings of anger that may otherwise be inaccessible for reasons of fear, lack of trust, codependency, or a threat to safety (Hinz, 2009a). Addiction psychiatrist Dr. Visala Dandamudi emphasizes the importance of somatic processing of trauma. She states that art therapy clients often "don't even know how much they've processed" when they manifest their issues in an art product:

> A patient may not always be able to put feelings into words, but that doesn't mean they don't feel them. Patients have no control over the physical symptoms of PTSD. It's invaluable for them to process their somatic symptoms in order to understand what's causing them so they can unlearn that fear-based response.
>
> (V. Dandamudi, personal communication, January 21, 2017)

When clients are able to access their genuine feelings in a nonthreatening environment, the most vital work of recovery can begin.

Somatic Experiencing and New Realms in Trauma Treatment

Brighton Center for Recovery began offering art therapy in 2014, when it became clear that the integration of art therapy with the treatment of trauma offered unique opportunities to provide a more global approach to addressing clients' goals. By integrating concepts and processes of the ETC (Hinz, 2009a), with the pioneering neuroscience of the polyvagal theory (Porges, 2011), interventions designed to help clients stabilize in treatment allowed them more focused opportunities to learn and adapt. The polyvagal theory presents an elegant explanation of the body's role in addressing traumatic stress. The somatic and psychiatric disturbances that occur when one uses a mind- and mood-altering substance over time can leave individuals feeling 'at war' with both their internal and external worlds. Addressing these disturbances is key to helping the person achieve stability and self-efficacy, thus returning to the 'home' of his or her body.

Porges (2011) coined the word 'neuroception' to describe the reciprocal relationship between the brain and the autonomic nervous system. Once believed to be a 'top down' processing model, with the brain informing the body and the body responding, Porges' research revealed that the Vagus nerve carries vital information to and from the viscera of the body, assisting the neural circuits to instinctively distinguish whether people and situations are safe, dangerous, or life-threatening in nature (Porges, 2011). A primary component of the autonomic nervous system, the Vagus nerve comprises several branches and functions, with two main branches dedicated to behavioral strategies. In simplistic terms, the older, branch of the Vagus functions in the subdiaphragmatic region (stomach, intestines) of the body and is the branch that tells the body to 'shut down' when under attack (Figure 15.3). To have a 'gut feeling' in the polyvagal sense invokes a very genuine, and ancient, representation of the body's wisdom regarding survival. When the brain and body perceive an environment or event as unmanageable or life-threatening, neuroception causes the individual to involuntarily freeze as a 'last ditch' survival strategy (Levine, 1997). In mammals, this is generally the final stage before death and serves two functions: it helps the individual 'numb' if death is immanent, and to conserve energy if an opportunity for escape becomes available (Levine, 1997). The ability to access, and recover from, this primordial numbing state enables the individual to reduce the pain and terror of the overwhelming trauma at hand. Physical and emotional numbing is a key feature in SUD and permits the progression of the disease despite the threat of grave consequences. The emptiness and hopelessness that frequently accompanies active addiction mimics the strategy of unconsciously preparing for death, as the individual has lost the ability to abstain from the destructive behaviors that threaten his or her life and well-being.

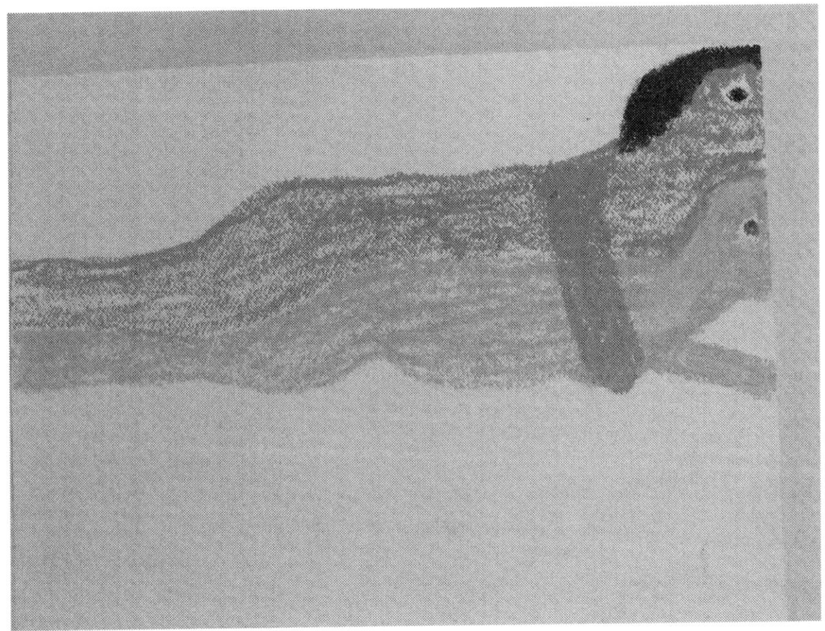

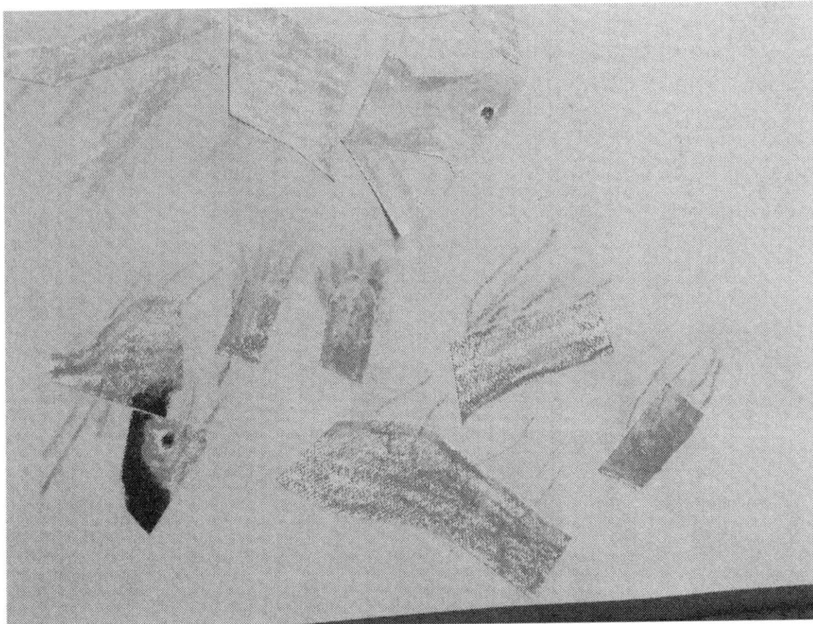

Figure 15.3 Violation of 'Relationship Abstraction' Experiential, Created by Alcohol-dependent Male in an Enmeshed Relationship with a Married Woman

The newer part of the Vagus is the 'mammalian' branch, which is associated with bonding and assessing for safety and attachment. This newer branch is highly developed in humans and exists in the supradiaphragmatic region of the body, regulating the heart and lungs. Porges (2011) called this the 'Vagal brake' for its ability to, when activated, disinhibit the instinct to freeze or numb, allowing alternative adaptive responses to challenging stimulus. It is the body's social engagement system and responds to sensory aspects of neuroception, including eye contact, facial expression, sound/prosody of voice, gesture, proximal relationships with others, and synchronous behavior and activity (Porges, 2011). Think of a mother's gaze, a dancer's internal rhythm with a partner, a herd of gazelle all bowing their heads at once to drink when a watering hole is deemed free of predators, or of making art with others in a group.

The work of van der Kolk (2015) has brought to light the brutal, long-term effects of trauma on those who lose the ability to have domain over their safety. van der Kolk argues that if clients do not possess an internal model for safety that permits a 'friendly' relationship with the body, they must rely on external means such as drugs and alcohol to provide regulation of autonomic social engagement systems. Stabilizing somatic symptoms and reducing sensory cues for threat must be a primary goal when attempting to influence and educate people who require new tools for adaptive functioning:

> Neuroscience shows that very few psychological problems are the result of deficits in understanding. Most originate in pressure from deeper regions of the brain that drive our perception and attention. When the alarm bell of the brain keeps signaling danger, no amount of insight will silence it.
>
> (van der Kolk, 2015, p. 64)

In short, traditional talk-therapy practices such as 'active listening,' which involve eye contact, verbal probes, and body language that put full focus on the client, could be more intimidating than helpful for people who are experiencing symptoms associated with SUD-related trauma or PTSD. Porges, van der Kolk, and other leaders in trauma research and treatment are now advocating for modalities that support autonomic regulation and integration with opportunities to safely explore adaptive social functioning (Figure 15.4).

Art therapy is an ideal modality in this regard as it presents a safe way for clients to identify with others when working on challenging emotions related to SUD, such as guilt, shame, and remorse (Rotgers, Morgenstern, & Walters, 2003). Group art therapy settings mimic the synchrony of primal mammalian bonding, as clients work in concert with each other in a setting that promotes nonthreatening proximal interactions and can allow for selective eye contact (Wadeson, 2010). The kinesthetic or sensory process of art-making provides a necessary physical outlet to reduce stress, emotional tension, depression, and anxiety (Haluzan, 2012; Hinz, 2009a; Lauer & van der Vennet, 2015). Treatment schemas can also be more flexible in art

Figure 15.4 Violation of 'String Painting' Experiential by Alcohol-dependent Male Presenting with Traumatic Brain Injury and Co-occurring Diagnoses of PTSD and Bipolar Disorder

therapy, allowing for movement, sound, gesture, and other somatic experiences that are unlikely to occur in a talk-therapy setting. Vance and Wahlin (as cited in Hass-Cohen & Carr, 2008), describe the integration of movement and music in her sessions as "opening a necessary door" (p. 159). The nonverbal aspects of art therapy assist clients in organizing their perceptions in a way that may reflect the sensory experience more accurately than traditional therapeutic modalities (Wadeson, 2010), and the ability of the clients to control and contain emotional content in an art product reduces the likelihood that they will lapse into a state of hyperarousal.

While clients typically struggle with emotional regulation and disturbed mood and affect during detox, those who engage in art therapy practices can be taught to use art as a safe platform for expressing psychic and emotional pain instead of acting on destructive or antisocial impulses (Hinz, 2009a). Clients will sometimes violate the directive of an experiential to enact a self-soothing intervention or to express volatile emotional or trauma-related experiences in a safe, self-directed way (see Figures 15.3 and 15.4). Clients are also surprisingly adept at spontaneously representing the organicity of polyvagal function in experientials that feature renderings of the human body (Figure 15.5). As an art therapist, it is important to recognize and appreciate the client's innate understanding of how stress is impacting his or her ability to engage in treatment. The client is the expert, our role is to design and make available interventions that can best respond to that individual's needs.

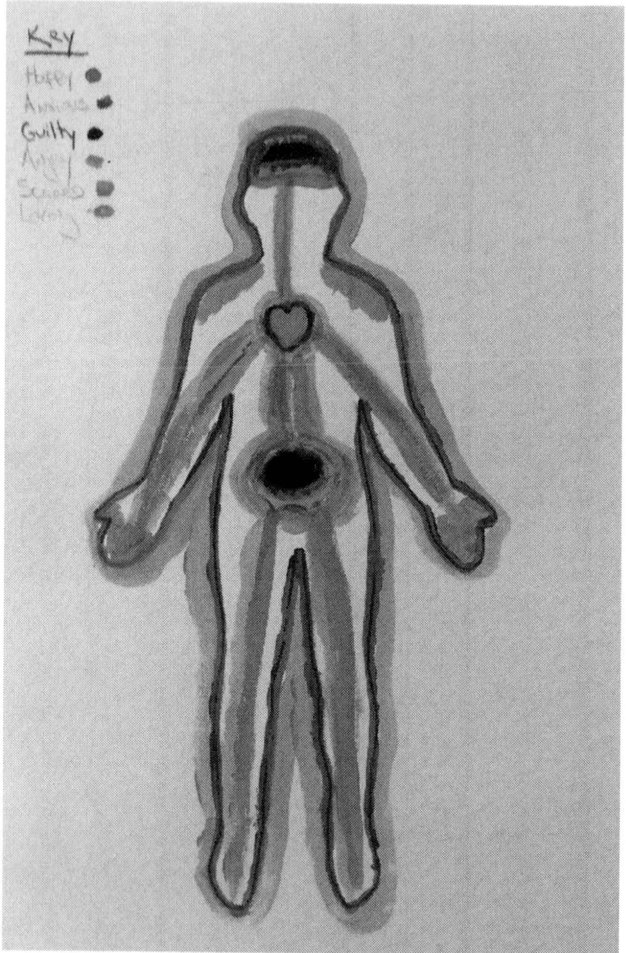

Figure 15.5 Client's rendering demonstrates an innate understanding of polyvagal function, despite no previous education on the relationship between the brain, heart, and gut in regulating autonomic response to stress

Conclusion

Valuing addiction treatment is about valuing people. It is about saving lives, limiting the need for emergency hospitalization, reducing the social impact of SUD, and restoring the individual's freedom to make life-affirming choices and set life-enhancing goals (DeRoche, 2016). Through the intersection of cognitive, kinesthetic, sensory-motor, and social interactions, art therapy counteracts the biochemistry of trauma, improves motivation, and contributes to resilience, hope, stabilization, and integration; this offers fellowship and connection with others.

References

Adedoyin, C., Burns, N., Jackson, H. M., & Franklin, S. (2014). Revisiting holistic interventions in substance abuse treatment. *Journal of Human Behavior in the Social Environment, 24*, 538–546. doi: 10.1080/10911359.2014.914718.

Aletraris, L., Paino, M., Edmond, M. B., Roman, P. M., & Bride, B. E. (2014). The use of art and music therapy in substance abuse treatment programs. *Journal of Addiction Nursing, 25*(4), 190–196. doi: 10.1097/JAN.0000000000000048.

American Psychiatric Association. (2013). *Diagnostic and statistical manual of mental disorders (DSM-5)* (5th ed.). Washington, DC: American Psychiatric Association.

American Society of Addiction Medicine. (2011). *Public statement: Definition of addiction. Short definition of addiction*. Retrieved from www.asam.org/quality-= practice/definition-of-addiction.

Bierut, L. J., Dinwiddie, S. H., Begleiter, H., Crowe, R. R., Hesselbrock, V., Nurnberger, J. I., . . . Reich, R. (1998). Familial transmission of substance dependence: Alcohol, marijuana, cocaine, and habitual smoking. A report from the collaborative study on the genetics of alcoholism. *Archives of General Psychiatry, 55*, 982–988. doi: 10.1001/archpsyc.55.11.982.

Case, W. (2016, October). *Art therapy as a primary modality in the treatment of trauma*. In Addiction Treatment: Moving the Field Forward. Conference sponsored by St. John Providence and Brighton Center for Recovery, Novi, MI.

DeRoche, C. (2016, October). *Solving addiction*. Keynote presented at the conference of Addiction Treatment: Moving the Field Forward. St. John Providence Brighton Center for Recovery, Novi, MI, USA.

Feen-Calligan, H. (2007). The use of art therapy in detoxification from chemical addiction. *Canadian Art Therapy Association Journal, 20*, 16–28. doi: 10.1080/08322473.2007.11432289.

Gantt, L., & Tinnin, L. (2009). Support for a neurobiological view of trauma with implications for art therapy. *The Arts in Psychotherapy, 36*, 148–153. doi: 10.1016/j.aip.2008.12.005.

Gielen, N., Havermans, R. C., Tekelenburg, M., & Jansen, A. (2012). Prevalence of posttraumatic stress disorder among patients with substance use disorder: It is higher than clinicians think. *European Journal of Psychotraumatology, 3*(0), 1–9. doi: 0.3402/ejpt.v3i0.17734.

Haluzan, M. (2012). Art therapy in the treatment of alcoholics. *Alcoholism, 48*(2), 99–105.

Hass-Cohen, N., & Carr, R. (2008). *Art therapy and clinical neuroscience*. Philadelphia, PA: Jessica Kingsley Publishers.

Hinz, L. (2009a). *Expressive therapies continuum: A framework for using art in therapy*. New York, NY: Routledge.

Hinz, L. (2009b). Order out of chaos: The expressive therapies continuum as a framework for art therapy interventions in substance abuse treatment. In S. Brooke (Ed.), *The use of creative therapies with chemical dependency issues* (pp. 51–68). Springfield, IL: Charles Thomas Publisher, LTD.

Jellinek, E. M. (1960). *The disease concept of alcoholism*. New Haven, CT: Hillhouse.

Lauer, M., & van der Vennet, R. (2015). Effect of art production on negative mood and anxiety for adults in treatment for substance abuse. *Art Therapy: Journal of the American Art Therapy Association, 32*(4), 177–183. doi: 10.1080/07421656.2015.1092731.

Levine, P. A., & Frederick, A. (1997). *Waking the tiger-healing trauma*. Berkeley, CA: North Atlantic Books.

Matto, H. (2005). A bio-behavioral model of addiction treatment: Applying dual representation theory to craving management and relapse prevention. *Substance Use & Misuse, 40*, 529–541. doi: 10.1081/1A-20030707.

Matto, H., Corcoran, J., & Fassler, A. (2003). Integrating solution focused and art therapies for substance abuse treatment: Guidelines for practice. *The Arts in Psychotherapy, 30*(5), 265–272.

Mauro, P. M., Furr-Holden, C. D., Strain, E. C., Crum, R. M., & Motjabai, R. (2016). Classifying substance use disorder treatment facilities with co-located mental health services: A latent class analysis approach. *Drug and Alcohol Dependence, 163*, 108–115. doi: 10.1016/j.drugalcdep.2016.04.001.

McCauley, K. (2009). *Pleasure unwoven: A personal journey about addiction*. DVD. Retrieved from www.instituteforaddictionstudy.com.

Miller, W. R., Forcehimes, A. A., & Zweben, A. (2011). *Treating addiction: A guide for professionals*. New York, NY: The Guilford Press.

Miller, W. R., & Rollnick, S. (2002). *Motivational interviewing: Preparing people for change* (2nd ed.). New York, NY: The Guilford Press.

Moore, R. W. (1983). Art therapy with substance abusers: A review of the literature. *The Arts in Psychotherapy, 10*(4), 251–260.

Morrison, J. A., Berenz, E. C., & Coffey, S. F. (2014). Exposure-based, trauma-focused treatment for comorbid PTSD-SUD. In P. Ouimette & J. Read (Eds.), *Trauma and substance abuse: Causes, consequences, and treatment of comorbid disorders* (2nd ed., pp. 253–279). Washington, DC: American Psychological Association.

Najavits, L. M., Sullivan, T. P., Schmitz, M., Weiss, R. D., & Lee, C. S. N. (2004). Treatment utilization by women with PTSD and substance dependence. *The American Journal on Addictions, 13*, 215–224. doi: 10.1080/10550490490459889.

Pifalo, T. (2007). Jogging the cogs: Trauma focused art therapy and cognitive behavioral therapy with sexually abused children. *Art Therapy: Journal of the American Art Therapy Association, 24*(4), 170–175. doi: 10.1080/07421656.2007.10129471.

Porges, S. W. (2011). *The polyvagal theory: Neurophysiological foundations of emotions attachment communication self-regulation*. New York, NY: W. W. Norton & Company.

Prescott, M. V., Sekendur, B., Bailey, B., & Hoshino, J. (2008). Art making as a component and facilitator of resiliency in homeless youth. *Art Therapy: Journal of the American Art Therapy Association, 25*(4), 156–163. doi: 0.1080/07421656.2008.10129549.

Robinson, T. E., & Berridge, K. C. (2003). Addiction. *Annual Review of Psychology, 54*, 25–53. doi: 10.1146/annurev.psych.54.101601.145237.

Rotgers, F., Morgenstern, J., & Walters, S. T. (2003). *Treating substance abuse: Theory and technique* (2nd ed.). New York, NY: The Guilford Press.

Shu, J. E., Lin, A., & Chang, G. (2015). Alcohol withdrawal treatment in the medically hospitalized patient: A pilot study assessing predictors for medical or psychiatric complications. *Psychosomatics, 56*(5), 5467–555. doi: 10.1016/j.psym.2014.12.002.

Simmons, S., & Suarez, L. (2016). Substance abuse and trauma. *Child & Adolescent Psychiatric Clinics of North America, 25*(4), 723–734. doi: 10.1016/j.chc.2016.05.006.

van der Kolk, B. (2015). *The body keeps the score: Brain, mind and body in the healing of trauma*. New York, NY: Penguin Books.

Vickers, L. (2004). One-off art therapy in in-patient detoxification. In B. Reading & M. Weegmann (Eds.), *Group psychotherapy and addiction* (pp. 117–132). London, UK: Whurr Publishers Ltd.

Volkow, N. D., Koob, G. F., & McLellan, A. T. (2016). Neurobiologic advances from the brain disease model of addiction. *New England Journal of Medicine, 374*(4), 363–371. doi: 10.1056/NEJMra1511480.

Wadeson, H. (2010). *Art psychotherapy* (2nd ed.). Hoboken, NJ: John Wiley & Sons.

16 Art Therapy Applications and Substance Abuse

Libby Schmanke

The human experience of compulsive drug-taking has been viewed in myriad ways over the course of history. The current biomedical understanding of addiction as a disease is supported by neuroscience research. Art therapists may work with people diagnosed with substance use disorders in a setting where the medical model predominates. This chapter will note a few of the issues encountered in such settings, while emphasizing the importance of a biopsychosocial treatment approach that aligns with the individual client. A foundational protocol for psychoeducational art therapy groups is provided; case vignettes exemplify individual art therapy within a substance abuse treatment (SAT) program.

The Disease Concept and SAT Settings

The American Society of Addiction Medicine (ASAM) is a leader in articulating research findings and providing guidelines for assessment and treatment. An excerpt from its definition states:

> Addiction is a primary, chronic disease of brain reward, motivation, memory and related circuitry. Dysfunction in these circuits leads to characteristic biological, psychological, social and spiritual manifestations . . . reflected in an individual pathologically pursuing reward and/or relief by substance use.
>
> (American Society of Addiction Medicine, 2017a, para. 1)

Addiction is clearly framed as a disease of the brain; yet the definition includes other biological as well as psychological, social, and even spiritual symptomology. Although brain dysfunction can be treated medically to a certain extent (i.e., with pharmacotherapy), a broader treatment approach is required to ensure recovery from addiction. In addition, people with substance use disorders (SUD) are a vastly heterogeneous group; effective treatment is tailored to the individual.

The ASAM has categorized treatment settings along a continuum of care in its client placement system, which is widely used in managed care settings in the United States. Persons seeking substance abuse treatment are screened according to the ASAM criteria, which assess characteristics such as need for medical detox and readiness to change. The placement assessment matches the client to the optimal level of service on the continuum. The most intensive level of care, Level IV, is usually located in a medical center or psychiatric hospital; most referrals have co-occurring disorders and/or biomedical needs. In addition to SAT, these settings provide 24-hour medical care and psychiatric services (American Society of Addiction Medicine, 2017b). Persons in these settings may have co-occurring mental diagnoses, such as schizophrenia, and have gone off their medication regimen or combined medications with illicit substances or alcohol to ill effect. Diseases frequently seen in conjunction with SUD that may require medical attention during treatment include hepatitis B, hepatitis C, and HIV/AIDS (Stevens & Smith, 2017).

Dominant Considerations in Medical Settings

Co-occurring Disorders

The abbreviation MICA (mental illness–chemical addiction) or the terms 'co-occurring disorders' or 'dual diagnosis' refer to the presence of one or more psychiatric diagnoses in addition to the SUD. The most commonly encountered codiagnoses include mood disorders, anxiety disorders, schizophrenia, and personality disorders (in particular, antisocial and narcissistic) (Stevens & Smith, 2017). People with dual diagnoses who present for treatment at hospital settings are usually in crisis; frequently they have gone off an established pharmacotherapy regimen and have substituted alcohol or illicit drug use. Such 'self-medicating' may seem to be an attractive alternative to people whose prescribed medications are not working effectively, have troublesome side effects, or are too expensive.

Identification of the best pharmacological options for stabilization and ongoing treatment is the primary purpose of crisis hospitalization, but accurate diagnosis and prescribing for co-occurring disorders can be complicated by illicit drug use. By assessing and comparing art products made over time, art therapists can assist in differential diagnosis and in charting the degree or direction of change as clients detoxify. In addition, building commitment to medication compliance and abstinence from other drugs is a primary goal; art therapists can support medication compliance by customizing generic directives such as pro–con collages, past–present–future images, and incident drawings (e.g., draw what happened when you went off your medication).

Opioid Addiction

Opioid addiction occurs with prescription pain killers as well as with illicit opioids such as heroin, and has reached epidemic status in the United States

(Stevens & Smith, 2017). Medication-assisted treatment (MAT) refers to the use of opioid agonists and partial agonists, such as methadone and buprenorphine, or antagonists, such as naltrexone, to reduce cravings or otherwise prevent relapse within an opioid addiction treatment protocol. These drugs are considered safe to use as part of a medically monitored, long-term maintenance plan.

Management of ongoing physical pain is an additional issue that must be addressed for some people with opioid use disorders. Off-label use of low-dose naltrexone is showing promise for treating chronic pain (Younger, Parkitny, & McLain, 2014). Nonpharmacological methods of pain management include hypnosis, mindfulness, biofeedback, and guided imagery. Creative therapies also show promise for pain management (Angheluta & Lee, 2011; Pavlek, 2008). When taught to the client, tools from these approaches provide a sense of empowerment, in addition to reducing the perception of pain.

Self-Help Groups in Aftercare

For people assessed at the higher ASAM placement levels, abstinence from alcohol and other nonprescribed drug use is essential for recovery as well as for successful management of any comorbid condition. Clients will be referred to professional services in the community upon discharge, but also should be encouraged to participate in a 12-step or alternative support group in the community. Self-help groups provide benefits such as promoting recovery and abstinence without the presence of authority figures; providing socialization and mutual encouragement; offering a range of meeting times, including evenings and weekends; and being free of charge.

Although occasionally someone in a self-help recovery meeting may be heard to disparage the practice of 'using drugs to treat drug abuse,' the founders of Alcoholics Anonymous (AA) and its literature recognize that underlying conditions such as depression pose challenges to recovery that can be alleviated through pharmacotherapy (Kurtz, 2008). Most participants in traditional self-help meetings like AA and Narcotics Anonymous (NA) do support peers who take medication for co-occurring disorders. Self-help groups designed specifically for persons with dual disorders include Dual Recovery Anonymous and Double Trouble in Recovery. Clients should be encouraged to shop around for the best fit in a self-help group.in order to feel comfortable and want to return.

Incorporation of Art Therapy into SAT Groups

A recent review of the literature concerning art therapy and substance abuse (Schmanke, 2017) found that social (group) and spiritual (including 12-step) applications predominated. Art therapy can be employed in a variety of ways in substance abuse settings, from pictographic worksheets incorporated into manualized protocols, to a studio approach that enriches treatment in a milieu setting. This flexibility is a boon to whatever model of addiction and SAT is dominant at a particular setting.

Art therapists working in substance abuse programming in Level IV settings will most likely be providing groups. A warm facilitator style and an emphasis on hope, motivation, and compliance are essential, especially with clients who have co-occurring disorders or who experience multiple treatment episodes due to relapse (Montrose & Daley, 1995). In settings with a rapidly changing participant roster, group therapists must work continually to build norms of engagement in the art-making process and support for each other's efforts. Enthusiasm and belief in the power of the art are essential attributes for the art therapist.

A group art therapy protocol that I designed to match one setting's open-entry curricular requirements is shown in the table (Table 16.1). Six topics were covered in 6 weeks, via twice-weekly, 3-hour group sessions. In each session, I first provided a lecturette and guided discussion; then clients worked individually on art responses; we concluded by coming back together for verbal processing of the art. I had the luxury of 6 hours to cover each topic, but I usually chose only one or two of the suggested directives for each week in order to allow for more in-depth art responses. Sometimes I rotated in other art tasks not shown on the chart, when it seemed indicated by group dynamics in a particular session. An art therapist who can become comfortable with extemporaneous decision-making will avoid a cookie-cutter approach that may not address client needs in the moment.

Examples of Individualized Art Therapy

Research to identify best practices in substance abuse treatment has indicated that therapy must address the whole person (Capuzzi & Stauffer, 2016). Therapists should maintain awareness that every person is different and has unique needs. Within a SAT program, personalized planning is most readily addressed in case management and in individual therapy. The following case vignettes demonstrate that effective individual art therapy aligns with the client.

Art Cuts to the Chase: The Case of Harold

Harold was a nurse who had become dependent on prescription pain relievers while recovering from a back injury. Although he and his personal physician were well aware of the dangers of prolonged use of opioids, the path to his addiction was insidious, as it is for most people. By the time his physician refused to continue to refill his prescription, Harold had already planned how to divert a supply from the small nursing home where he was employed. In fact, the reason for his entry into treatment was that his behavior was suspected at work; he had been given the choice of providing a clean UA or being reassigned to a lesser position without access to medications. Somewhat to his own surprise as well as to his employer's, Harold confessed, and requested to go on leave for treatment.

Table 16.1 A Flexible Protocol for Group Art Therapy in a Substance Abuse Psychoeducational Curriculum

Psychoeducational Topic	*Directive*	*Prompt for Processing*
Disease concept: Review the medical/disease/neuroscience basis of addiction as well as the bio-psycho-social-spiritual (BPSS) aspects. Discuss origins of addiction and various explanatory models (see Capuzzi & Stauffer, 2016; Stevens & Smith, 2017)	(A) Depict your addiction as a character or abstract image. (B) Make a postcard to send to your disease of addiction. (C) Make a symbolic "pie chart" for the bio, psycho, social, spiritual aspects of your addiction (see Schmanke, 2017).	(A) & (B) How did you view your addiction before learning the disease model? Now? How does it feel to know that addiction is not due to character weakness? (C) Which of the BPSS aspects are prominent in your situation?
The developmental path of addiction: A classic, client-accessible biopsychosocial chart of addiction progression known as the Jellinek curve can serve as a jumping-off point and is available at: www.hazeldenbettyford.org/articles/jellinek-curve **The developmental path of recovery:** See client-accessible Gorski (1997), and other work by this author, the stages of change (e.g., Connors, DiClemente, Velasquez, & Donovan, 2015)	(A) Make a road drawing that depicts the history of your addiction; consider the kind and condition of the road, detours, environment, signage (see Hanes, 1995). (B) Make a pro–con drawing for stopping to use, may also make a pro–con drawing for continuing to use, which can add insight (see Horay, 2006). (C) Make a past–present–future collage.	(A) How did you first step onto your path of addiction? When did you first realize you were not on a good road? Did you have options along the way? (B) What do you like about using your drug? More than anything else, what has kept you using it? Do the benefits of quitting outweigh losses? (C) What would you like to see happen in this treatment experience? In your future?
Denial and other ego defenses: • Explain the role of defenses in the development and maintenance of addiction, such as avoiding feelings of shame and guilt. • Focus on denial, acting out, rationalization, minimization, and compartmentalization. • Provide examples, then ask for personal examples.	(A) 'Draw your problem' (give no other directions) (B) Make a storyboard to depict a time you used drugs and behaved immaturely. (C) Make an inside–outside object (collaged or mixed-media, box, mask, or paper bag) to depict excuses have you used for your substance abuse problem.	(A) How did you identify your problem? Did you demonstrate responsibility? (B) How do you feel about your using behavior? How would you deal with a similar situation when sober? (C) Have others "bought into" the excuses or rationalizations you've made? Have you?
Identifying and handling emotions: • Discuss how most people who have abused drugs have buried their feelings.	(A) Depict a troublesome feeling in three drawings: 1. Depict it as a monster.	(A) Have you felt your feelings were somehow outside of you at times? Did you try to control them with drugs? What is a healthy way to deal with them?

(*Continued*)

Table 16.1 (Continued)

Psychoeducational Topic	*Directive*	*Prompt for Processing*
• Repressed feelings can trigger relapse. • Normalizing "negative" feelings and learning to tolerate uncomfortable feelings is a developmental task that is delayed by substance use. • Continued abstinence and social support enables the development of mature handling of feelings.	2. Depict the monster as it interacts with you. 3. Depict a time you overcame it, without drugs. (B) Calling out an emotion one at a time as clients use eight separate cards, ask them to abstractly (not symbolically) depict feeling sad, excited, ashamed, chill (or mellow), angry, blissful, and irritated; then for the eighth card, ask them to depict the feeling they have when using their drug.	(B) How do your depictions differ from your peers for the same feelings? Which one of your seven feeling cards looks most like your "high" card? Is it positive or negative feeling? If positive, do you prefer being excited or relaxed? Describe the relationship of your drug use to your feelings.
Healthy relationships and communication • Codependency patterns may be found in users, too. • People may cling to or take advantage of others out of need for approval, financial need, or from habit. • Discuss ways to formulate and establish healthy boundaries. • Recognize the need for 'me time' and how improved self-esteem can arise from feeling personally capable.	(A) Use a large sheet of paper and miniature plastic animals to create a sociogram to depict the identity, relative importance and closeness of others in your life. (B) Make a self-portrait by drawing or using collage images to depict a time when you felt good about yourself and had healthy behaviors. (Caveat: know your clients to prevent backfire—some may not remember such a time.)	(A) Are you satisfied with the relationships in your life right now? Rearrange to show how they were different in the past and describe the change. Would the animals you chose differ? Take this further by depicting environments on the paper. (B) When you look at this image, how do you feel? How can you help that "you" emerge again? Will you keep this piece to inspire you?
Relapse prevention: Identify personal triggers: • Cravings/drug related • Environmental triggers • Stress/internal triggers Identify healthy behaviors: • Responses to triggers • Healthy daily preventative personal behaviors • Ongoing treatment components (aftercare group, med check, 12-step sponsor)	(A) BPSS Pie redux: Make a pie depicting relapse prevention or recovery tactics for each area. (B) Use graphic or cognitive mapping techniques to depict your relapse prevention plan. (C) Make a set of pocket-sized recovery cards with tips for handling stress or craving, or morale-boosting quotations.	(A) How will you need to address your personal BPSS elements to ensure recovery? (B) Can you spin off new ideas or directions on your map? (C) Encourage group members to share ideas for cards; have each draw a name and make a card of encouragement for that person.

Harold's initial work with me in an individual art therapy session revealed that he was relatively advanced in terms of the stages of change (SOC). The SOC paradigm, part of the larger integrative model of behavioral health change known as the transtheoretical model, is frequently used to describe clients' readiness for change and identify appropriate treatment (Connors, DiClemente, Velasquez, & Donovan, 2015). The earliest stages, precontemplation and contemplation, are characterized by denial, disinterest in change, or ambivalence about the need and desire to change. Harold's emotional meeting with his employer seemed to have purged any lingering ambivalence he may have had about addressing his drug use. By taking an actual step toward change (asking for leave to go into treatment), Harold moved into the stage of preparation; and now, by refraining from further use and engaging in treatment, he was well into the action stage.

Harold's readiness for change was reflected in his first drawing, made in response to my three-word prompt to *Draw your problem*. He depicted a bust of himself in his scrub shirt, his pupils *pinned* as in one who is high on an opioid (Figure 16.1). An x-ray view of his forehead shows faulty cognitive

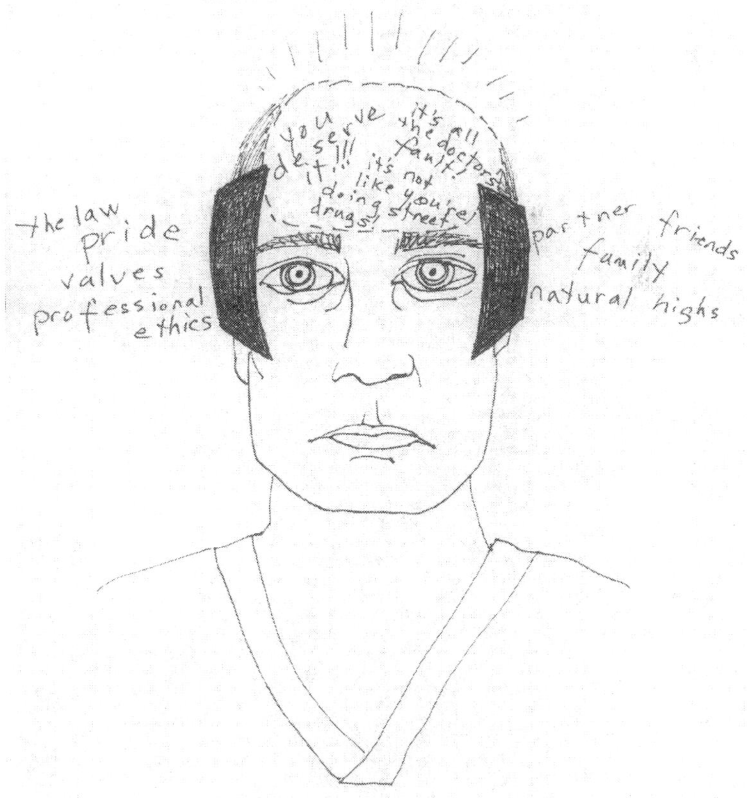

Figure 16.1 Harold's Problem Drawing

processes, such as thinking he *deserved* to steal drugs and get high. He added blinders to depict how he had ignored his personal values and relationships in the pursuit of his drug.

Many clients, when given this simply worded directive, will depict their drug of choice; they may even depict another person such as a spouse or probation officer, or a life situation, such as pending legal charges. Harold was unequivocal in his assessment that his problem was himself. It was exciting for both of us to observe that his problem drawing generated its own solutions, which we incorporated into his art therapy treatment plan: cognitive behavioral therapy–style reframing of the seductive and destructive self-talk via storyboards and a mixed-media board book with prompts designed to depict and honor values and relationships. Harold's SAT program treatment plan included MAT, substance abuse psychoeducation, and referral to a peer recovery mentor from a nursing association. The combination of approaches, in concert with his action-stage immersion in treatment, resulted in a positive prognosis and feelings of optimism for Harold at discharge.

Art Provides a Satisfying Substitute: The Case of Carolyn

I worked with Carolyn in a forensic MICA setting where she was incarcerated for felony drug possession. In a group art therapy session, she had participated in a joint mixed-media project to create a *garden of strengths* paper quilt. A brightly colored seed catalog provided inspiration, and each member chose a plant to depict a personal strength she could bring to the community. The method was to use intensely applied crayon, folding the paper randomly to crack the crayon wax, and painting over with black ink, which left a black background and a crackled batik effect. Each quilt square was then mounted on a mural-sized sheet of background paper.

Carolyn had depicted a scarlet flower, which she said represented herself as both strong and beautiful. I interpreted this to be a welcome sign of her growing self-esteem. Prior to the group when we would assemble the wall quilt, she showed her piece to the psychologist on the unit. The next day I learned she had been put in segregation on suicide watch, because he had interpreted the intense red and black colors as an indication that she was going to find a way to self-harm.

After she was released from segregation, Carolyn told me she was angry at the psychologist and had felt shamed for the drawing, which she had shown him out of pride. Although I was strongly tempted to concur with her indignation, I asked her if we could examine whether there was any truth to the concerns. In addition to the red color signaling self-harm behaviors, I had recalled Spring's (1985) identification of single red flowers an image frequently drawn by women with substance abuse problems who had been sexually abused. Carolyn did have this in her history, and I wondered if it needed further processing. Still, she had not come up with this symbol randomly; the project directions had dictated floral or vegetable content, the intense application of color, and the ink black background.

Carolyn was an insightful person, and I told her I trusted her ability to be honest with herself and with me: Could she identify a reason for choosing the scarlet red flower? Carolyn reflected for a moment, then shared that she had enjoyed the sensory process of building up the red color as thickly as she could, per the instructions. She stated, *it was like I had permission to play in the red. I don't think it would have felt so good if it was blue or purple. But it didn't trigger me, in fact, I think it felt like I was like doing the 180 of cutting. It still took me outside myself while I was doing it, but I didn't feel bad about myself afterward!* Carolyn's description made me think of the flow state, which has qualities of dissociation from the external world in a positive sense. I affirmed Carolyn's ability to use this task to see herself as beautiful and strong despite her stigmatized diagnoses, abuse experience, and the behaviors for which she was accustomed to feel ashamed.

This experience inspired an addition to Carolyn's art therapy treatment plan. It seemed clear that her habitual response to emotional pain or life difficulties had been to seek oblivion through dissociation, whether by cutting or the use of drugs that were sedating or had dissociative properties. Now that we had discovered a healthy alternative to those coping mechanisms, she could learn to enter the flow state. The formula for achieving flow relies on identifying a proactive activity (e.g., not a passive one such as watching television) that is attractive to the individual, and then refining it so that the challenge level of the particular task is balanced with the individual's ability to perform it. The flow state is achieved at the midpoint between frustration and boredom, when the task is neither too difficult nor too easy (Csikszentmihalyi, 1990).

Carolyn's search for flow-inducing activities also reflected upward movement from a sensory-based to a cognitive process in terms of the ETC (see Hinz, 2009). After we had experimented with various media and techniques, it was Zentangle-style drawing that became Carolyn's choice for coping with stress and other triggers. The final product she made in art therapy was an intricate black and white revision of her red flower drawing, in which stars and planets floated in arcs emanating from the flower's petals. This piece was stylistically more complex than the original; it was more emotionally contained, and yet emotionally satisfying. Carolyn reported that she felt more capable and in control when creating the final drawing, a state she preferred to the more disorganized experience with the red crayon. Her narcissistic sensory involvement with the red flower could now be seen as symbolic of her passage through a necessary stage in development, one that would lead to a more mature and balanced self in recovery.

Conclusion

Art therapy is a powerful way to address problematic substance use within a comprehensive medical treatment model. When incorporated in a typical psychoeducational curriculum, art therapy in groups can illuminate concepts clients are expected to learn and help them personalize their new understanding of addiction. Further, professional art therapists can readily tailor their approach to meet clients' needs in individual sessions. In the case of Harold, an initial assessment drawing quickly identified problems and held the key to solutions. This enabled effective treatment planning at the very start, which is essential for someone like Harold who is at the peak of readiness for change. For Carolyn, being in long-term treatment allowed for development of the therapeutic relationship, which, in turn, enabled deep exploration of art products. The art therapy approach evolved with her developmental progress, and led to the identification of the potential for art-making as an alternative to self-harm and substance abuse behaviors.

References

Angheluta, A.-M., & Lee, B. (2011). Art therapy for chronic pain. *Canadian Journal of Counseling and Psychotherapy*, *45*(2), 112–131.

American Society of Addiction Medicine. (2017a). *Definition of addiction*. Retrieved from www.asam.org/resources/definition-of-addiction.

American Society of Addiction Medicine. (2017b). *The ASAM criteria*. Retrieved from www.asamcontinuum.org/knowledgebase.

Capuzzi, D., & Stauffer, M. (2016). *Foundations of addictions counseling*. Boston, MA: Pearson.

Connors, G., DiClemente, C., Velasquez, M., & Donovan, D. (2015). *Substance abuse treatment and the stages of change* (2nd ed.). New York, NY: Guilford Press.

Csikszentmihalyi, M. (1990). *Flow: The psychology of optimal experience*. New York, NY: Harper & Row.

Gorski, T. (1997). *Passages through recovery*. Center City, MN: Hazelden.

Hanes, M. (1995). Utilizing road drawings as a therapeutic metaphor in art therapy. *American Journal of Art Therapy*, *34*(1), 19–23.

Hinz, L. (2009). Order out of chaos: The expressive therapies continuum as a framework for art therapy interventions in substance abuse treatment. In S. L. Brooke (Ed.), *The use of creative therapies with chemical dependency issues* (pp. 51–68). Springfield, IL: Charles Thomas Publisher, LTD.

Horay, B. J. (2006). Moving towards gray: Art therapy and ambivalence in substance abuse treatment. *Art Therapy: Journal of the American Art Therapy Association*, *23*(1), 14–22. doi: 10.1080/07421656.2006.10129528.

Kurtz, E. (2008). *The collected Ernie Kurtz*. New York, NY: Authors Choice.

Montrose, K., & Daley, D. (1995). *Celebrating small victories: A counselor's manual for treating chronic mental illness and substance abuse*. Center City, MN: Hazelden.

Pavlek, M. (2008). Paining out: An integrative pain therapy model. *Clinical Social Work Journal*, *36*(4), 385–393. doi: 10.1007/s10615–007–0136-y.

Schmanke, L. (2017). *Art therapy and substance abuse: Enabling recovery from alcohol and other drug addiction*. London, UK: Jessica Kingsley Publishers.

Spring, D. (1985). Symbolic language of sexually abused, chemically dependent women. *American Journal of Art Therapy*, *24*, 13–21.

Stevens, P., & Smith, R. (Eds.). (2017). *Substance use counseling* (6th ed.). Upper Saddle River, NJ: Pearson.

Younger, J., Parkitny, L., & McLain, D. (2014). The use of low-dose naltrexone as a novel anti-inflammatory treatment for chronic pain. *Clinical Rheumatology*, *33*(4), 451–459. doi: 10.1007/s10067-014-2517-2.

17 Material Considerations to Providing Art Therapy Within a Medical Model

Morgan Gaydos

Introduction

Through its cathartic and expressive properties, art therapy within a medical model naturally lends itself to the multidimensional healing process. Kinesthetic experiences during the art-making process have been observed to aid medically ill patients in finding a sense of relief from physical and emotional symptoms, and restoring a sense of control within a diagnosis. This chapter will discuss the benefits of art therapy with medical populations, specifically through media choice, material applications, and adaptive directives. Material considerations are an essential part of the art therapy process, and hold additional therapeutic value when engaged in by a patient in need of a kinesthetic, fully immersed experience. It is important to note that this chapter discusses medical patients on a broad spectrum, and not just those who are hospitalized; therefore, it will provide multiple applications that can apply to inpatient hospitalizations, outpatient clinics, and medical patients residing within the community.

Aspects to Consider when Selecting Art Therapy Materials

Art therapy alone is an extremely explorative process, as it allows a patient to process feelings, thoughts, and work through personal hardships. For individuals diagnosed with a medical illness, the choice in art materials by the art therapist can be as crucial as, if not more than, the directive itself. Despite a wide range in diagnoses, medical patients experience some sort of physiological and/or physical change; it is essential to choose an art material that not only adapts to changes in physical well-being, but also taps into the emotional response derived from the diagnosis.

Within a medical model, one can suggest that the connection between the mind and the body can become compromised, as symptoms occur that the mind, itself, cannot control or alter. Czamanski-Cohen and Weihs (2016) discussed the importance of restoring, and strengthening, the mind–body connection through active engagement in art therapy, with an emphasis on kinesthetic and tactile engagement. Art-making itself can be viewed as a sensory experience; an individual is required to directly interact and physically manipulate materials to engage in the process. The added experience of a kinesthetically driven material can provide sensory responses, soothing stimulation, and result in an emotional response that is healing in nature (Czamanski-Cohen & Weihs, 2016; Elkis-Abuhoff & Gaydos, 2016). The value of both kinesthetic and sensory materials when working within the medical realm can be further understood by examining the expressive therapies continuum and how it specifically applies to art media.

Incorporating the Expressive Therapies Continuum in Material Selection

The expressive therapies continuum (ETC) was first published in 1978 by Kagin and Lusebrink to understand and define art-based assessment in direct relation to art therapy media. Despite its many art therapy applications, there is an emphasis on the choice of art media, as well as the participant's interaction with the materials, within the therapeutic environment (Hinz, 2009; Lusebrink, Mārtinsone, & Dzilna-Šilova, 2013). The ETC model was in part designed to help art therapists determine which art materials are appropriate for the specific needs of a patient, making it useful as a point of reference when working with medical populations (Hinz, 2009).

The ETC functions on four distinct levels, which describe different modes of information processing during art engagement: (1) kinesthetic/sensory (K/S; gratification within movements and/or focus on stimulation), (2) perceptual/affective (P/A; expressive and emotional), (3) cognitive/symbolic (C/S; conscious planning and interactions within the individual's world), and 4) creative (CR; intersects through, or transcends above, the prior three levels; fulfillment in the process) (Kagin & Lusebrink, 1978; Lusebrink, 2010). Each level is a step-up process; individuals progress through the K/S, P/A, C/S, and end with CR level interconnected through all for a sense of wholeness and well-being (Lusebrink, 2010).

Appropriate and therapeutic choices in art materials can heavily determine a medically ill individual's ability to progress through the four ETC levels. Especially when faced with an initial diagnosis, invasive treatment, and/or chronic symptoms, initial engagement with an art material in the K/S level can set the stage for the therapeutic intervention to occur. Kinesthetic engagement (satisfaction through physical movements) and sensory stimulation (satisfaction through touch and other senses) are on both ends of the K/S level, and can also go hand-in-hand depending on the material of choice. For example, an individual can gain satisfaction in the physical movement of pounding a ball of clay, but can also be soothed by the soft, malleable, and warm feeling of overworked clay. Another example can be seen with the use of thickened paint; an individual can find stimulation through the repetitive arm movement of swirling the paint on the paper with their fingers, and can also enjoy the direct feeling of the paint against their skin. Especially when faced with an overwhelming diagnosis, the act of drawing itself can often be difficult to engage in, making the choice in art therapy materials essential in not only making the individual more comfortable, but providing them with a sense of structure and control (Pénzes, van Hooren, Dokter, Smeijsters, & Hutschemaekers, 2014).

Medical patients, experiencing a disconnect with their body, loss of control/independence within their diagnosis, undergoing invasive treatment, and/or facing life-threatening factors, can more intimately engage with a kinesthetic and sensory art material on an emotional level (Lusebrink, 2010). For example, a material such as clay allows an individual to take direct control—manipulating the form as they see fit, while simultaneously releasing inner physical and emotional tension through the repetitive nature of kneading and shaping clay. In addition to immediately engaging a medical patient on a physical and stimulating level, individuals can also experience a sense of therapeutic distraction from their diagnosis and a relief in symptoms within the moment (Elkis-Abuhoff & Gaydos, 2016). This can allow an individual to become fully immersed in the art therapy process, and transition into the P/A, C/S, and CR stages for a sense of mastery and fulfillment. It can be suggested that this phenomenon can also be partly due to the neurological properties of kinesthetic and sensory materials, and the brain's response when manipulating an art product.

Neurological Responses to Kinesthetic and Sensory Art Materials

Although still a relatively new concept within the field of art therapy, current research within the medical model has lent itself to understanding the neurological affects that art materials have on the brain. Elkis-Abuhoff and Gaydos (2016, 2018) have explored the use of kinesthetic materials, specifically within the category of clay, and state that active brain stimulation begins at the fingertips. Direct engagement with an art material begins with the sense of touch; the periphery area of the body, such as the fingertips, is sensitive to sensory experiences and can relay tactile stimulation to areas of the brain (Elkis-Abuhoff & Gaydos, 2018). Areas such as the somatosensory cortex, basal ganglia, and frontal cortex, to name a few, have the potential to become activated through the sense of touch—more specifically, the immersion of kinesthetic and sensory materials (Elkis-Abuhoff & Gaydos, 2016, 2018; Longo, Azañón, & Haggard, 2010).

Art therapy with neurological conditions can be described as action oriented, as the direct engagement in art-making involves both physical movements and tactile manipulation. (Lusebrink, 2010). The direct, fingertip contact with a kinesthetic and sensory material can therefore benefit medical conditions such as Parkinson's disease, Alzheimer's disease, multiple sclerosis, and individuals who suffered a seizure or stroke, and even improve symptomology during the process through active brain stimulation.

The process and application of art therapy is innately known to be a healing and generally relaxing process; individuals engaged in the materials and directive can metaphorically step outside of their internal selves (thoughts/feelings) and look at a medical concern and/or crisis in a different light (Hass-Cohen & Clyde Findlay, 2015; Lusebrink, 2010). Specifically, with neurological disorders, there can be a disconnect in an individual's ability to verbally express and communicate his or her thoughts and feelings, making the nonverbal aspect of the art therapy process ever more crucial. The use of kinesthetic and sensory materials for expression and stimulation can excite areas of the brain that have been compromised by a medical diagnosis, producing a positive change in physical movement as the individual continues to manipulate and become immersed in the art material (Koch & Fuchs, 2011). Furthermore, individuals can experience a reconnection of the mind and body through an art material, gaining a stronger sense of control over physical symptomology and finding the words, or art image, to better convey their experiences despite neurological barriers (Elkis-Abuhoff & Gaydos, 2018; Hass-Cohen & Clyde Findlay, 2015).

Understanding the Therapeutic Properties of Art Materials

Although there is an emphasis on kinesthetic and sensory materials within this chapter, it is important to clarify that nonkinesthetic/nonsensory materials also possess therapeutic benefits that can help address the needs of a medical patient. It is the responsibility of the art therapist to evaluate and gain any relevant information on medical/interpersonal history of the patient, prior to selecting art materials and tools. The following depicts a variety of considerations when selecting art therapy materials within a medical model (Table 17.1) and serves as a general point of reference to the most frequently used materials. Material selection will depend on the specific application and capability of the individual and/or aptitude of a group.

As referenced within Table 17.1, some materials have contradictory properties, such as being both fluid and resistive. A significant therapeutic property of any art material is its ability to transform its substance and/or aesthetic by altering the application or technique. For example, altering the consistency of paint, or providing untraditional painting tools, can result in a more textured application and an alternative approach to painting. This can be done in the moment, and is often based off the expressive needs of an individual and the progression of the session. This characteristic can greatly benefit a medical patient, and can further provide them with a sense of control and personal exploration within their artwork.

Table 17.1 Therapeutic Properties of Commonly Used Art Materials

Clay forms
Variations: Ability to set (kiln, air-dry, nondrying), color (glaze, precolored dough), technique (slip and score, molds), and accessibility (modeling dough, less traditional forms, little residue)
Therapeutic properties: Three-dimensional, physical, malleable, transformative, soothing, tactile, repetitive, resistive, earthy, sense of mastery, portable if in a less traditional form
Kinesthetic/sensory components: Range in surface texture (smooth, carved, grooved), warms when overworked, incorporation of water (if applicable), stimulating, use of fingers, palms, hands, and full arm movements if desired (kneading, pounding of clay), olfactory aspect
Psychological responses: Regressive, emotional, symbolic

Drawing
Variations: Markers (broad/thin tip), colored pencils, lead pencils, crayons, oil pastels, chalk pastels, charcoal, pens
Therapeutic properties: Controlled, structured, orderly, creation of symbolic or realistic imagery, resistive (pencils) or fluid (pastels), portable
Kinesthetic/sensory components: Use of small or large hand/arm movements, variations can offer sensory aspects; watercolor pencils (incorporation of water and transformation of medium), oil/chalk pastels (more textured, material residue can be felt between the fingertips and physically blended by hands)
Psychological responses: Organization, imagination

Painting
Variations: Oil, acrylic, tempera, fingerpaint, watercolor (liquid and cakes), painting pens, ink, variations in accompanied tools (pallet, paintbrush size, sponge, easel)
Therapeutic properties: Fluid, loose, can be resistive (i.e., combination of oil pastels and watercolors), colorful and expressive, relaxing, stimulating, olfactory aspect, variations in surface (canvas vs. paper), ability to transform, layer, and blend colors
Kinesthetic/sensory components: Use of arm/body movements, use of fingers, can be thickened for texture (i.e., sand), tactile if used on a textured surface
Psychological responses: Affective, symbolic, can be regressive

Collage
Variations: Precut, option to cut, images, words, shapes, textured and/or smooth paper, three-dimensional objects, use of adhesive (tape, glue stick, liquid glue, art glaze)
Therapeutic properties: Controlled application, materials are loose in presentation, ability to layer, symbolic, sense of mastery, can provide structure and order, free expression, multimedia, requires less skill
Kinesthetic/sensory components: Tactile application, contrasting textures, sorting and mixing the collage materials, ripping of the paper
Psychological responses: Representation, symbolic

Material Safety and Limitation

Especially within the medical model, where art therapists come in contact with a wide range of diagnoses, physical and adverse symptoms, and sensitivity within the treatment process, it is important to be aware of the safety and restriction of materials. In most hospital facilities, references such as the Material Safety Data Sheet (MSDS) are readily available to help educate the handling of any and all materials, and encourage the use of nontoxic materials for patient care. Other resources, such as art material safety guides, can be accessed online and printed for designated art therapy spaces within medical settings (Horovitz, 2018; Malchiodi, 2013). Material guides also serve as a reference to cleaning/wiping down supplies; some supplies, such as modeling dough, cannot be wiped down and should be discarded after initial use for infectious control purposes (Malchiodi, 2013).

The type of medical environment, such as direct treatment areas, bedside programming, and clinics, will determine the range of art materials that the therapist can incorporate into their work. On an inpatient unit, or clinic, the art therapist's relationship with interdisciplinary treatment team members can help designate a given space, specifically for patients who are unable to leave their room. Mobile art therapy at bedside allows the therapeutic process to be brought directly to the patient in need, and the art therapist follows the infectious control and isolation medical protocols of the unit for themselves and the art materials (McNutt, 2013). Although some art materials may still be restricted due to the given medical condition, mobile art therapy sessions allow for a greater flexibility in range as the materials are in a controlled and highly supervised setting. In less restricted areas, such as community settings and private practice, the art therapist can incorporate a wider selection of materials suited to the medical and emotional needs of the patient.

Careful consideration of a medical diagnosis, and its accompanied symptoms, can help determine which materials are appropriate, and which materials should be restricted (Horovitz, 2018; Malchiodi, 2012). For example, if an art therapist is working with an individual who has a respiratory concern, a material such as raw plaster or powdered paint would not be appropriate due to the risk of inhalation. Another example can be seen in referencing individuals diagnosed with Parkinson's disease; although considered a safe and controlled material, the selection of colored pencils may be inappropriate if the individual has lost his or her fine motor ability, and therefore could become frustrated with their inability to hold the material. The use of adaptive tools can aid individuals in working with a material deemed difficult by their symptomology, and help the patient overcome a preconceived limitation within the art therapy process (Malchiodi, 2013). Furthermore, it is important to understand that within the medical model, the sense of mastery is automatically a main goal for the patient. Whether through the use of an adaptive and assistive tool/technique, or providing materials that are without limitation, a medical patient will experience and feel a greater sense of control through mastering the art material and final product. Providing a medically ill patient with control over an art material can become a symbolic representation of regaining a sense of control over their life, medical diagnosis, and any procedures that have negatively impacted their quality of life.

Maintaining a Medically Clean Environment

Some limitations, such as the need to maintain a clean and 'sterile' environment of an inpatient medication setting, cannot be avoided. The value and therapeutic properties of a given art material can be quickly dismissed if it cannot be brought into a given medical space. Art therapists are known for their ability to adapt to a variety of limitations, whether patient or environment related, and can still provide therapy in restrictive areas.

With the presence of high-tech, and often large, medical equipment, overflow of staff, and need for scheduled treatment interventions, inpatient medical settings are often viewed as a restrictive area for art therapy. Some patients are unable to leave their bed, and for those who can, some may rely on or be accompanied by equipment attached to a part of their body. In addition, some treatment interventions can weaken the immune system or provide increasing sensitivity to the senses, making it more important to maintain a clean environment and more difficult to engage a patient with an art material that could be viewed as 'messy.' Even with the wiping down of materials, many intensive and invasive treatment areas, such as chemotherapy rooms, prohibit any material from being brought into the environment (Elkis-Abuhoff, Gaydos, & Goldblatt, 2017).

Continuing to emerge as an art therapy application within the medical realm, the use of technology has revealed its ability to provide patients with creativity and expression while leaving no material 'mess' or residue. The use of technology allows art therapy to gain accessibility in areas known to be medically restrictive, and treat a wider range of patients—specifically those facing invasive and potentially life-threatening treatments.

The Use of Technology as a Happy Medium

Whether to provide art therapy in medically restrictive areas or to take advantage of its portable nature, technology can be used as a cutting-edge approach within the art therapy process. As technology itself continues to add a sense of realism with enhanced graphics, commands, and direct interaction, the use of a tablet can allow a medical patient to create a piece of art with a variety of digitalized art materials at their disposal. This not only allows art therapy to become more portable within medical settings, but also alleviates any concern about 'messy' materials in sterile environments.

Through drawing, painting, and even sculpture applications, use of one's fingers and/or a stylus can mimic brush strokes, pencil lines, and three-dimensional indentations with a material of choice, on a surface of choice, all on the tablet (Elkis-Abuhoff et al., 2017; Waller, 2015). The use of a tablet also provides a sensory aspect, such as holding a stylus, the feeling of one's finger on the smooth, cool surface, and experiencing slight vibrations or sound effects with given action. In addition, the use of a tablet can help individuals create a piece of artwork with ease, and possibly more initial confidence, as it does not involve the use of traditional materials and automatically engages the individual through the digital manner (Choe, 2017).

The use of tablet technology can allow art therapy into a previously restricted area, such as a chemotherapy room, where the patient can engage during direct treatment. This application allows not only the art therapist to work with a medical patient in a different light, but also allows physicians to evaluate the psychological needs of an individual undergoing invasive treatment for their diagnosis (Elkis-Abuhoff et al., 2017). Although art applications are not designed, as of yet, for the purpose of art therapy, the use of tablets have been found to be a valuable tool in the art therapist's possession (Choe, 2014) and can further expand the range in treatment within the medical model.

Conclusion

This chapter aimed to illustrate the wide range in material considerations with the medical model, taking environmental factors into account, and how material selection is a crucial aspect of both a medical patient's diagnosis and the art therapy process. Art materials have a significant impact on the engagement, creativity, and expression of a medical patient undergoing direct treatment, recovering, and/or adapting to the changes in lifestyle of a given diagnosis. Material considerations can also allow an art therapist to better understand medical symptoms, and the diagnosis itself, creating a stronger sense of cohesion within the therapeutic application.

References

Choe, S. (2014). An exploration of the qualities and features of art apps for art therapy. *The Arts in Psychotherapy, 41*(2), 145–154.

Choe, N. S. (2017). Using digital tools and apps in art therapy sessions. In R. Garner (Ed.), *Digitial art therapy: Material, methods, and applications* (pp. 54–66). Philadelphia, PA: Jessica Kinsley Publishers.

Czamanski-Cohen, J., & Weihs, K. L. (2016). The bodymind model: A platform for studying the mechanisms of change induced by art therapy. *The Arts in Psychotherapy, 51*, 63–71. doi: 10.1016/j.aip.2016.08.006.

Elkis-Abuhoff, D., & Gaydos, M. (2016). Medical art therapy applied to the trauma experienced by those diagnosed with Parkinson's disease. In J. L. King (Ed.), *Art therapy, trauma, and neuroscience: Theoretical and practical perspectives* (pp. 195–210). New York, NY: Routledge.

Elkis-Abuhoff, D., & Gaydos, M. (2018). Medical art therapy research moves forward: A review of clay manipulation with Parkinson's disease. *Art Therapy: Journal of the American Art Therapy Association, 35*(2). In Press. doi: 10.1080/07421656.2018.1483162.

Elkis-Abuhoff, D., Gaydos, M., & Goldblatt, R. (2017). Using tablet technology as a medium for art therapy. In S. L. Brooke (Ed.), *Combining the creative therapies with technology: Using social media and online counseling to treat clients* (pp. 53–73). Springfield, IL: Charles C. Charles Publishers.

Hass-Cohen, N., & Clyde Findlay, J. (2015). *Art therapy and the neuroscience of relationships, creativity, and resiliency: Skills and practices*. New York, NY: W.W. Norton & Company.

Hinz, L. D. (2009). *Expressive therapies continuum: A framework for using art in therapy*. New York, NY: Routledge.

Horovitz, E. G. (2018). *A guide to art therapy materials, methods, and applications*. New York, NY: Routledge.

Kagin, S. L., & Lusebrink, V. B. (1978). The expressive therapies continuum. *Art Psychotherapy, 5*(4), 171–180.

Koch, S. C., & Fuchs, T. (2011). Embodied arts therapies. *The Arts in Psychotherapy, 38*(4), 276–280.

Longo, M. R., Azañón, E., & Haggard, P. (2010). More than skin deep: Body representation beyond primary somatosensory cortex. *Neuropsychologia, 48*(3), 655–668. doi: 10.1016/j.neuropsychologia.2009.08.022.

Lusebrink, V. B. (2010). Assessment and therapeutic application of the expressive therapies continuum: Implications for brain structures and functions. *Art Therapy: Journal of the American Art Therapy Association, 27*(4), 168–177. doi: 10.1080/07421656.2010.10129380.

Lusebrink, V. B., Mārtinsone, K., & Dzilna-Šilova, I. (2013). The expressive therapies continuum (ETC): Interdisciplinary bases of the ETC. *International Journal of Art Therapy, 18*(2), 75–85. doi: 10.1080/17454832.2012.713370.

Malchiodi, C. A. (2012). Art therapy materials, media, and methods. In C. A. Malchiodi (Ed.), *The handbook of art therapy* (2nd ed., pp. 27–41). New York, NY: The Guilford Press.

Malchiodi, C. A. (Ed.). (2013). *Art therapy and health care*. New York, NY: The Guilford Press.

McNutt, J. V. (2013). An open art studio model. In C. C. Malchiodi (Ed.), *Art therapy and health care* (pp. 281–290). New York, NY: The Guilford Press.

Pénzes, I., van Hooren, S., Dokter, D., Smeijsters, H., & Hutschemaekers, G. (2014). Material interaction in art therapy assessment. *The Arts in Psychotherapy, 41*(5), 484–492. doi: 10.1016/j.aip.2014.08.003.

Waller, D. (2015). *Group interactive art therapy: Its use in training and treatment* (2nd ed.). New York, NY: Routledge.

18 TTAP Method® Applied to Individuals with Alzheimer's Disease

Linda Levine Madori

Research reports that an estimated 5.5 million individuals are currently diagnosed with Alzheimer's dementia within the United States; the prevalence of Alzheimer's disease continues to be on the rise, with a new diagnosis developing approximately every 66 seconds (Alzheimer's Association, 2017). Alzheimer's disease ranks as the fifth leading cause of death in the country, and preventative efforts regarding cognitive impairments have been on the forefront of research efforts (Madori, Melville, Stickney, Padoto, & Rodriguez, 2016).

The prevention of cognitive impairments and promotion of increased cognitive functioning has remained on the forefront of social science research; clinicians have identified the importance of emotional, social, and mental stimulation improvements in enhancing the cognition of individuals diagnosed with Alzheimer's disease (Madori et al., 2016). Multimodal interventions, defined as a variety of interventions that stimulate affect, behavior, sensation, imagery, and interpersonal/intrapersonal relationships within regions of the brain, have proven to be extremely successful in decreasing cognitive symptoms of Alzheimer's disease (Burgener, Buettner, Beattie, & Rose, 2009). Such interventions are designed to provide a wide variety of stimuli, positively affecting and increasing neuronal activity, responses, and plasticity within the Alzheimer's disease brain (McKinney, Antoni, Kumar, Tims, & McCabe, 1997; Santos et al., 2015).

Therapeutic Thematic Arts Programming for Older Adults Method (TTAP Method®) is a multimodal, art/recreation group therapy process that engages creative recreation activity within a nine-step structure to inhibit the progression of Alzheimer's disease (AD) (Madori & Bendel, 2013). The TTAP Method® maximizes interaction among participants, stimulates all aspects of brain functioning, addresses social and emotional needs, and integrates opportunities for life review (Baune, Suslow, Engelien, Arolt, & Berger, 2006). The TTAP Method® therefore provides the early intervention needed to assist older adults in retaining cognitive and psychosocial abilities (Madori, 2009; Madori et al., 2016).

What Is the TTAP Method®?

The TTAP Method®, along with the 12 steps, was first published in 2007. Since the material was written with descriptive language for standard practice by this author, it was made accessible to clinicians in the form of an Internet resource, along with other publications that followed (Madori, 2007, 2009, 2012, 2013; Madori & Alders, 2010; Madori & Bendel, 2013; Madori et al., 2016). For applying the TTAP Method® to the medical parameters of this text, a review of the standard material is as follows, and can also be accessed in its entirety through the TTAP Madori website (http://levinemadoriphd.com).

12 Steps of the TTAP Method®

By utilizing the 12 steps, it has been proven in clinical studies that the therapist, healthcare professional, social worker, and all others can facilitate structured and person-centered programming. The TTAP Method's 12-step intervention directs the focus of therapy on a proven factor helping cognition: the reinforcement and utilization of remaining strengths, such as accessing long-term memory or controlling motor coordination (Madori, 2007). The 12 steps are as follows: group discussion, music/guided imagery, drawing/painting, sculpture, movement, poetry, food, themed event, photography, sensory stimulation, drama therapy, and evaluation (Madori, 2013).

The second step is the most significant in assisting participants to identify their own personal needs. Step 2 brings together music, body relaxation, and guided meditation into the session, allowing for moments of introspection followed by increased social interactions through discussions. Meditation has been linked to an increased likelihood of a later experience, as it allows for increased levels of concentration, creates complete absorption in the cognitive experience, and distracts from the external environment (Brewer et al., 2011). Table 18.1 shows the 12 steps, their progression, the type of stimulation that each step provides to the participants, as well as the region of the brain stimulated throughout the TTAP Method.

Due to the multiple points of engagement, the TTAP Method's® 12 steps have been recognized as a proven therapeutic intervention that goes beyond pharmaceuticals (Madori et al., 2016). Since 2007, clinical research collected on the TTAP Method® has demonstrated its ability to stimulate brain function, resulting in increased cognition and significant improvements in mood, social, emotional needs for those diagnosed with AD (Madori & Bendel, 2013; Madori et al., 2016). In addition, the expressive properties within this therapeutic method provide increased communication between patients and clinicians, an important part of any medical model, and has led to feelings of connectedness within the larger medical community (Madori & Bendel, 2013).

Objectives of the TTAP® Approach

The TTAP Method® encompasses a series of therapeutic objectives to stimulate brain functioning and increase cognition. Furthermore, these objectives are intended to aid an older individual in enhancing emotional, social, and physical capacities within one's quality of life (Madori et al., 2016).

Table 18.1 12 Steps of the TTAP Method®

Step	*Process*	*Stimulation*	*Brain Region*
1	Individual thought to group ideas	Linguistic	Broca's area
2	Group ideas to music/guided imagery	Musical/visual	Frontotemporal lobe
3	Music/guided imagery to 2D image	Visual	Parietal/posterior parietal lobe
4	Image into 3D image/sculpture	Spatial	Motor cortex, temporal lobe, cerebellum
5	Sculpture into movement	Kinesthetic	Motor cortex, temporal lobe, cerebellum
6	Movement into words/poetry/stories	Linguistic	Broca area, Wernicke's area, frontal lobe
7	Words into food for thought	Linguistic/spatial	Sensory cortex, reticular formation
8	Food for thought into theme event	All learning styles intra-interpersonal	Broca area, Wernicke's area, reticular formation
9	Themed event phototherapy	Visual intra-interpersonal	Reticular formation
10	Phototherapy to sensory stimulation	All learning styles intrapersonal	All regions
11	Sensory stimulation to drama therapy	Kinesthetic	Motor cortex, frontal lobe, temporal lobe
12	Drama therapy into feedback	Intrapersonal	Broca area, Wernicke's area, frontal lobe

Stimulate Optimal Brain Functioning

Previous research on brain plasticity, neural regeneration, and the phenomena of cognitive reserve demonstrates that positive changes in neural activity can be activated by visual, auditory, and sensory stimulation (Burgener et al., 2009; Concerto et al., 2016; Hass-Cohen & Clyde Findlay, 2015). During the TTAP Method® program, participants are provided a replicable creative arts approach stimulating visual, auditory, and sensory systems as well as stimulation to three distinct brain systems: the affective system, the strategic system, and the recognition system. The challenge for the art therapist, working with all levels and abilities of those diagnosed with AD, is to identify activities that meet the needs of their patients at *every level*. The TTAP Method® approach identifies, through the assessment forms, which areas of the brain are being stimulated, and structures programming to provide challenging activities based on *life themes*, such as loved ones, for mental and emotional well-being.

The use of multiple forms of interaction is essential in the TTAP Method®. Bloom's taxonomy of learning is incorporated into the TTAP Method® approach, and each of the 12 steps is designed to stimulate the visual, musical, linguistic, interpersonal, intrapersonal, kinesthetic, and spatial learner (Cooper et al., 2003; Hass-Cohen & Carr, 2008). The integration of various artistic activities (i.e., body relaxation accompanied with conversation and painting) elicits an integration of higher cortical thinking, such as attentiveness and problem solving, to promote faster cognitive and emotional processing and facilitate learning (Koelsch, 2015). Guided imagery, synchronized with music, is one of the most unique and significant steps in the methodology in that it allows the individual to access positive long-term memory (Baune et al., 2006; Koelsch, 2015). Guided imagery has also been shown to significantly decrease cortisol levels, thereby enhancing mood and subsequent cognitive performance (Madori & Alders, 2010). Figure 18.1 provides an example of the regions of the brain stimulated during a TTAP Method session of Madori and Alders' (2010) intervention (Miles & Loughlin, 2011).

Maximizing Interaction Among Participants

The TTAP Method® employs dynamic interaction by incorporating avenues for both nonverbal and verbal communication in a group context, which has been shown to regulate functions within the cerebral cortex (Miles, 2011), promoting brain wellness and skill retention among older adults (Plassman et al., 2007). As with other medical diagnoses, there is a tendency for AD individuals to become socially withdrawn as cognition and memory decline. Participation within a creative and self-expressive modality has been found to enhance feelings of confidence and self-worth, leading to increased motivation for therapeutic involvement and decreased social isolation (Madori et al., 2016).

Through the 12-step structure, the TTAP Method® increases the total time a participant spends in programming, and exposes the participant to longer levels of increased stimulation. In stimulating participants for longer periods of time, through person-centered recreational/art therapy, the TTAP Method® activates mental, physical, and social domains. By activating these domains, the TTAP Method® can protect against cognitive decline and dementia, as well as promoting positive social interactions that can become lost in a diagnosis such as AD (Madori, 2007, 2009).

Addressing Social and Emotional Needs

The TTAP Method® was created and designed to address a range of emotional and social needs by increasing opportunities to engage participants in positive individualized and person-centered social involvements (Baune

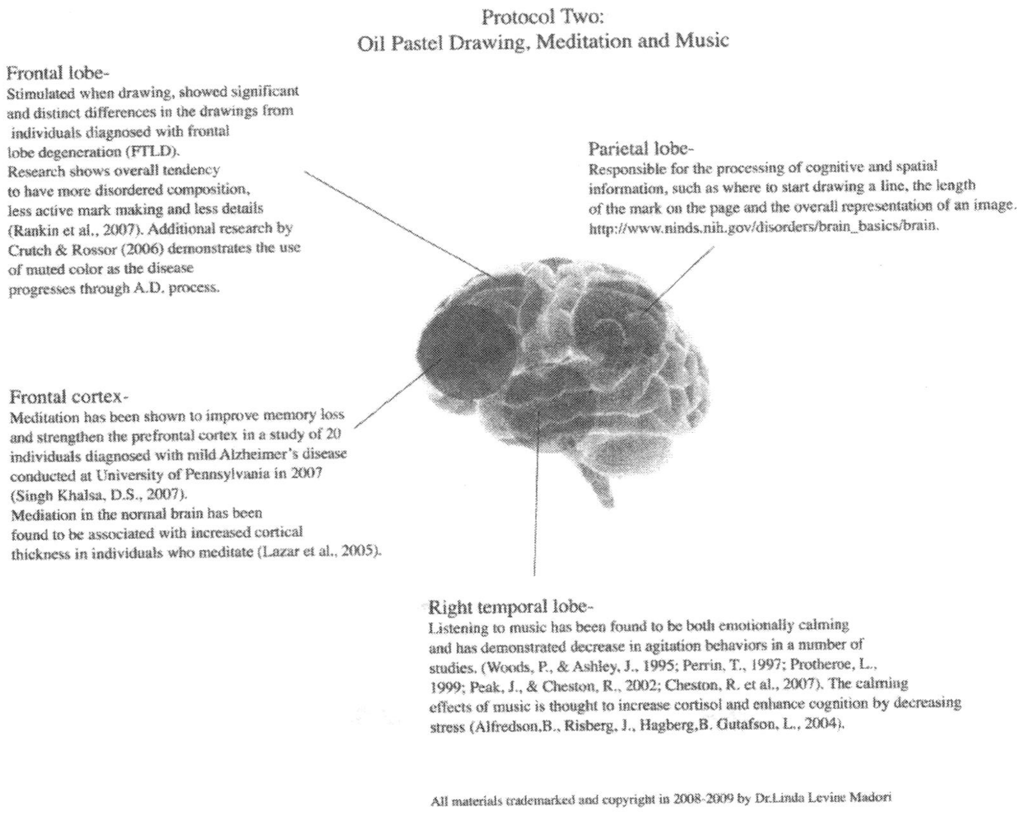
Protocol Two:
Oil Pastel Drawing, Meditation and Music
Frontal lobe-
Stimulated when drawing, showed significant and distinct differences in the drawings from individuals diagnosed with frontal lobe degeneration (FTLD).
Research shows overall tendency to have more disordered composition, less active mark making and less details (Rankin et al., 2007). Additional research by Crutch & Rossor (2006) demonstrates the use of muted color as the disease progresses through A.D. process.
Parietal lobe-
Responsible for the processing of cognitive and spatial information, such as where to start drawing a line, the length of the mark on the page and the overall representation of an image. http://www.ninds.nih.gov/disorders/brain_basics/brain.
Frontal cortex-
Meditation has been shown to improve memory loss and strengthen the prefrontal cortex in a study of 20 individuals diagnosed with mild Alzheimer's disease conducted at University of Pennsylvania in 2007 (Singh Khalsa, D.S., 2007).
Mediation in the normal brain has been found to be associated with increased cortical thickness in individuals who meditate (Lazar et al., 2005).
Right temporal lobe-
Listening to music has been found to be both emotionally calming and has demonstrated decrease in agitation behaviors in a number of studies. (Woods, P., & Ashley, J., 1995; Perrin, T., 1997; Protheroe, L., 1999; Peak, J., & Cheston, R., 2002; Cheston, R. et al., 2007). The calming effects of music is thought to increase cortisol and enhance cognition by decreasing stress (Alfredson,B., Risberg, J., Hagberg,B. Gutafson, L., 2004).
All materials trademarked and copyright in 2008-2009 by Dr.Linda Levine Madori

Figure 18.1 Regions of the Brain Stimulated Through Madori and Adler's 2010 Intervention

et al., 2006). In its thematic orientation, The TTAP Method® structures sessions to meet the specific needs of persons with AD, including the exploration and verbalization of feelings ranging from hope, to love, to sorrow (Madori, 2009, 2013).

Cognitive difficulties, specifically short-term memory loss, are a defining feature of AD and are one of the central problems experienced daily (Dubois et al., 2007). For a person with early stage AD, memory loss can have a major impact on daily living skills, which impedes self-confidence and can lead to anxiety, depression, and withdrawal from activities and other social involvements (Alzheimer's Association, 2017; Elferink, van Tilborg, & Kessels, 2015). Social withdrawal, in turn, can result in a general increase in symptoms, including enhanced memory loss. This increase in symptoms beyond those attributable to the disease process is an example of what has been termed 'excess disability' (Madori et al., 2016). The TTAP Method®, through its person-centered approach, naturally enhances feelings of self-worth, which has a direct correlation to motivation levels directed toward creating enhanced social support systems, thus decreasing the likelihood of withdrawal among participants. Additionally, it has been clinically documented that subgroups form through the therapeutic group process and continue long after the therapist is gone. These subgroups further enhance socialization and increased social networks in those diagnosed with AD.

Depression coupled with feelings of hopelessness can have a detrimental impact on cognitive functioning. Cognitive evaluation tests have shown that cognitive performance can be significantly impaired during depressive states (Baune et al., 2006). Emotions directly affect cognition and, therefore, subsequent motor coordination, memory, self-esteem, and the perception of one's own health (Madori et al., 2016; Mather, 2012). Successful depression treatment, using multimodal interventions such as the TTAP Method®, has been correlated to significant alleviation of cognitive impairments and therefore an overall improvement in independent functioning (Ristau, 2011).

Integrating Opportunities for Life Review

The TTAP Method® utilizes, during the group art/recreation therapy sessions, a continual process of life review at each of the 12 steps, which is a naturally occurring process (Madori, 2007). This process is structured within the method in which the individual looks back on his or her life with reflection, and revisits positive events and unresolved difficulties and/or conflicts (Rentz, 2002). The continual ability for reminiscence and life review to occur as a therapeutic approach allows individuals to revisit profound life events, thus serving as a useful intervention for depression and as a promising intervention among older adults with dementia (Ristau, 2011). In consideration of cognitive, emotional, and physical needs, a self-reflective approach during art/recreation therapy sessions can provide healing, comfort, and closure to previous life issues.

The TTAP Method® provides a structured and systematic approach to life review which has shown to help the older adult adjust to the many life changes and challenges positively affecting well-being (Madori, 2012). Moreover, the TTAP Method® incorporates life review in successive steps (Baune et al., 2006), which has been shown to promote memory retention, perceived social values of self, decreased disorientation, reduced fear and anxiety, and improved self-esteem and social interaction (Madori, 2012).

Therapeutic Applications of the TTAP Method®

Having explored the multimodal interventions and objectives, the therapeutic application of the TTAP Method® can be understood through a summary of a standard session. Each session is structured to offer a 1-hour creative experience for individuals within a group therapy setting.

A TTAP Method® session begins with a basic introduction of both the therapist and the group participants. The therapist will then discuss the goals of the TTAP Method® session, such as mind–body connection and brain stimulation, relaxation and meditation, reminiscing, and the expression of thoughts and ideas. This dialogue helps orient participants to the group process, and allows them to feel more comfortable within the group as the goals are tailored to their cognitive, social, and emotional needs.

Participants will then begin a guided imagery meditation (time can range depending on the group), beginning with each participant getting into a comfortable position while the lights dim. Accompanied music will be described, and participants are invited to partake in this meditative journey. The therapist will then talk the group through the guided imagery meditation, for example *visualize being in the woods*, or *visualize yourself walking on a beach*. Once complete, participants will be invited to discuss what they saw in their minds eye, and will be asked questions such as, *What details did you notice in your vision? Who did you see? Did you smell anything?* and *What memories came to you?* Participants will then be handed objects that relate to the guided imagery and further stimulate conversation, such as seashells and sand.

The therapist will then lead the group into one of the 12 steps of creative arts to further promote self-expression and processing within the group (refer to Table 18.1). For example, participants can be provided with clay to create a sculpture related to their guided imagery medication experience (step 4), which provides for spatial brain stimulation and engagement in kinesthetic movement. Once the art directive is complete, participants will be asked to join in an open dialogue to share both their creative work and personal experience within the group.

Conclusion

In using the TTAP Method®, all aspects of life are explored through the use of personal or environmental themes, which make social interaction easier in the group setting. In addition, the TTAP Method® includes dynamic interactions by integrating both verbal and nonverbal communication within a group environment, which is beneficial to the cerebral cortex to maintain brain wellness and skill retention. Due to the loss of socialization and memorization when an individual starts to decline, the disease process can be rapid. What we see regarding the TTAP approach is enhanced person-centered programming. This approach naturally enables the individual/patient to engage in art/therapeutic interventions for longer periods of time, which activates the social, mental, and physical domains (Burgener et al., 2009). However, the memory loss can really become a burden on an individual and impact their self-esteem, and may lead to anxiety, depression, and loss of interest in activities. Because there is the chain reaction to the disease, the TTAP Method® was developed to enhance feelings of self-worth, which then increases all individuals' domains, motivates them to participate in art/recreational activities, and increases their quality of life through a person-centered approach. The outcomes the TTAP Method® have also been shown to be a proven procedure to restore, remediate, or rehabilitate functional abilities, such as those supported by neuroscience research.

References

Alzheimer's Association. (2017). 2017 Alzheimer's disease facts and figures. *Alzheimer's & Dementia, 13*(4), 325–373. doi: 10.1016/j.jalz.2017.02.001.

Baune, B. T., Suslow, T., Engelien, A., Arolt, V., & Berger, K. (2006). The association between depressive mood and cognitive performance in an elderly general population—The MEMO study. *Dementia and Geriatric Cognitive Disorders, 22*(2), 142–149. doi: 10.1159/000093745.

Brewer, J. A., Worhunsky, P. D., Gray, J. R., Tang, Y. Y., Weber, J., & Kober, H. (2011). Meditation experience is associated with differences in default mode network activity and connectivity. *Proceedings of the National Academy of Sciences, 108*(50), 20254–20259. doi: 10.1073/pnas.1112029108.

Burgener, S. C., Buettner, L. L., Beattie, E., & Rose, K. M. (2009). Effectiveness of community-based, nonpharmacological interventions for early-stage dementia: Conclusions and recommendations. *Journal of Gerontological Nursing, 35*(3), 50–57. doi: 10.3928/00989134-20090301-03.

Concerto, C., Infortuna, C., Mineo, L., Pereira, M., Freedberg, D., Chusid, E., . . . Battaglia, F. (2016). Observation of implied motion in a work of art modulates cortical connectivity and plasticity. *Journal of Exercise Rehabilitation, 12*(5), 417. doi: 10.12965/jer.1632656.328.

Cooper, L., Gonzalez, J., Gallo, J. J., Rost, K. M., Meredith, L. S., Rubensyein, L. V., . . . Ford, D. E. (2003). The acceptability of treatment for depression among African-American, Hispanic, and White primary care patients. *Medical Care, 41*(4), 479–489. doi: 10.1097/01.MLR.0000053228.58042.E4.

Dubois, B., Feldman, H. H., Jacova, C., DeKosky, S. T., Barberger-Gateau, P., Cummings, J., . . . Scheltens, P. (2007). Research criteria for the diagnosis of Alzheimer's disease:

Revising the NINCDS—ADRDA criteria. *The Lancet Neurology*, *6*(8), 734–746. doi: 10.1016/S1474-4422(07)70178-3.

Elferink, M.W. O., van Tilborg, I., & Kessels, R. P. (2015). Perception of emotions in mild cognitive impairment and Alzheimer's dementia: Does intensity matter? *Translational Neuroscience, 6*(1), 139–149. doi: 10.1515/tnsci-2015-0013.

Hass-Cohen, N., & Carr, R. (Eds.). (2008). *Art therapy and clinical neuroscience*. London, UK: Jessica Kingsley Publishers.

Hass-Cohen, N., & Clyde Findlay, J. (2015). *Art therapy and the neuroscience of relationships, creativity, and resiliency: Skills and practices*. New York, NY: W.W. Norton & Company.

Koelsch, S. (2015). Music-evoked emotions: Principles, brain correlates, and implications for therapy. *Annals of the New York Academy of Sciences, 1337*(1), 193–201. doi: 10.1111/nyas.12684.

Madori, L. (2007). *Therapeutic thematic arts programming for older adults*. Baltimore, MD: Health Professions Press.

Madori, L. L. (2009). Uses of therapeutic thematic arts programming (TTAP Method) for enhanced cognitive and psychosocial functioning in the geriatric population. *American Journal of Recreation Therapy*, *8*(1), 25–31.

Madori, L. L. (2012). *Transcending Dementia through the TTAP Method: A new psychology of art, brain and cognition*. Baltimore, MD: Health Professions Press.

Madori, L. L. (2013). Utilizing a thematic approach to art therapy with seniors: Enhancing cognitive abilities and social interactions. In P. Howie, S. Prasad, & J. Kristel (Eds.), *Using art therapy with diverse populations: Crossing cultures and abilities* (pp. 317–327). Philadelphia, PA: Jessica Kingsley Publishers.

Madori, L. L., & Alders, A. (2010). The effect of the TTAP Method on cognitive performance in Hispanic elderly. *Art Therapy: Journal of American Art Therapy Association, 3*, 1–18.

Madori, L. L., & Bendel, T. (2013). Research to practice: The TTAP Method® a new psychology of art, brain and cognition. *Alzheimer's & Dementia: The Journal of the Alzheimer's Association, 9*(4), P293. doi: 10.1016/j.jalz.2013.05.595.

Madori, L. L., Melville, L., Stickney, G., Padoto, D., & Rodriguez, J. (2016). Meditation and TTAP Method® with residents diagnosed with early stage Alzheimer's disease. *Journal of Alzheimer's Parkinsonism & Dementia, 1*(1), 1–6.

Mather, M. (2012). The emotion paradox in the aging brain. *Annals of the New York Academy of Sciences, 1251*(1), 33–49. doi: 10.1111/j.1749-6632.2012.06471.x.

McKinney, C. H., Antoni, M. H., Kumar, M., Tims, F. C., & McCabe, P. M. (1997). Effects of guided imagery and music (GIM) therapy on mood and cortisol in healthy adults. *Health Psychology, 16*(4), 390.

Miles, A. (2011). On the need for person-centered medicine. *International Journal of Person Centered Medicine, 1*(4), 1–10.

Miles, A., & Loughlin, M. (2011). Models in the balance: Evidence-based medicine versus evidence-informed individualised care. *Journal of Evaluation in Clinical Practice, 17*(4), 531–536. doi: 10.1111/j.1365-2753.2011.01713.x.

Plassman, B. L., Langa, K. M., Fisher, G. G., Heeringa, S. G., Weir, D. R., Ofstedal, M. B., . . . & Wallace, R. B. (2007). Prevalence of dementia in the United States: The aging, demographics, and memory study. *Neuroepidemiology, 29*(1–2), 125–132. doi: 10.1159/000109998.

Rentz, C. A. (2002). Memories in the Making: Outcome-based evaluation of an art program for individuals with dementing illnesses. *American Journal of Alzheimer's Disease & Other Dementias®, 17*(3), 175–181. doi: 10.1177/153331750201700310.

Ristau, S. (2011). People do need people: Social interaction boosts brain health in older age. *Generations*, *35*(2), 70–76.

Santos, G. D., Nunes, P.V., Stella, F., Brum, P. S.,Yassuda, M. S., Ueno, L. M., . . . Forlenza, O. V. (2015). Multidisciplinary rehabilitation program: Effects of a multimodal intervention for patients with Alzheimer's disease and cognitive impairment without dementia. *Archives of Clinical Psychiatry*, *42*(6), 153–156. doi: 10.1590/0101–60830000000066.

19 The Use of Clinical Assessments Within Medical Art Therapy

Identifying the Level of Emotional and Physical Symptoms

Deborah Elkis-Abuhoff and Morgan Gaydos

Introduction

Within the realm of medicine, clinical art therapy assessment can offer tangible evidence into the physical and emotional symptomology of a diagnosis. Art therapy assessment within the medical milieu takes on a different approach than typically found in mental health. An individual experiencing medical illness is often unable to fully express his or her thoughts, feelings, pain, and/or physical state within a diagnosis. This chapter will discuss how art therapy assessments can be utilized to tap into these areas, in addition to providing better insight into a medical patient's overall state.

A Brief Overview on Art Therapy Assessment

The origin of art therapy assessment is heavily rooted in the projective testing realm, with instruments such as the House-Tree-Person (HTP) test, Draw-A-Person (DAP) test, and the Thematic Apperception Test (TAT) (Betts, 2016). Through a psychoanalytic framework, it was believed that the use of projective-based art assessments could reveal inner conflicts to better articulate the psychological forces behind a patient's behavior (Gilroy, 2012). Although assessments such as the HTP, DAP, and TAT became benchmark instruments for assessing the mental and emotional processes of a patient, they relied on the symbolic interpretation of the therapist and suggested a need for stronger validity (Betts, 2016; Penzes, van Hooren, Dokter, Smeijsters, & Hutschemaekers, 2014). Furthermore, it was emphasized that art therapy assessments remain distinct psychological instruments used as a systematic way to identify important information needed to best treat the patient (Kapitan, 2017).

Art therapy assessments still possess psychodynamic interventions that are similar to psychological assessments; however, art assessments have

transformed from origin to offer a unique approach to gathering information on a patient. The incorporation of art materials, compared to pencil-and-paper methods, offer patients a sensory experience with their artwork and can provide an interpersonal connection within the assessment tool (Gilroy, 2012). Furthermore, patients can express their symptoms, emotions, and treatment needs through various artistic and formal elements through the use of materials.

Clinical art therapists have been working towards objective standardization methods in assessment and evaluation, incorporating evidenced-based knowledge on elements such as color, line quality, and line consistency (Goldblatt, Elkis-Abuhoff, Gaydos, Rose, & Casey, 2011; Kapitan, 2017). Assessments such as the Diagnostic Drawing Series (DDS) and Person Picking an Apple from a Tree (PPAT), in accordance with the Formal Elements Art Therapy Scale (FEATS), are examples of more objective standardized evaluations (Penzes, van Hooren, Dokter, Smeijsters, & Hutschemaekers, 2014); however, the majority of evidence-based research on these assessments lies within mental health, with few to no studies involving medically ill patients.

The Need for Assessments in Medical Art Therapy

The complex symptom management present within the realm of medical illness can make it difficult for clinicians to determine a patient's level of physical and emotional functioning through medical testing alone. The onset and progression of physical symptoms can hinder a patient's quality of life and lead to emotional distress, which can have a negative impact on the patient's ability to engage in necessary, and oftentimes invasive, treatment. The use of art therapy assessments can provide physicians with a noninvasive approach to broadening medical interventions and instilling a sense of comfort within treatment (Elkis-Abuhoff, Gaydos, Goldblatt, Rose, & Chen, 2009).

Art therapy assessments possess the ability to obtain diagnostic and symptomatic information, which can further aid the treatment team in determining both the patient's status and course of treatment (Gilroy, 2012). Research on the impact of art assessments within medicine, although lacking, have found that the use of drawings could depict both physical and emotional change in response to treatment (Elkis-Abuhoff et al., 2009; Thomas & Dufresne, 2014). Individuals with a medical illness have the opportunity to use art therapy assessment to highlight specific areas of the body affected by their diagnosis and/or treatment (Thomas & Dufresne, 2014), providing physicians with increased awareness into the overall state of patients.

The Use of Art Therapy Assessments Within the Medical Realm

The needs of the medically ill person brings to light a unique set of concerns related to physical challenges that target the body and mind connection. These include understanding the patient's perception of his or her own illness, and how he or she can express his or her inner concerns and physical understanding. Assessments targeted for the medically ill need to allow for freedom of visual expression, as well as the identification of conflicts that an illness inflicts on the body/mind and the strength a person may possess through hope and resilience. The following are three developing assessments that can assist the art therapist in evaluating the state of the patient both emotionally and physically.

Mandala Assessment with Those Diagnosed with Breast Cancer

Mandalas as an assessment tool with women diagnosed with breast cancer (Elkis-Abuhoff et al., 2009) incorporates the theoretical work of Susan Bach (1990), Elizabeth Kübler Ross (1981), and Bernie Siegel (1990), who all believed that drawings could help uncover specific physical and/or emotional states even prior to reported symptomology. Bach (1990) and Kübler-Ross (1981) both focused on spontaneous drawings, and evaluated colors, shapes, numbers, and motifs that they believed visually expressed the unconscious. In fact, Kübler-Ross (1981) believed that not only do these drawings unveil the physical and emotional state, but could even indicate of a person's position within their life span. The incorporation of the mandala, Sanskrit word for *circle* or *center*, has supported the visual journey of illness and recovery through providing a visual map for a person (Elkis-Abuhoff et al., 2009).

The focus of this study was to develop an assessment tool to monitor breast cancer patients in a noninvasive manner. The mandala, a circle, was chosen as a natural shape to mirror the breast, allowing the patient's drawing to give indication of the location and state of the illness. Through line quality, line usage, position of visual, shape, and color, the art therapist could extrapolate information that to give indication regarding the patient's present state. Based on the outcome, the art therapist could communicate to the physician the need to explore the patient's physical state.

The researchers observed the journey of breast cancer patients from diagnosis through treatment (surgery, chemotherapy, and/or radiation), collecting mandala drawings at each physician visit. After being brought into the treatment room, patients were given a mandala outline and a set of color-specific pencils (Bach 1990). Each patient was asked to *color in the circle*, and was given time to explore and create. The researchers hypothesized that "patients diagnosed with breast cancer will depict a correlation between physical state and mandala drawings" (p. 233), as assessed through their developed assessment tool (Elkis-Abuhoff et al., 2009) (Appendix 19.A).

Approximately 6 months later, each patient's medical chart was reviewed for information related to present diagnosis and whether the patient's physical state coincided with the created mandala drawings. The results supported that the created mandala drawings could give indication of physical state as documented in the patient's medical chart. Figure 19.1 depicts an example of created mandalas assessed as healthy with physically positive outcomes.

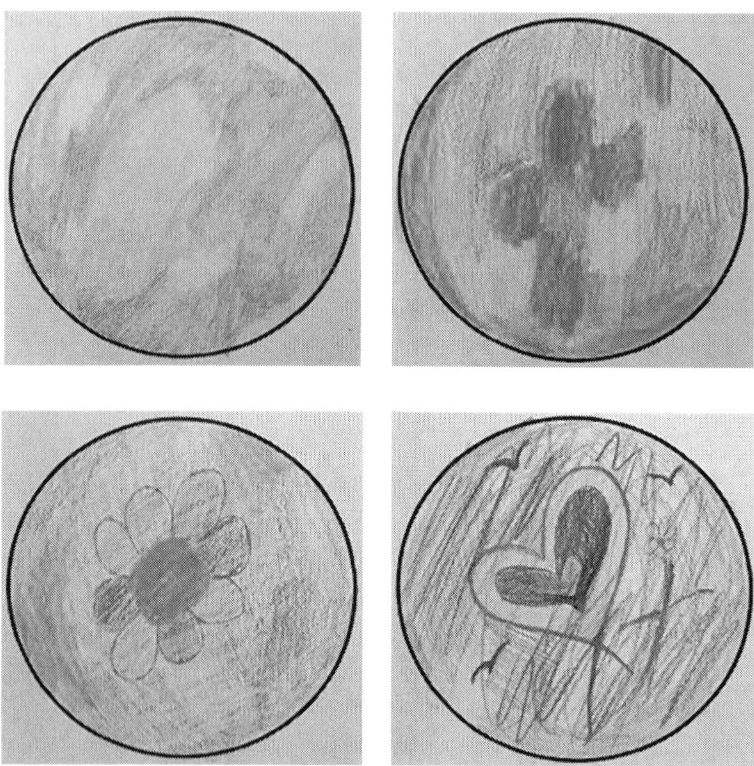

Figure 19.1 Example of Mandalas Created by a Participant Assessed as Healthy with a Positive Outcome

Source: Elkis-Abuhoff et al., 2009

Although newly developed, this assessment could bring insights into a patient's medical treatment. Many times words are not available, or medical tests are inconclusive; the artwork created through this mandala assessment could help speak for the patient, and his or her body.

Assessing Conflict Within the Body Through Cooper's Conflict Ladder

Upon receiving a medical diagnosis, a person is faced with a sense of conflict. Conflict, in this regard, can be described as an escalating or deescalating concept of opposing forces within an individual's needs, emotions, and/or principals (Goldblatt et al., 2011). Within medical illness, the body becomes the adversary, and the person must face this conflict in order to come to terms with the diagnosis—and the new 'normal.'

Conflict within a medical diagnosis can be dealt with in a way that allows the individual to engage in personal growth and reflection; however, negative coping skills or avoidant behavior can contribute to increased emotional stressors and maladaptive behaviors that can be detrimental to the individual's experiences and environment (Paletz, Miron-Spektor, & Lin, 2014). By addressing conflicts within a medical diagnosis an individual can be given the opportunity to face confrontation and regain a sense of inner peace through creative expression (Goldblatt et al., 2011; Landgarten, 2013).

Art therapy within medicine has strived to promote insight into an individual's inner thoughts, emotions, and experiences in the midst of conflicts that arise due to a diagnosis. The use of Cooper's Conflict Ladder (Goldblatt et al., 2011) could play a role in gaining insights into the personal and internal struggle that a medical diagnosis creates. The 14-rung ladder was developed by Alan K. Cooper, self-taught philosopher and social scientist. Although Cooper based his observations on interpersonal interactions, his concept can be applied to the emotional and physical relationship within a medically ill person.

The approach describes conflict as a 14-rung ladder; conflict rises from the bottom, where there is no conflict, and gradually escalates to moderate, and finally severe (Appendix 19.B). To aid the clinician in assessing the level of conflict, as well as the appropriate approach necessary to diminish the conflict, Cooper described and titled each rung on the ladder. The goal, as identified by Cooper, is to assist the individual in minimizing the effects of perceived conflict. Rungs 0 to 6 of Cooper's Conflict Ladder comprise unconscious and involuntary responses that are outside of the person's awareness. Line drawings completed by patients during the first seven rungs depicted more free-flowing, curved, and squiggled lines. The higher rungs of the ladder, 7 to 13 are conscious and voluntary to the individual and identify a more severe level of conflict. Line drawings completed by individuals during these levels depicted more sporadic, jagged, pointed, and pressured lines. Using Cooper's Conflict Ladder, Goldblatt, Elkis-Abuhoff, Gaydos, Rose, and Casey (2011) asked college students to "remember a time in your life when you were involved in either a positive or negative relationship with a person or institution. Please create a line drawing using your marker to illustrate this relationship" (p. 106) (Figure 19.2).

As an assessment tool, it is important to note that a person may jump, accelerate, or simply skip rungs. Within a medical diagnosis, any sudden change in symptomology can greatly affect both an individual's level of functioning and quality of life. The definition of an individual's level of conflict is a reflection of the person's thoughts, feelings, and behaviors, which in most cases become compromised when experiencing severe conflict. With Cooper's Conflict Ladder, the goal of the clinician is to use line drawings to identify the severity of conflict, and then determine

Figures 19.2 Example of a Low-conflict Line Drawing (a) and a High-conflict Line Drawing (b)

Source: Goldblatt et al., 2011

the appropriate treatment intervention to reduce the negative feelings, thoughts, or behaviors regarding the conflict. Specifically within medical illness, it is important to always move in the direction of peace, or decrease conflict, when both undergoing treatment and coping with progressive symptoms.

Hope Scale and Draw a Person in the Rain (DAPR)

Hope is an important aspect related to body–mind connection. It has been shown that having hope allows for the development of multiple routes to achieving goals, increased optimism, improved sense of control, positive affect, enhanced self-esteem, and positive goal expectations (Snyder, 1994). Hope, through the Draw a Person in the Rain (DAPR) assessment, has been administered to medical students to identify how stress is visually expressed within the standardized DAPR (Rose, Elkis-Abuhoff, Goldblatt, & Miller, 2012). Each participant's drawing was evaluated through the developed DARP Scoring System of Hope (Appendix 19.C) and compared to the standardized Dispositional Hope Scale (DHS) (Rose et al., 2012). The findings support that the projective assessment of the DAPR, when properly evaluated, could identify indicators of hope as defined by the DHS (Figures 19.3a and 19.3b) (Snyder et al., 1991). Figure 19.3a shows high hope and Figure 19.3b shows low hope of the DAPR assessed outcome.

In support of the use of the DAPR with the DARP Scoring System of Hope, clinicians can identify levels of hope within the medically ill patient in a time-efficient and noninvasive manner. A positive attitude related to hope plays a major role in the perception of illness (Krause & Edles, 2014). By asking the patient to *draw a person in the rain*, the patient is able to communicate feelings through visual expression. The projective drawing

Figures 19.3 Example of High Hope (a) and Low Hope (b) DAPR

Source: Rose et al., 2012

and evaluation system alleviates the need for the patient to find words, especially when experiencing difficulty within illness. This allows the art therapist to address strengthening the patient's level of hope related to the illness, which, in turn, could lead to increased coping and quality of life.

Conclusion

It is important to support medically ill patients throughout their journey from diagnosis through treatment. The inclusion of a noninvasive means of monitoring patients both physically and emotionally could bring insight to assist the art therapist in supporting the patient to process, incorporate coping skills, and create a new 'normal.' The three assessments highlighted in this chapter all allow the art therapist to gain a glimpse into the strengths and needs of the medically ill patient.

References

Bach, S. (1990). *Life paints its own span: On the significance of spontaneous pictures by severely ill children*. Einsiedeln, Switzerland: Daimon Verlag.

Betts, D. (2016). Art therapy assessments: An overview. In D. E. Gussak & M. L. Rosal (Eds.), *The Wiley handbook of art therapy* (pp. 501–513). Malden, MA: John Wiley & Sons.

Elkis-Abuhoff, D., Gaydos, M., Goldblatt, R., Rose, S., & Chen, M. (2009). Mandala drawings as an assessment tool for women with breast cancer. *The Arts in Psychotherapy, 36*(4), 231–238. doi: 10.1016/j.aip.2009.04.004.

Gilroy, A. (2012). What's best for whom? Exploring the evidence base for assessment in art therapy. In A. Gilroy, R. Tipple, & C. Brown (Eds.), *Assessment in art therapy* (pp. 11–27). New York, NY: Routledge.

Goldblatt, R., Elkis-Abuhoff, D., Gaydos, M., Rose, S., & Casey, S. (2011). Unlocking conflict through creative expression. *The Arts in Psychotherapy, 38*(2), 104–108. doi: 10.1016/j.aip.2010.12.006.

Kapitan, L. (2017). *Introduction to art therapy research*. New York, NY: Routledge.

Krause, J. S., & Edles, P. A. (2014). Injury perceptions, hope for recovery, and psychological status after spinal cord injury. *Rehabilitation Psychology, 59*(2), 176–182. doi: org.ezproxy.hofstra.edu/10.1037/a0035778.

Kübler-Ross, E. (1980). *Living with death and dying: How to communicate with the terminally ill*. New York, NY: Macmillan Publishing Co., Inc.

Landgarten, H. B. (2013). *Clinical art therapy: A comprehensive guide*. New York, NY: Routledge.

Paletz, S. B., Miron-Spektor, E., & Lin, C. C. (2014). A cultural lens on interpersonal conflict and creativity in multicultural environments. *Psychology of Aesthetics, Creativity, and the Arts, 8*(2), 237–252. doi: 10.1037/a0035927.

Pénzes, I., van Hooren, S., Dokter, D., Smeijsters, H., & Hutschemaekers, G. (2014). Material interaction in art therapy assessment. *The Arts in Psychotherapy, 41*(5), 484–492. doi: 10.1016/j.aip.2014.08.003.

Rose, S., Elkis-Abuhoff, D., Goldblatt, R., & Miller, E. (2012). Hope against the rain: Investigating the psychometric overlap between an objective and projective measure of hope in a medical student sample. *The Arts in Psychotherapy, 39*(4), 272–278. doi: 10.1016/j.aip.2012.04.003.

Siegel, B. (1990). *Peace, love and healing: Body mind communication and the path to self-healing: An exploration*. New York, NY: Harper and Row, Publishers.

Snyder, C. R. (1994). Hope and optimism. In V. S. Ramachandran (Ed.), *Encyclopedia of human behavior* (pp. 535–542). Orlando, FL: Academic Press.

Snyder, C. R., Harris, C., Anderson, J. R., Holleran, S. A. Irving, L. M., Sigmon, S. T., . . . Harney, P. (1991). The will and the ways: Development and validation of an individual-differences measures of hope. *Journal of Personality and Social Psychology, 60*, 570–585. doi: 10.1037/0022-3514.60.4.570.

Thomas, A. D., & Dufresne, D. (2014). The influence of osteopathic treatment on children's drawings. In L. Handler & A. D. Thomas (Eds.), *Drawings in assessment and psychotherapy: Research and application* (pp. 95–106). New York, NY: Routledge.

Appendix 19.A

Mandala Assessment Tool

Mandala Drawings as an Assessment Tool for Women with Breast Cancer

Mandala Assessment

1) What are the predominant color(s) used in this artwork? Please check:

CATEGORY I	CATEGORY II	CATEGORY III
Light Green _______	Red _________	Dark Green ________
Light Brown_______	Orange_______	Dark Brown________
Mauve ___________	Black ________	Dark Blue _________
Light Blue ________	Gray _________	Deep Yellow ______
Pale Yellow _______	White ________	
Violet ___________		

If any color(s) is/are checked off in Category II would you perceive the color's usage in a positive or negative manner?

Negative ___________ Undefined __________ Positive ___________

2) Please indicate the amount of color(s) used by participant. Circle the appropriate number

1 2 3 4 5 6 7 8 9 10 11 12 13 14 15

Below please circle the appropriate answer for each question:

3) How would you describe the line quality in the artwork?

1	2	3	4	5
Extremely Light	Light	Medium	Heavy	Extremely Heavy

4) How would you describe the consistency of the line usage in the artwork?

1	2	3	4	5
Curved	Slightly Curved	Mixed Representation	Slightly Jagged	Jagged

5) How would you rate the use of drawing space?

20% 40% 60% 80% 100%

6) Where is the artwork located within the circle?

1	2	3	4	5
Lower Left	Upper Left	Upper Right	Lower Right	Entire Page

7) Where is the focal point of the artwork located within the circle?

1	2	3	4	5
Lower Left	Upper Left	Upper Right	Lower Right	Entire Page

8) Is the artwork appropriate in fitting into the directive "Color in the entire circle?" Yes_____ No_____

9) What is your overall impression of the artwork? Healthy_______ Unhealthy______

Appendix 19.B

Cooper's Conflict Ladder

Cooper's Conflict Ladder

- ⋆ Rungs 0–7 are usually unconscious, but could be brought to an individual's attention.

  0—Zero Level Conflict—("Peace")
  1—Disagreement—("The Mask")
  2—Hostility—(The Twitch or Nonverbal Flick)
  3—Dissent—Movement Back—("Increase Distance")
  4 —Confrontation—Verbal Words—("What are you so upset about?")
  5—Debate—("Compromise or Not")
  6—Disobedience—("NO")
  7—Games—("Negotiation")

- ⋆ Rungs 7–13 are usually conscious and voluntary.

  8—Flight—Quit—("Flees") Drugs and alcohol are usually at this stage.
  9—Fight—Bodily Harm—("Invasion of Life Space")
  10—War—("Mobilize the Community")
  11—Coup d'état—("Overthrow of Property")
  12—Rebellion—(Riot "Destruction of Property")
  13—Kill—("Out for Blood")

Appendix 19.C

DAPR Scoring System for Hope

DAPR Scoring System for Hope

Variable 1

Relevant Essential Details: Body Characteristics

Descriptions: These are the primary or basic body characteristics. The absolute minimum features needed to identify the figure as that of a human being. The person must have: a head, trunk, two legs, two arms, hands and feet—unless the position is such that only one of each can be seen. For facial characteristics the major ones are: eyes, nose, mouth, and ears. If the head is turned and only one ear or eye is shown, then reassume that is a symmetrically in the figure. If the figure drawn shows a back view and there are indications of a well-integrated human figure, then credit is given for the major features but at somewhat lower level.

Scoring:

5 = ALL major details listed above are present.
4 = ALL major details but back turned and we can assume facial characteristics of drawings are well integrated.
3 = One major characteristic is missing.
2 = Two major characteristics are missing.
1 = More than two major characteristics are missing.

Variable 2

Essential Details: Secondary Characteristics

Descriptions: These are the secondary basic details that enrich and complete the drawing. Included here are articles of clothing (i.e., hat, rain jacket, boots, shirt, pants, and umbrella).

Scoring:

5 = Four or more details
4 = Three details
3 = Two details
2 = One details
1 = No details

Variable 3

Relevant Details: Environmental Characteristics

Descriptions: This category refers to objects and aspects of the environment in close proximity to the drawn figure. Some major examples are puddles, rain, sun, clouds, and lightening.

Scoring:

5 = Four or more details
4 = Three details
3 = Two details
2 = One details
1 = No details

Variable 4

Essential Details: Environmental Characteristics

Descriptions: This category refers to objects and aspects of the environment that are not in close proximity to the drawn figure. Examples include mountains, skyline, horizon scene, distant trees, airplanes, birds, etc.

Scoring:

5 = Four or more details
4 = Three details
3 = Two details
2 = One details
1 = No details

Variable 5

Body Proportion

Descriptions: This refers to proportions of the major body characteristics, such as head to trunk, legs to trunk, etc.

Scoring:

5 = Highly rated for proportion
4 = Moderately high
3 = Moderate
2 = Moderately poor
1 = Very poor

Variable 6

Dimensionality of Body

Descriptions: This refers to the portrayal of the dimensions of length and width in the figure (i.e., figure vs. full figure including elaboration of musculature and facial features).

Scoring:

5 = Very high elaboration
4 = Moderately high elaboration
3 = Moderate degree of elaboration
2 = Moderately poor elaboration
1 = Very poor elaboration

Variable 7

Perspective of the Spatial Relationship—Success

Descriptions: The spatial relationship of the figures and objects on the page.

Scoring:

5 = Quadrant #5
4 = Quadrant #4
3 = Quadrant #3
2 = Quadrant #2
1 = Quadrant #1

Variable 8

Perspective of the Geometric Placement—Success

Descriptions: Objects on the page in terms of their relationship to each other and to the geometric midpoint of the page.

Scoring:

5 = Placement C
4 = Placement D
3 = Placement B
2 = Placement E
1 = Placement A

Variable 9

Rain in the Environment

Descriptions: This category refers to boldness and darkness of the strokes to produce effects of rain.

Scoring:

5 = Very high degree of stokes, lines, dots—usually associated with heavy strokes 80%
4 = Moderately high degree of stokes 60%
3 = Moderate degree of stokes 40%
2 = Minimal amount of stokes—quick, light stokes, dots 20%
1 = Few or no marks or portrayal 0%

Variable 10

Movement of the Human Figure

Descriptions: This category refers to the amount of movement of the change of position in the major human figure.

Scoring:

5 = Very high degree of movement or change (i.e., running)
4 = Moderately high degree of movement (i.e., walking fast)
3 = Moderate degree of movement (i.e., walking slowly)
2 = Slight movement (i.e., tilting, bending, or swaying of body)
1 = No movement (i.e., standing straight, rigid body position)

Variable 11

Constriction of Drawing—Problem Solving

Descriptions: This category refers to the degree to which the subject has utilized the entire space of the page for his or her drawing.

Scoring:

5 = 80% or more of the page has been used
4 = 60% of the page has been used (approx.)
3 = 40% of the page has been used
2 = 20% of the page has been used
1 = Less than 20% of the page has been used

Variable 12

Indications of Hope

Descriptions: This category refers to aspects of the human figure or the environment that are indicative of hope. Includes evidence of facial expression (i.e., smile), loose posture, laughing, happiness, feeling of satisfaction portrayed in the figure, pleasant environment, unconcerned, sun etc.

Scoring:

5 = Very high degree of hope
4 = Quite high degree of hope
3 = Moderate degree of hope
2 = Slight degree of hope
1 = Minimal indication of Hope

Variable 13

Indications of Depression

Descriptions: This category refers to signs in the environment or in the major drawn figure of sadness, depression, pessimism, etc. A high degree of depression would be indicated by a downcast figure, extreme sadness in the face, bleak scene, heavy dark clouds, etc.

Scoring:

5 = Minimal indication of depression
4 = Moderate degree of satisfaction or happiness
3 = Neutral degree of satisfaction
2 = Moderate degree of depression
1 = High degree of depression

Variable 14

Indications of Realism of Drawing—Hope

Descriptions: This category refers to the degree to which the drawing as a whole indicates a realistic portrayal of a scene or a figure, or on the other hand, the extent to which it is distorted or highly bizarre, pathological.

Scoring:

5 = Highly realistic
4 = Moderately realistic
3 = Somewhat realistic
2 = Somewhat unrealistic
1 = Highly unrealistic

The Following Categories Are Scored Either Present or Absent

Variable 15

Drawing of Page Margins

Descriptions: Refers to the amputation of a part of the figure by one or more of the page margins.

Score: **1** = Present **0** = Absent

Variable 16

Paper Chopping

Descriptions: The figure or scene touches the top of the page and does not appear to extend beyond it.

Score: **1** = Present **0** = Absent

Variable 17

Paper Siding—Using Margins of Some Kind

Descriptions: Refers to one part or more of the whole extended to the page's lateral margin, but apparently does not extend beyond it.

Score: **1** = Present **0** = Absent

Variable 18

Paper Basing

Descriptions: Refers to the bottom margin of the paper being used as the baseline of the whole.

Score: **1** = Present **0** = Absent

Variable 19

Transparency

Descriptions: Refers to the occurrence of some object ordinarily being covered by something still being visible.

Score: **1** = Present **0** = Absent

Variable 20

Baseline

Descriptions: Is there an indication of a drawn baseline/grounding?

Score: **1** = Present **0** = Absent

20 Culturally Responsive Care for Art Therapists in Medical Settings

Yasmine J. Awais and Mariya Keselman

Art therapy within medical settings requires unique considerations to fully address the treatment needs of diverse patients. This chapter provides the frameworks of cultural humility and structural competency to work with patients who are medically ill to address structural racism in medical settings. These concepts go beyond the awareness of self and others to address the systems of inequality that impact the individuals we serve. While this chapter speaks specifically to art therapists, we intend for this chapter to be useful for expressive therapists and creative arts therapists from other fields of practice and disciplines.

Medical Art Therapy

Commonly understood as "the use of art expression and imagery with individuals who are physically ill, experiencing trauma to the body or who are undergoing aggressive medical treatment such as surgery or chemotherapy," the observed benefits of arts in medicine dates back to 1945 when British artist Adrian Hill claimed its benefit for patients being treated for tuberculosis (Malchiodi, 1999, p. 13). Since then, medical art therapists have worked to consider psychosocial implications of an illness to best support patients receiving treatment.

It is recommended that medical art therapists be aware of patient's physical abilities, limitations, and possible somatic differences while facilitating the client's process of using art media for self-expression (Councill, 2012). The main stressors for pediatric patients are being away from primary caregivers, feelings of helplessness, lack of independence, and fear regarding medical procedures and possibility of death (Malchiodi, 1999). Due to advancements made in healthcare, babies born with chronic illness in industrialized countries live longer than ever and an increased life expectancy requires greater knowledge of adolescents with medical concerns (Luginbuehl-Oelhafen, 2009).

Unlike younger children for whom family members have more involved and decisive roles in treatment, adolescents are encouraged to be active participants when deciding on matters related to their treatment plan

(Luginbuehl-Oelhafen, 2009). Art therapy can be an appropriate intervention as the emotions that arise may be difficult for adolescents to express verbally (Luginbuehl-Oelhafen, 2009). Art can offer adolescents a sense of autonomy, and an opportunity to express their own truth while simultaneously gaining self-awareness, allowing for positive verbal and nonverbal expression, identity development and self-esteem, and coping tools.

Similarly to children and adolescents, adults can gain support with coping and rehabilitation through participation in art therapy (Malchiodi, 1999). Carr (2014) considered that art therapy for adults who are medically ill struggle with losing one's sense of self, which, in turn, can lead to loss of ability to cope. Medical art therapy can provide adult patients with a sense of empowerment and control, which can be lost at the onset of an illness (Carr, 2014).

Understanding and Acknowledging Culture

Improvements made in medicine when treating patients cross-culturally (Metzl & Hansen, 2014) promote an emphasis to address patient's language, spiritual and religious beliefs, dietary, ethnic, and psychosocial needs in treatment (Joint Commission on Accreditation of Healthcare Organizations [JCAHO], 2010). Professional organizations in healthcare and social service professions have included cultural competency as part of their educational curriculum, standards of care, and ethics (see Fisher-Borne, Cain, & Martin, 2015), including those of art therapy (American Art Therapy Association [AATA], 2011; Art Therapy Credentials Board [ATCB], 2016).

Cultural competence is the awareness of the counselor's own assumptions and biases, actions needed to understand worldviews of diverse clients, and active measures essential for ensuring culturally appropriate practices, which are understood as ongoing and aspirational, not attainable, as it is impossible to be knowledgeable about every culture and experience (Sue & Sue, 2016). Art therapist Doby-Copeland (2013) discussed cultural proficiency similarly as an endeavor that requires self-awareness, including the recognition of one's privilege, oppression, and own limitations, and awareness of external matters such as social systems and inequalities. In other words, cultural competence is enacted through the actions, attitudes, and policies that allow professionals "to work effectively in cross-cultural situations both in prevention and treatment contexts" (Giannet, 2003, p. 118).

Cultural Humility

The concept of competence, however, has led to the misconception that learning about cultures equates to having mastery of clients' cultural experiences (see critiques by Furlong & Wight, 2011; Gregg & Saha, 2006; Tervalon & Murray-García, 1998). While agreement on cultural humility as a replacement (Fisher-Borne et al., 2015) or enhancement (Prasad et al., 2016) of cultural competence is lacking, there is consensus that cultural humility proposes a view that is fluid, evolving, and addresses and challenges inequalities on individual and organizational levels (Tervalon & Murray-García, 1998). This involves taking into account the power differentials that exist on macro and micro levels (Chang, Simon, & Dong, 2012; Fisher-Borne et al., 2015; Foronda, Baptiste, Reinholdt, & Ousman, 2016).

Medical professionals who practice cultural humility allowed for better relationships with patients and resulted in better health prognosis for those patients (Chang et al., 2012). Juarez et al. (2006) found that inclusion of cultural humility into medical curriculum led to greater patient involvement in care and attention to care for medical students. In the therapeutic relationship, cultural humility was considered to be important when working with clients who experienced marginalization, increasing the possibility that clients would continue treatment, resulting in positive therapeutic alliances and the way clients viewed their progress in therapy (Sue & Sue, 2016). Similarly, Hook, Davis, Owens, Worthington, and Utsey (2013) found that clients who perceived their counselor to have greater cultural humility reported fewer experiences of macroaggressions in the counseling setting.

Power and Structure

Structural racism is defined as "the totality of ways in which societies foster racial discrimination through mutually reinforcing systems of housing, education, employment, earnings, benefits, credit, media, healthcare, and criminal justice," which are factors that promote equity in healthcare (Bailey et al., p. 1453).

Metzl, Petty, and Oluwantuse (2017) state, "structural competency emphasizes diagnostic recognition of the economic and political conditions that produce health inequalities in the first place" (p. 190). Thus, structural competence asks practitioners to strive for collective responsibility and advocacy. To acknowledge structural racism inherent in medical settings structural competency was offered as an approach, a movement, and a framework in health care (Ali & Sichel, 2014; Hansen & Metzl, 2016). Metzl and Hansen (2014) propose five steps to achieve structural competency: understanding political and societal structures' impact on clinical care and healthcare decisions; building on clinical language to include knowledge of structures that impact treatment of individuals served; integrating cultural learning with structural learning; recognizing that structures are contextual and a reflection of that particular moment; and developing the practice of structural humility, which includes recognition of the limitations of practitioner's knowledge and an openness to learning from patients. This last point does not necessarily mean asking clients to teach therapists about their culture, but an openness to consider a shift in hierarchy of who holds the knowledge.

Incorporating Culture into Practice

Issues of diversity and cultural humility have increasingly been raised in medicine. With the critique of the ways in which culture and cultural competence are defined, including the lack of consideration of privilege and social positioning, scholars in medicine are advocating for deeper understanding of practice with diverse populations (Kumaş-Tan, Beagan, Loppie, MacLeod, & Frank, 2007). The current political and social conditions and injustices further signify the importance of incorporating cultural humility with consideration of structural competence when working with marginalized populations (Foronda et al., 2016; Hays, 2008; Prasad et al., 2016).

Talwar (2010), an art therapist, stressed the importance of utilizing the framework of intersectionality in the field of art therapy. However, this has not been explicitly considered for medical settings, which add an additional dimension. As noted in the critiques in medicine mentioned earlier, cultural identities and psychosocial needs and challenges have not been well integrated into the medical model. While the focus on physical illness is of course necessary, the lack of attention to the identities of patients may result in increased psychological stress, impacting their physical and mental well-being (Councill & Tedeschi, 2016; Taylor, 2003).

Multiculturalism and diversity have been areas of discussion in the field of art therapy and, most recently, issues have been raised as to who is authorized to advocate for the profession through scholarly discourse (see Kaiser, 2017; Talwar, 2017). Coursework specific to multiculturalism was integrated into art therapy graduate programs in 1994, following the revision of AATA's Educational Standards (Potash et al., 2015). Art therapists committed to the issue of multiculturalism propose ways in which individuals in the field of art therapy can build a more culturally sensitive practice through engaging in multicultural work on individual and collective levels. Calish (2003) has reiterated that the primary steps in cultural sensitivity for art therapists are self-reflexivity (being aware of one's own views and biases) and ethnorelativity (involving analysis of relational hierarchies, privileges and oppressions and, most important, relational thinking). These are important considerations, as minorities are less likely to seek services from mental health clinicians, and that providing services that are culturally sensitive can result in the increase of use of services (Awais & Yali, 2015; Gipson, 2015).

Gerity (2000) discussed ways for art therapists to embrace diversity and exploration of the client's cultural heritage in their practice as opposed to encouraging assimilation as a healing mechanism and a way to bypass cultural differences. She observed the need expressed by individuals receiving services (and further reinforced by service providers) to assimilate into the dominant culture, pushing aside their cultural and mental health histories (Gerity, 2000). Patients wanted to be just like their white counselors, who they perceived as healthy; therefore, equating being white to being healthy

(Gerity, 2000). Gerity proposed that there should be greater respect for client's inner world and desires as opposed to external demands (2000). A push for assimilation may cause denial of this inner world. Contrary to this, appreciation for multiculturalism and individual differences, can lead to better health (Gerity, 2000).

Power dynamics impact therapist's perception and value orientations and can be a source of conflict and disempowerment when interacting with persons presenting with conflicting perceptions. Ways to mitigate such misconceptions include acknowledging and collaborating on differences (Freeman & Lobovits, 1993; Malchiodi, 1999) and developing efforts through creating a conarrative and bringing into session multiple subjective perspectives in an exploratory, rather than judgmental, fashion (Gerity, 2000, p. 205). This has been preferred over ignoring the conflict as integrating art therapy with an egalitarian therapeutic relationship can result in transformation, healing and strength (Gerity, 2000).

Art therapists working with diverse populations require research on culturally appropriate art therapy interventions, particularly in medical art therapy. Yet we do not understand how cultural humility is promoted by medical art therapists, which would be beneficial before medical art therapy interventions are suggested. As a way to address this gap, we conducted a study that aimed to better understand how medical art therapists employ cultural humility (Keselman & Awais, manuscript accepted). Our study highlighted the relevance of multicultural considerations in medical settings and the lack of formalized training for medical art therapists.

Medical Art Therapy Interventions

When developing or adapting existing interventions in medical art therapy, we recommend that art therapists consider the patient's medical condition, developmental level, and psychosocial needs in relation to treatment goals (Awais, 2013; Malchiodi, 1999). Interventions can focus on goals involving healthy coping strategies, feelings of control and empowerment (Malchiodi, 1999), and the medical condition itself. Although art therapists working in medical settings reinforce the importance of culture on development of art therapy interventions (Councill, 2012; Malchiodi, 1999), there is lack in the literature on the development of culturally sensitive interventions.

The use of adaptive equipment, such as devices that allow patients to hold paintbrushes, to completely forgoing how media is traditionally employed (e.g., painting with wheelchairs or blowing paint through a straw), has been used by both authors in their art therapy practice in medical settings. In addition to using typical materials such as paints, mixed media, mosaic, and yarn, art therapists in medical settings have employed medical tools such as tongue depressors and bandages. Material choice has been identified as vital when working across cultures (Prasad, 2013), which includes medical settings.

Suggestions for International Practice

When beginning an art therapy program internationally, it is necessary for art therapists who are viewed as 'outsiders' to get connected to the culture, cultural customs, and sometimes even community leaders of individuals with whom they are trying to work. Ottemiller and Awais (2016) offer a model for developing competent art therapy practice for community settings that may also be applicable to international work. Their model calls for common goals and outcomes, the importance of identifying inherent power differences, and the need for trust and relationship building. Suggestions to achieve these recommendations include partnering with participants to develop treatment goals, engaging in open and clear communication about each other's roles and limitations, and continued collaboration with participants throughout treatment (Ottemiller & Awais, 2016). Aspects of this model can be applied in creating a medical art therapy program in communities of which the art therapist is not considered a member.

It is arguable that art therapists who have engaged in work abroad become more immersed in the culture of people who are different from themselves. For the art therapist trained in America working abroad, it may be useful to adapt strategies that have been suggested when working in these communities. For example, in the first author's work in a rehabilitation hospital in Saudi Arabia, Awais (2013), an American art therapist, demonstrated the importance of utilizing art therapy with both the patients' and therapists' culture in mind. Nondirective interventions were influenced by the awareness of client's culture and of herself in relation to the culture. Through remaining open to clients' views, Awais worked across ethnic and gender boundaries to incorporate metaphors that were valued in collectivist cultures as well as in the field of art therapy (2013).

Envisioning Medical Art Therapists as Social Justice Advocates

As a subspecialty of art therapy, medical art therapy is impacted by conditions in both art therapy and medicine. Therefore, it acts as a microcosm of society and current political movements. As art therapists, the profession, our clients, and society benefit if we practice cultural humility, structural competence, and intersectionality. We are responsible for educating ourselves and practicing individual, cultural, and structural awareness, staying mindful of the impact of institutions and systems in which we operate on our clients and our practice.

Nadal (2017) has raised the need for a new paradigm in psychology, particularly around the view of political neutrality, which often conflicts with the ethical standpoint of minimizing harm for clients. This approach may also be useful for medical art therapists to consider. Akin to the concept of practitioner-scholar, Nadal proposes the psychologist-activist, as the balance between both roles needed to appropriately serve diverse populations (2017). On institutional levels, this includes holding intergroup dialogues and diversity trainings and responding to injustices. On individual level, this includes challenging societal inequalities, seeking to learn about other's experience from them, drawing from liberation psychology, inflicting social consciousness by using their position to challenge inequality, practicing self-awareness, teaching and learning, and realizing that this learning is a lifelong process (Nadal, 2017).

Patients seen in medical settings may experience disempowerment due to the intersections of their medical and social conditions and physical limitations. Medical art therapists can use the art process for empowerment, emancipation, and social action. Art materials and interventions can be chosen and practiced through the framework of cultural humility with structural competence, and applying feminist theory and intersectionality. In this way, medical art therapists can collaborate with patients to allow for a reclaiming of their voice through portraying themselves and experiences that may be difficult to put into words. Incorporating cultural humility into cross-cultural interactions with patients we serve allows for a stronger therapeutic alliance. Studies have shown that a strong therapeutic relationship increases the likelihood of patients seeking and continuing treatment (Bailey et al., 2017). Being mindful of the cultural background, multiple aspects of identity and current and past experiences of individuals we serve should guide our choices of materials to make them relevant and therapeutic to the client populations.

Medical art therapists can incorporate structural competency into their clinical practice by approaching it from the five angles suggested by Metzl and Hansen (2014). This can be achieved by keeping abreast of local and national policies that impact medical care. In accordance with structural competency, medical art therapy trainees and practitioners are encouraged to get involved on individual and institutional levels to create the changes necessary to ensure equity in healthcare. It is also possible for art therapists working with diverse populations to gain knowledge of their client's culture and develop culturally appropriate approaches in addition to utilizing Western-based methods (Calisch, 2003). Incorporating local art customs like calligraphy and textiles or imagery such as sea life or the desert may seem obvious; however, when art therapists are trained to employ assessments that are culturally bound (i.e., Draw a Person Picking an Apple from a Tree, or House-Tree-Person) these become processes that must be carefully considered.

We also suggest an intersectional framework for art therapists working in medical settings. Kuri (2017) argues that medical art therapists must be aware of how aspects of one's identity and lived experience impact their medical care and medical art therapy services. Furthermore, there is a responsibility to examine and confront institutions that result in further oppression and marginalization of our clients (Kuri, 2017), including when developing treatment interventions, is another step for medical art therapists.

Conclusion

In summary, multicultural considerations for medical art therapists include:

1. Practice cultural humility either in place of or in addition to cultural competence. Be dedicated to lifelong learning.
2. Avoid making generalizations. Utilize past knowledge, but remain open to individual's experience of his/her/their culture.
3. Be open to utilizing gatekeepers and culturally familiar objects and images as appropriate and as directed by patient.
4. Understand how power and structure are inherent and enacted in medical settings. Particularly, how hierarchy is enacted, such as prioritizing medical treatments and eliminating illnesses over psychosocial needs and how access to care is impacted by societal inequalities. Be active and consider social activism and justice as part the medical art therapist's role.
5. Consider utilizing the framework of intersectionality. Learn about individual patient's cultures, which include regional, religious, and familial norms and expectations. Explore how different aspects of their identities interact to inform their experiences in medical settings. Other viewpoints worth considering include how therapy (or speaking to strangers about personal matters) is viewed, and how the arts are viewed and utilized. Education is obtained by learning from all sources—formalized (e.g., trainings and books) and from patients and personal interactions with individuals and groups.

The above multicultural considerations, coupled with culturally responsive care, provides therapists with a heightened awareness on how to better treat culturally diverse patients within medical settings.

References

Ali, A., & Sichel, C. E. (2014). Structural competency as a framework for training in counseling psychology. *The Counseling Psychologist, 42*(7), 901–918. doi: 10.1177/0011000014550320.

American Art Therapy Association. (2011). *Art therapy multicultural/diversity competencies.* Retrieved from www.arttherapy.org/upload/multiculturalcompetencies2011.pdf.

Art Therapy Credentials Board. (2016). *Code of ethics, conduct, and disciplinary procedures* [PDF file]. Greensboro, NC: ATCB. Retrieved from www.atcb.org/resource/pdf/2016-ATCB-Code-of-Ethics-Conduct-DisciplinaryProcedures.pdf.

Awais, Y. J. (2013). Reframing identity: Art therapy in Saudi Arabia. In P. Howie, S. Prasad, & J. Kristel (Eds.), *Using art therapy with diverse populations: Crossing cultures and abilities* (pp. 267–276). London, UK: Jessica Kingsley Publishers.

Awais, Y. J., & Yali, A. M. (2015). Efforts in increasing racial and ethnic diversity in the field of art therapy. *Art Therapy: Journal of the American Art Therapy Association, 32*(3), 112–119. doi: 10.1080/07421656.2015.1060842.

Bailey, Z. D., Krieger, N., Agénor, M., Graves, J., Linos, N., & Bassett, M. T. (2017). Structural racism and health inequities in the USA: Evidence and interventions. *The Lancet, 389*(10077), 1453–1463. doi: 10.1016/S0140–6736(17)30569-X.

Calisch, A. (2003). Multicultural training in art therapy: Past, present, and future. *Art Therapy: Journal of the American Art Therapy Association, 20*(1), 11–15. doi: 10.1080/07421656.2003.10129632.

Carr, S. M. D. (2014). Revisioning self-identity: The role of portraits, neuroscience and the art therapist's 'third hand'. *International Journal of Art Therapy, 19*(2), 54–70. doi: 10.1080/17454832.2014.906476.

Chang, E. S., Simon, M., & Dong, X. (2012). Integrating cultural humility into health care professional education and training. *Advances in Health Sciences Education, 17*, 269–278. doi: 10.1007/sl0459-010-9264-1.

Councill, T. (2012). Medical art therapy with children. In C. A. Malchiodi (Ed.), *Handbook of art therapy* (2nd ed., pp. 222–240). New York, NY: Guilford Press.

Councill, T., & Tedeschi, K. (2016). *Culture, medicine and art therapy: Building a practice that works.* American Art Therapy Association Annual Conference Presentation, Personal recollection of T. Councill and K. Tedeschi, American Art Therapy Association, Baltimore, MD, USA.

Doby-Copeland, C. (2013). Practicing multiculturally competent art therapy. In P. Howie, S. Prasad, & J. Kristel (Eds.), *Using art therapy with diverse populations: Crossing cultures and abilities* (pp. 114–125). London, UK: Jessica Kingsley Publishers.

Fisher-Borne, M., Cain, J. M., & Martin, S. L. (2015). From mastery to accountability: Cultural humility as an alternative to cultural competence. *Social Work Education, 34*(2), 165–181. doi: 10.1080/02615479.2014.977244.

Foronda, C., Baptiste, D., Reinholdt, M. M., & Ousman, K. (2016). Cultural humility: A concept analysis. *Journal of Transcultural Nursing, 27*(3), 210–217. doi: 10.1177/1043659615592677.

Freeman, J., & Lobovits, D. (1993). The turtle with wings. In S. Friedman (Ed.), *The new language of change: Constructive collaboration in psychotherapy* (pp. 188–225). New York, NY: The Guilford Press.

Furlong, M., & Wight, J. (2011). Promoting "critical awareness" and critiquing "cultural competence": Towards disrupting received professional knowledges. *Australian Social Work, 64*(1), 38–54. doi: 10.1080/031207X.2010.537352.

Gerity, L. A. (2000). The subversive art therapist: Embracing cultural diversity in the art room. *Art Therapy: Journal of the American Art Therapy Association, 17*(3), 202–206. doi: 10.1080/07421656.2002.10129683.

Giannet, S. (2003). Cultural competence and professional psychology training: Creating the architecture for change. *Journal of Evolutionary Psychology, 24*(3–4), 117–128.

Gipson, L. R. (2015). Is cultural competence enough? Deepening social justice pedagogy in art therapy. *Art Therapy: Journal of the American Art Therapy Association, 32*(3), 142–145. doi: 10.1080/07421656.2015.1060835.

Gregg, J., & Saha, S. (2006). Losing culture on the way to competence: The use and misuse of culture in medical education. *Academic Medicine, 81*(6), 542–547.

Hansen, H., & Metzl, J. (2016). Structural competency in the US healthcare crisis: Putting social and policy interventions into clinical practice. *Journal of Bioethical Inquiry, 13*(2). doi: 10.1007/s11673–016–9719-z.

Hays, P. A. (2008). *Addressing cultural complexities in practice: Assessment, diagnosis, and therapy* (2nd ed.). Washington, DC: American Psychological Association. doi: 10.1037/11650–000.

Hook, J. N., Davis, D. E., Owen, J., Worthington, E. L., Jr., & Utsey, S. O. (2013). Cultural humility: Measuring openness to culturally diverse clients. *Journal of Counseling Psychology, 60*, 353–366. doi: 10.1037/a0032595.

Joint Commission on Accreditation of Healthcare Organizations [JCAHO]. (2010). *Cultural and linguistic care in area hospitals*. Retrieved from www.jointcommission.org/assets/1/18/FINAL_REPORT_MARCH_2010.pdf.

Juarez, J. A., Marvel, K., Brezinski, K. L., Glazner, C., Towbin, M. M., & Lawton, S. (2006). Bridging the gap: A curriculum to teach residents cultural humility. *Family Medicine, 38*, 97–102.

Kaiser, D. H. (2017). What do structural racism and oppression have to do with scholarship, research, and practice in art therapy? *Art Therapy: Journal of the American Art Therapy Association, 34*(4), 154–156. doi: 10.1080/07421656.2017.1420124.

Keselman, M., & Awais, Y. J. (2018). Exploration of cultural humility in medical art therapy: A multiple-case study. *Art Therapy*, 1–11.

Kumaş-Tan, Z., Beagan, B., Loppie, C., MacLeod, A., & Frank, B. (2007). Measures of cultural competence: Examining hidden assumptions. *Academic Medicine, 82*(6), 548–557. doi: 10.1097/ACM.0b013e3180555a2d.

Kuri, E. (2017). Towards an ethical application of intersectionality in art therapy. *Art Therapy: Journal of the American Art Therapy Association, 34*(3), 118–122. doi: 10.1080/07421656.2017.1358023.

Luginbuehl-Oelhafen, R. R. (2009). *Art therapy with chronic physically ill adolescents; Exploring the effectiveness of medical art therapy as a complementary treatment*. Portland, OR: Book News, Inc.

Malchiodi, C. A. (1999). *Medical art therapy with adults*. London, UK: Jessica Kingsley Publishers.

Metzl, J. M., & Hansen, H. (2014). Structural competency: Theorizing a new medical engagement with stigma and inequality. *Social Science & Medicine, 103*, 126–133. doi: 10.1016/j.socscimed.2013.06.032.

Metzl, J. M., Petty, J., & Oluwantuse, V. O. (2017). Using a structural competency framework to teach structural racism in pre-health education. *Social Science & Medicine, 199*, 189–201. doi: 10.1016/j.socscimed.2017.06.029.

Nadal, K. L. (2017). "Let's get in formation": On becoming a psychologist—Activist in the 21st century. *American Psychologist, 72*(9), 935–946. doi: 10.1037/amp0000212.

Ottemiller, D. D., & Awais, Y. J. (2016). A model for art therapists in community-based Practice. *Art Therapy: Journal of the American Art Therapy Association, 33*(3), 144–150. doi: 10.1080/07421656.2016.1199245.

Potash, J. S., Doby-Copeland, C., Stepney, S. A., Washington, B. N., Vance, L. D., Short, G. M., & Maat, M. B. (2015). Advancing multicultural and diversity competence in art therapy: American Art Therapy Association multicultural committee 1990–2015. *Art Therapy: Journal of the American Art Therapy Association, 32*(3), 146–150. doi: 10.1080/07421656.2015.1060837.

Prasad, S. (2013). The impact of culture and the setting on the use and choice of materials. In P. Howie, S. Prasad, & J. Kristel (Eds.), *Using art therapy with diverse populations: Crossing cultures and abilities* (pp. 76–84). Philadelphia, PA: Jessica Kingsley Publishers.

Prasad, S. J., Nair, P., Gadhvi, K., Barai, I., Danish, H. S., & Philip, A. B. (2016). Cultural humility: Treating the patient, not the illness. *Medical Education Online, 21*, 1–2. doi: 10.3402/meo.v21.30908.

Sue, D. W., & Sue, D. (2016). *Counseling the culturally diverse: Theory and practice* (7th ed.). Hoboken, NJ: John Wiley & Sons.

Talwar, S. (2010). An intersectional framework for race, class, gender, and sexuality in art therapy. *Art Therapy: Journal of American Art Therapy Association*, *27*(1), 11–17. doi: 10.1080/07421656.2010.10129567.

Talwar, S. (2017). Ethics, law, and cultural competence in art therapy. *Art Therapy: Journal of American Art Therapy Association*, *34*(3), 102. doi: 10.1080/07421656.2017.1358026.

Taylor, J. S. (2003). Confronting "culture" in medicine's "culture of no culture". *Academic Medicine*, *78*(6), 555–559. doi: 10.1097/00001888–200306000–00003.

Tervalon, M., & Murray-Garcia, J. (1998). Cultural humility versus cultural competence: A critical distinction in defining physician training outcomes in multicultural education. *Journal of Health Care for the Poor and Underserved*, *9*(2), 117–125.

21 Special Issues for the Art Therapist Working in a Medical Setting

Irene Rosner David

Introduction

This edited volume contains information on various applications of medical art therapy wherein my colleagues admirably describe many subspecialties. Each arena warrants particular attention, as clinical goals and interventions vary depending on the medical condition, etiology, diagnosis, prognosis, treatment, and age. The common thread among these arenas is existence with our patients on the precarious border of illness and health, life and death. Issues are tapped for clinicians who work in medical art therapy that are unlikely to be experienced by others in the field.

The constant confrontation with the finiteness of well-being is a dimension unlike any other. Surely countertransference, self-awareness, and the incumbent processing of emotions evoked are core to successful work and universal for all healthcare providers. However, the inevitability of physical and cognitive change is relentlessly apparent and must be regularly dealt with. We must process our emotions in response to our patients' losses while dealing with our own feelings of vulnerability. Moreover, the medical art therapist working with contagious patients must protect his or her physical health. This evokes feelings in response to real risk, adding a layer of personal emotion over responses to our patients' ordeals. Overall, the stage is set in the medical realm for exposure to myriad emotions.

The Healthcare Setting Is the Therapist's World

In any field, it is common for one to become a player in a particular environment—it is an encapsulated world alien to most, but perceived by participants as the norm. Deeply entrenched in a hospital or medical setting, the atmosphere of tending to illness and awareness of life on its edge becomes natural. On a practical level, the implementation of art therapy often means to be present for medical interventions and treatment, to negotiate between ventilators, respirators, pharmacologic pumps, and intravenous poles (David, 2015, p. 444). It is so familiar that such a therapist may be taken aback upon hearing from outsiders' comments such as *how can you handle that?* The question is likely to bring forth awareness to the medical art therapist as to how unusual it is to feel natural in the throes of such experiences and surroundings. My response has always been one of surprise, as the ongoing confrontation with impairment and illness actually serves to affirm life.

In the course of my career, I have worked with patients with severely disabling conditions and ominous disease prognoses, including those with paralysis, amputations, stroke, dementia, traumatic brain injury, cancer, HIV/AIDS, infectious disease, chronic and end-stage illness in palliative care, as well as those traumatized by world events such as 9/11. This has placed me in a variety of settings within the medical milieu from inpatient rehabilitation treatment rooms, acute care bedsides, and intensive care cubicles, to outpatient conference and clinic waiting rooms. Each is a realm unto itself and has called for modified styles in terms of the implementation of art therapy, awareness of patients' medical, psychological and cognitive issues, and related feeling evoked for the art therapist. Clinical elements and goals must be conceptualized within the particular domain so as to be viable for the patient (Rosner, 1982).

Moreover, there are unique features in caring for ourselves as we care for patients in the world of medicine. Paramount for a medical art therapist is the reality of human vulnerability to disability, disease, decline, and ultimately death. Hence, a therapist must be very self-aware as to one's capacity for sadness, exposure to reminders of the inevitable, attentive to feelings evoked and have opportunities to process them. Reflection upon the intimate experiences within the encapsulated world of medicine can transform into a personal world of well-being and enrichment.

Care to the Caregiver: Physical and Emotional

In addition to emotional vulnerability for the medical art therapist, there may be feelings related to risks of exposure to communicable disease, such as airborne infectious tuberculosis. This involves seeking education in order to understand the potency of disease entities and to ascertain guidelines for protected and safe patient contact. Medical patients may have conditions that warrant caregivers' use of protective garb such as gowns, gloves, or masks as barriers to the spread of infection. This donning of 'Personal Protective Equipment,' (United States Food & Drug Administration, 2018) may enter the realm of effective provision of care as the art therapist must compensate for appearing camouflaged, limited in expression, and perhaps inaccessible. The facial mask known as the 'Particulate N95 Respirator' must fit snuggly around the nose and mouth for proper filtration of airborne particles (United States Food & Drug Administration, 2017). The therapist should be aware that the patient may perceive this covering as guarding or distancing, which in reality it is. This makes for an unusual challenge in the effort to reach the patient in order to create a trusting therapeutic alliance conducive to art therapy (Conlon, 1995). There should be consideration of how the use of a protective shield may affect the therapeutic relationship, as well as initiation of compensatory techniques. One approach is to talk with the patient about the requirement to use the mask, in the hope he or she will still feel comfortable enough to engage despite it. It is also helpful to exaggerate one's facial expression, demeanor, gesture and body language so as to facilitate connection.

With proper training in the use of the respirator with a disease such as multidrug-resistant tuberculosis, generally one can administer treatment without concern. However, it would be prudent to consider the potential for contagion from patient to therapist if there are any personal health issues deeming the art therapist compromised, including discussion with one's physician or facility pulmonologists. Even with assurances regarding safety, there should be an exploration of feelings about working with infectious patients. In the early days of the AIDS epidemic, some caregivers feared for their health and refrained from taking care of patients. Being armed with up-to-date information is the most effective way to ameliorate anxiety, while remaining within the parameters of safety. I felt sufficiently assured by national guidelines, as well as my facility's medical leadership, that I was able to provide an active art therapy program without fear. However, if an art therapist harbors discomfort with any such patient, it would likely affect his or her presentation and could negatively impact the art therapy experience and preclude benefit for the participant.

There may also be reverse situations whereby the patient must be protected from the caregiver. Medical conditions such as immune suppression may cause heightened susceptibility to a caregivers' transmission of bacteria invoking contact precautions. This requires precautions such as wearing gowns and gloves (Centers for Disease Control and Prevention, 2016), eliciting the aforementioned challenges to readily forming a holding environment. Art materials should be pristine and new if possible, alternatively cleansed well. If there is any doubt with regard to materials, the input of a facility's epidemiologist could be sought. Also, the wearing of gloves may also compromise the art therapist's dexterity in managing art materials, something the art therapist must adjust for.

Medical art therapists need to consider the causes of impairment in order to understand patients' issues and artwork, as well as for understanding their own responses. There should be awareness of etiologies, ramifications, and psychological aspects of disease and disability. There may be loss of function, body parts, or the ability to think and reason due to illness, accident, or stroke. Deficits and ultimate decline may also be incurred by war disaster, blast injury, terrorist attack, or natural disaster. Disability and disease causation invariably conjure up clinicians' responses and emotions, which are to be confronted for effective job engagement and self-care. In medical art therapy one is regularly confronting risk and mortality, acutely aware of the reality of ill health, disability, and ultimate demise—major concepts to process in order to be professionally effective.

This poses risk to emotional well-being and an ongoing need to understand the feelings evoked. Hence, caregivers working with seriously compromised patients must be mindful of the need to take care of oneself in deliberate ways, lest they succumb to feeling emotionally frayed and exhausted. Striving for a balance between relentless nurturance toward those in our care and meaningful personal activity will lead to sufficient gratification and compassion satisfaction (Kearney, Weininger, Vachon, Harrison, & Mount, 2009). The feeling of enrichment versus depletion is reflected in a similar continuum whereby our patients progress toward reclaiming mastery instead of relinquishing the self and remaining victimized. As described by Wright (1960), people facing life-altering physical changes can be understood on a disability continuum of "coping versus succumbing" (p. 59). Medical art therapy invites the expression of the changed self and fortifies self-worth toward integrating the new reality. Thus, medical art therapists guide patients toward expression of their ordeals, ultimately contributing to enhanced coping and quality of remaining life; the art therapist, too, achieves gratification having guided the patient toward integrating the new realities.

Stretching the Boundaries

In medical art therapy, gratification is attained in the integration of a patient's disabilities, diseases, diagnoses, prognoses, procedures, and treatments. A core dimension is to contribute to enhanced coping abilities with their ordeals. The reward is in having provided an avenue toward expression and reclaiming quality of life despite what is gone.

Like art therapists working in other populations, medical art therapists deal with issues of treatment termination, closure, and separation. We practice art reviews and reinforce goals in the process and art termination. When medically compromised patients move on having regained a sense of mastery and improved quality of life, the art therapist experiences compassion satisfaction. However, in medicine, the tapering of treatment may not correlate with achievement of what had been conceptualized as art therapy goals. Art therapy terminates when medical or rehabilitation goals have been met and discharge to home or another facility have been arranged. The end of art therapy while having encouraged the integration of loss, will include witnessing the patient's loss of function, loss of limbs, loss of memory, and other cognitive deficits. It is common that patients may not significantly improve during medical treatment or upon discharge. Indeed, termination of art therapy may be at the end of the patient's life, or we may learn of a patient's demise post discharge. Death of patients is an ongoing reality in medicine, particularly in palliative care programs and hospice settings. Medical art therapists, by definition, work in a milieu of loss at every level.

In addition to the critical processing of emotions related to this phenomenon, there are measures for the clinician's coping that may go beyond what is typically practiced. The truncating of connection after discharge or demise may not allow sufficient winding down for the patient or the therapist. Death of a patient may preclude the opportunity to grieve. Although not a personal attachment, creating ways to detach, acknowledge our work, as well as pay tribute can be important.

With patients who leave an art therapist's care earlier than expected, not allowing for review or closure, a follow-up call or correspondence may serve to validate the experience. This may take the form of giving back any artwork left behind, which both validates the art therapy and encourages continuation of art-making. Such a contact may take place in a subsequent outpatient clinic or physician visit within the medical setting and be a singular terminating session or, if determined beneficial, may continue in an outpatient format.

Whether it is an anticipated death of a patient or not, the art therapist must find ways to feel the loss, especially as there may be multiple deaths and cumulative emotion. We need to experience our feelings, yet restore ourselves for our own lives and families. As professionals, we have to move on to other patients and shore up the resources and energy warranted for everyone in our care. The challenge is that during the provision of services, the art therapist had been integral within the circle of the patient; once the patient is deceased, that connection is over.

Maintaining communication with people in the patient circle for a while may be acceptable. This may take the form of extending oneself to loved ones, calling or writing a note of condolence, giving of art left behind, or offering bereavement session. I have also attended patients' funerals and memorial services, which conveys a message to loved ones that the work with the deceased was meaningful. Such experiences are reciprocal—once I paid tribute to the patient, I was able to more efficiently disconnect. As described by Winiarski (1991), this is a way "we can say our goodbyes, and give ourselves closure" (p. 140). This stretching of the boundaries should be selective and, as long as the relationships remain professional in dynamic and within ethical guidelines, can be highly effective.

Summary and Reward

The special issues for the art therapist in medicine run a spectrum of modified interventions, protective appearance, and selective extending of oneself for effective termination. With sufficient self-care, emotional and physical, there is particular compassion satisfaction regardless of the specific medical application. This gratification is brought forth in knowing the work helped to address and ameliorate the psychological and emotional aspects of medical conditions. Despite unrelenting sadness and loss, we feel uplifted when there are small gains in our patients' medical and personal processes. It is, indeed, a privilege to be with someone at such an intimate and deeply personal time, and to have met them through the eloquence and elegance of art therapy.

References

Centers for Disease Control and Prevention. (2016). *Protecting healthcare personnel: Sequence for donning and removing personal protective equipment*. Retrieved May 8, 2018, from www.cdc.gov/hai/prevent/ppe.html.

Conlon, S. (1995). TB, the mask, and me. *Art Therapy: Journal of the American Art Therapy Association, 12*(1), 72. doi: 10.1080/07421656.1995.10759129.

David, I. R. (2015). Art therapy in medical settings. In D. E. Gussak & M. L. Rosal (Eds.), *The Wiley Blackwell handbook of art therapy* (pp. 443–450). New York, NY: John Wiley & Sons.

Kearney, M. K., Weininger, R. B., Vachon, M. L. S., Harrison, R. L., & Mount, B. M. (2009). Self-care of physicians caring for patients at the end of life: "Being connected . . . a key to my survival." *Journal of the American Medical Association, 301*(11), 1155–1164.

Rosner, I. (1982). Art therapy with two quadriplegic patients. *American Journal of Art Therapy, 21*(4), 115–120. doi: 10.1001/jama.2009.352.

United States Food & Drug Administration. (2017). *Masks and N95 respirators*. Silver Spring, MD: U.S. F.D.A. Retrieved May 8, 2018, from www.fda.gov/MedicalDevices/Productsand MedicalProcedures/

United States Food & Drug Administration. (2018). *Personnel protective equipment for infection control*. Silver Spring, MD: U.S. F.D.A. Retrieved May 8, 2018, from www.fda.gov/MedicalDevices/Productsand MedicalProcedures/.

Winiarski, M. G. (1991). *AIDS-related psychotherapy*. New York, NY: Pergamon Press.

Wright, B. A. (1960). *Physical disability: A psychological approach*. New York, NY: Harper & Row.

Index

Note: Page numbers in *italic* indicate a figure and page numbers in **bold** indicate a table on the corresponding page.